IMAGES
of America

CHILDERSBURG

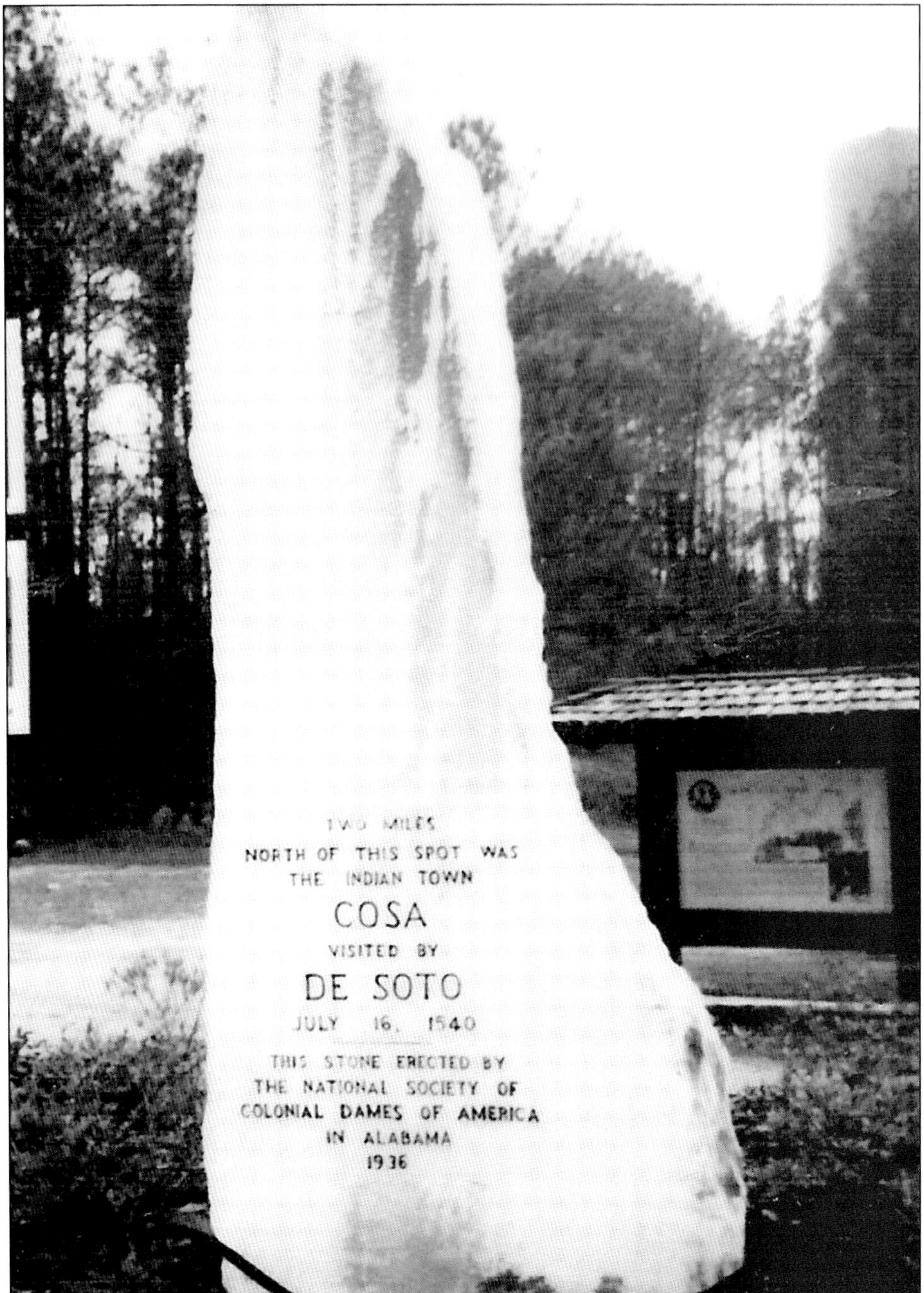

THE DE SOTO MONUMENT. Located at the intersection of Highway 280 and Highway 76, this monument was erected in 1936 by the National Society of Colonial Dames of America. It marks Childersburg as Chief Tushkalusa's political capital, Cosa, as well as commemorating the arrival of Hernando de Soto in the year 1540. (Courtesy of the Earle A. Rainwater Memorial Library.)

The cover image is courtesy of Jane Limbaugh Allen. See page 29 for information about this photograph.

IMAGES
of America

CHILDERSBURG

J. Leigh Mathis-Downs

ARCADIA
PUBLISHING

ISBN 978-0-7385-4221-8

Published by Arcadia Publishing
Charleston, South Carolina

Printed in the United States of America

Library of Congress Catalog Card Number: 2005933415

For all general information contact Arcadia Publishing at:
Telephone 843-853-2070
Fax 843-853-0044
E-mail sales@arcadiapublishing.com
For customer service and orders:
Toll-Free 1-888-313-2665

Visit us on the Internet at www.arcadiapublishing.com

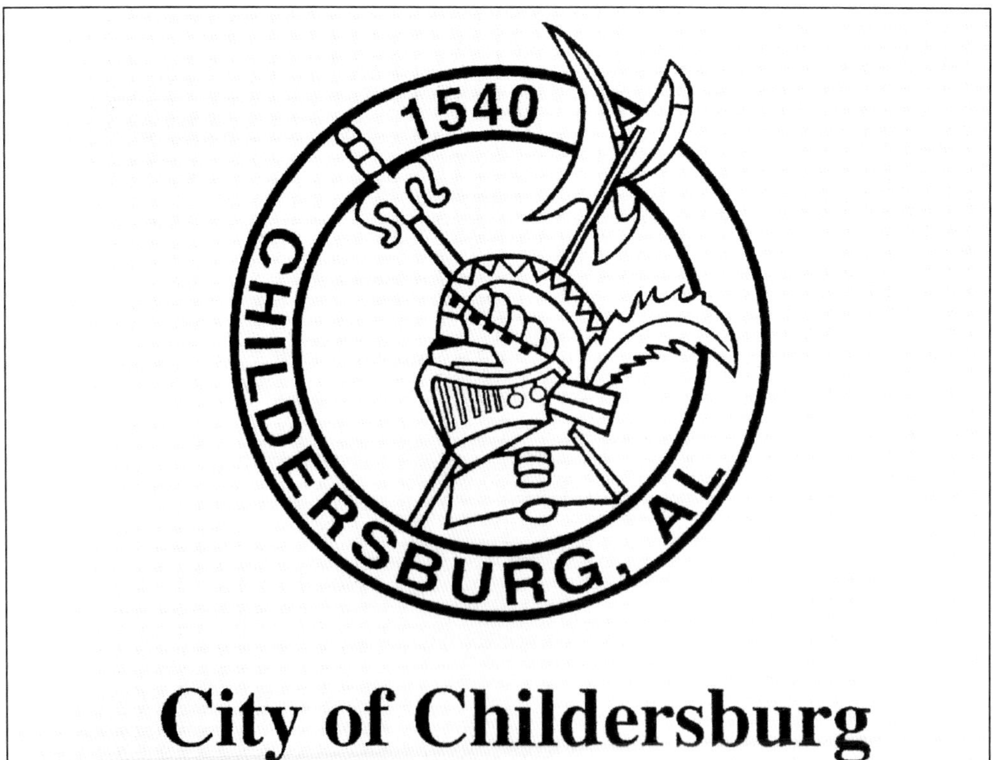

CHILDERSBURG SEAL. This is the official seal for the city of Childersburg. The date 1540 commemorates the year de Soto arrived in Cosa (Childersburg).

Contents

ACKNOWLEDGMENTS

This book was made possible by the good people of Childersburg, Alabama, who willingly shared their photographs with me as well as their memories. I thank them all. Their contributions will help educate future generations of Childersburg natives on the history of their city. In particular, I would like to thank my employer, Barbara Rich, director of the Earle A. Rainwater Memorial Library, as well as my co-worker Susan Carpenter for their help with this project. Much information, dedication, and photographs were given by Edwin "Mickey" Finn, Dr. Dee Moody, and Patricia Teague Wesley Godfrey. Special thanks go to Talladega County probate judge Billy Atkinson Sr., Childersburg's most dedicated historian and my friend. Special thanks also go to Mrs. Jane Limbaugh Allen for her generosity in sharing her knowledge and many photographs. Much appreciation is due to Katherine Frangopoulos Commander Blackerby, a prodigy with a camera, for her contribution of significant photographs that add a little something special to this book.

Special thanks go to Howard "Bucky" Riddle, Monty Powell, Frances Hudson, Beulah Garrett, Barbara Anderson, Gloria McGowan, Mrs. Judy McSween, Dean Ingram, Mr. Beasley Martin, Ralph and Dolly Finn, Mrs. Myrtle McDowell, and Mr. Allen W. Mathis III for their contributions and the passing on of oral history.

Most of all, I thank my family for giving me their full support and understanding of the time it took to create this book.

Finally, I would like to dedicate this book to my father, Erskine R. Mathis, who by word and example taught me the importance of preserving history, and to the people of Childersburg, Alabama, past and present.

INTRODUCTION

The oldest continuously occupied city in the United States, Childersburg, Alabama, is a place with an ancient and colorful past. This area, once known as Coosa (also spelled Coza, Cosa, Coca, and Coosee) was the political capital of Chief Tushkalusa's vast empire. Reports to the Spanish king referred to Tushkalusa as "Suzerain of vast territories and Lord of many peoples—equally feared by his vassals and the neighboring nations." Though Tushkalusa's own tribe, the Coosa, did not inhabit his entire nation, he ruled all the land south of the Ohio and east of the Mississippi, ruling other tribes within this territory like a Roman emperor would have ruled. Coosa's own population in 1540 was estimated to be between 30,000 and 40,000, according to Hernando de Soto's chroniclers.

There has been much controversy over the exact site of Coosa over the years, however irrefutable the evidence of its true location. Two state universities—Florida and California—collaborated to send Prof. Herbert Priestly to Spain to investigate records of the de Soto expedition. The ancient records were housed in the Spanish National Library at Seville. His report was accepted by the Final Report of the DeSoto Commission. Noted in those old documents is a description of Kymulga Cave, then in the suburbs of Coosa. Also noted is the description of the location of Coosa "on a beautiful plateau where two creeks, a half league apart, empty into a large river forming a barrier to an enemy on three sides." The two creeks are what is known today as the Tallasahatchee Creek and the Talladega Creek. In de Soto's time, these creeks were known as the Natchee and the Eufaulee. The chroniclers also said, "About two leagues distant is a range of mountains," which would be the Kahatchee Mountains between Childersburg and Sylacauga harboring Fulton Gap.

The Final Report of the DeSoto Expedition Commission (76th U.S. Congress, First Session, 1939, House Executive Document Number 71), chaired by John R. Swanton, stated emphatically that the site of Coosa was the area closest to Childersburg, Alabama. Dr. Swanton, a Harvard ethnologist, was appointed to chair this commission, as well as its fact-finding committee, by Pres. Franklin Delano Roosevelt. Many articles in support of the findings of this commission were written by Dr. Walter B. Jones, secretary of the DeSoto Commission and noted Alabama geologist.

Coosa was visited by other European explorers, namely Tristan de Luna y Arellano in 1560 and Capt. Juan Pardo in 1566, and the evidence for the location has been recorded in English in the more modern era by many. Between 1750 and 1760, a writer named James Adair visited Coosa and described it as being on the Tallasahatchee Creek. On March 29, 1772, David Taitt, a surveyor and cartographer for the British government, visited Tallasahatchee and stated its location to be about a half-mile from Coosa Old Town. On December 13, 1796, Benjamin Hawkins was appointed by George Washington as agent to the Creeks. He discusses the location of Coosa in his *Collection of the Historical Society of Georgia, Vol. IX*. Thomas Simpson Woodward stated in his *Reminiscences of the Creek, or Muscogee Indians* that this Indian village was the same one visited by de Soto in 1540.

Albert James Pickett stated in *History of Alabama and Incidentally of Georgia and Mississippi from the Earliest Period* that de Soto left two men in Coosa: Robles, "a Christian Negro, too sick to travel," and Feryada, a white Spaniard, thus giving the residents of Childersburg claim to the fact that the town has been continuously occupied since 1540 or earlier—first by Native Americans, then by the descendants of the first European settlers in Coosa, Robles and Feryada, and later by enterprising traders who lived among the Native Americans before the influx of pioneer settlers. In this book, Pickett asserts that Indian George Stiggins stated that the particulars of the route of de Soto were shared with him "during his boyhood from the lips of the oldest Indians" and that "the site of Coosa town was located along Tallasahatchee Creek." Pickett says that Stiggins asserts that the Abekas had at a late date a brass kettledrum and several shields that once belonged to the army of de Soto and that he has often seen them.

According to *Pioneer Talladega: Its Minutes and Memories* by Wellington Vandiver, the first bloodshed of the Creek Indian War in Alabama was shed at Coosa on June 27, 1813, known as "The Coosa Incident."

The Battle of Horseshoe Bend in 1814 between Gen. Andrew Jackson and the Creeks under William Weatherford, whose Indian name was Red Eagle, resulted in annihilation of the American Indian armies. Those who remained by 1836 were sadly rounded up and driven out west on the Trail of Tears to make room for white settlers who lived in fear of the American Indians. With the "threat of Indians" gone, more white settlers began settling the Coosa Valley area.

The first white community built their town on an area of high ground one and a half miles from Coosa Old Town. The greatest natural resource in the area was an abundance of longleaf yellow pine and various hardwoods. Logically the first industry here was a sawmill, and shortly after, charcoal was also being produced. Cotton gins, coke ovens, and brick manufacturing followed, and by 1864, Childersburgh (the first spelling) Town had a grist mill at Kymulga.

After the Civil War, even the wealthiest families of this area were struggling. Their Confederate money was worthless, and they no longer had their valuable slaves. It was a time for reconstruction, and a new South was born.

The settlers in the Coosa Valley area saw a need for a common village for trade, barter, and meetings to discuss and solve common problems. The founders of this common village were "The Four Johns:" John Oden, John Rawden (Rhoden), John Keith, and John Childers, as well as Tom Coleman. Together, they had decided to name their village Johnstown, when, according to Annie Louise Ryder-Bush, reportedly John Childers took it upon himself to go to the capital and had the town named Childersburgh after himself. The other Johns and the residents were in an uproar, and there was much buzz in the town over the incident. Childersburg wasn't actually incorporated until 1889.

Childersburg has deep religious roots. There were three original churches: the Methodist church, the Baptist church, and the Presbyterian church. Later the Church of Christ was established. With the start of World War II, Childersburg's population boomed, and there was need for a place for Catholics and Episcopals to worship. Out of that need, Holy Name of Jesus and St. Mary's were established.

By 1887, Childersburg had passenger trains serving north, south, east, and west. The Southern Depot was across the street from the New South (Finn) Hotel on what is now known as Southern Street. Two of the first trains that would lay over in Childersburg were the *Dude*, a passenger train between Childersburg and Rome, Georgia, and the *Goober*, which traveled between Childersburg and Columbus, Georgia. Many of the railroad men brought their families to settle in Childersburg. With this came more industry and more residents.

The town was later moved to lower ground to be near the railroad. On April 1, 1886, there was a three-day rain and the Coosa River flooded seven feet above any known high-water mark. The retail area of the town was flooded in five feet of water, above the countertops of the stores. The town suffered floods many times before the dam was built but never again to this extent.

On October, 21, 1887, Pres. Grover Cleveland, a relative of the local Cliett family, came to Childersburg with his wife, "Miss Frankie," on their way to Montgomery, where they attended the state fair. He made a speech off the balcony of the Exchange Hotel in which he aligned himself with the States Rights Southerners, solidifying the South politically. He said, "You have problems particularly your own, which must be solved without Federal Aid or Federal Interference."

In 1890, Sen. John Tyler Morgan delivered a speech in Childersburg that caused large numbers of Alabamians to remain in the Democratic Party instead of changing to the Populist Party.

According to Annie Louise Ryder-Bush, whose *Memoirs of Childersburg* preserved much town history that would have been lost otherwise, the first school was located in an old sawmill near the Town Branch, a stream that runs past the Methodist church. It was called Sunshine Academy. Mrs. Ryder-Bush stated that her mother attended that school. The second school was located near the first. About 1904, a new Childersburg School was built near the Central of Georgia Railway, not far from Fourth Street, SW. The students who attended these schools received a good education, and many went on to further their educations at universities. The public high school was built in 1922. Most of it burned in 1957 and later was rebuilt on the same spot. It was torn down, and a new school was built and finally occupied in 1999 on Faye S. Perry Road, where it is now located.

Blacks were schooled in tiny schoolhouses built near their churches; among these were Mount Olive School, Pinegrove, Enon, Tallasahatchee, Nottingham, and Cedar Creek. Eventually, they consolidated these schools when they built Childersburg Consolidated High School, which was located in the area of the Alabama Ordnance Works. Later it was moved to Childersburg-Fayetteville Road and renamed Phyllis Wheatley School. With the civil rights movement in Alabama, the schools slowly began integration. In 1967, Bertha Swain and Edith Moon became the first two blacks to graduate from Childersburg High School.

Through the 20th century, the sawmills and cotton gins continued to thrive. Childersburg was alive with industry and community life. Its population, being less than 500 in 1940, grew to almost 15,000 in just a year. On January 1, 1941, the War Department announced that they would be building a massive munitions plant, Alabama Ordnance Works (AOW), in Childersburg, and so they did. Even the housewives and farmers in Childersburg went to work for the plant.

People came from everywhere. Every house was taking boarders. Apartments, shack villages, dormitories, trailer parks, projects, and boarding houses were going up everywhere to accommodate the workers. Men were living in chicken and coal houses. Alabama Ordnance Works was not only a powder munitions plant but part of the Manhattan Project. Heavy water was manufactured there for use in the atomic bomb.

After the war, the munitions plant closed, leaving thousands out of work. Most of the families went back from whence they came. The farmers in this area continued to farm and now had other skills learned while working at the AOW that proved profitable for them.

Beaunit Mills, a rayon plant, and Coosa River Newsprint, a descendant of the old sawmills, opened on the uncontaminated property of the munitions plant (much of the AOW property was contaminated by nitrates), and local people once again had jobs. Coosa River Newsprint was sold to Kimberly Clark, then sold to U.S. Alliance, and later Bowater Newsprint, which still provides the most jobs in Childersburg. The Talladega County Board of Education, City of Childersburg, and Bates Enterprises provide many jobs for the residents as well.

Yes, Childersburg may look like a sleepy little town on first glance. But if you look a little closer, you'll see that it's a town brimming with history and a culture its very own. In these pages, you will find over 200 photographs documenting the history of Childersburg, America's oldest continuously occupied town.

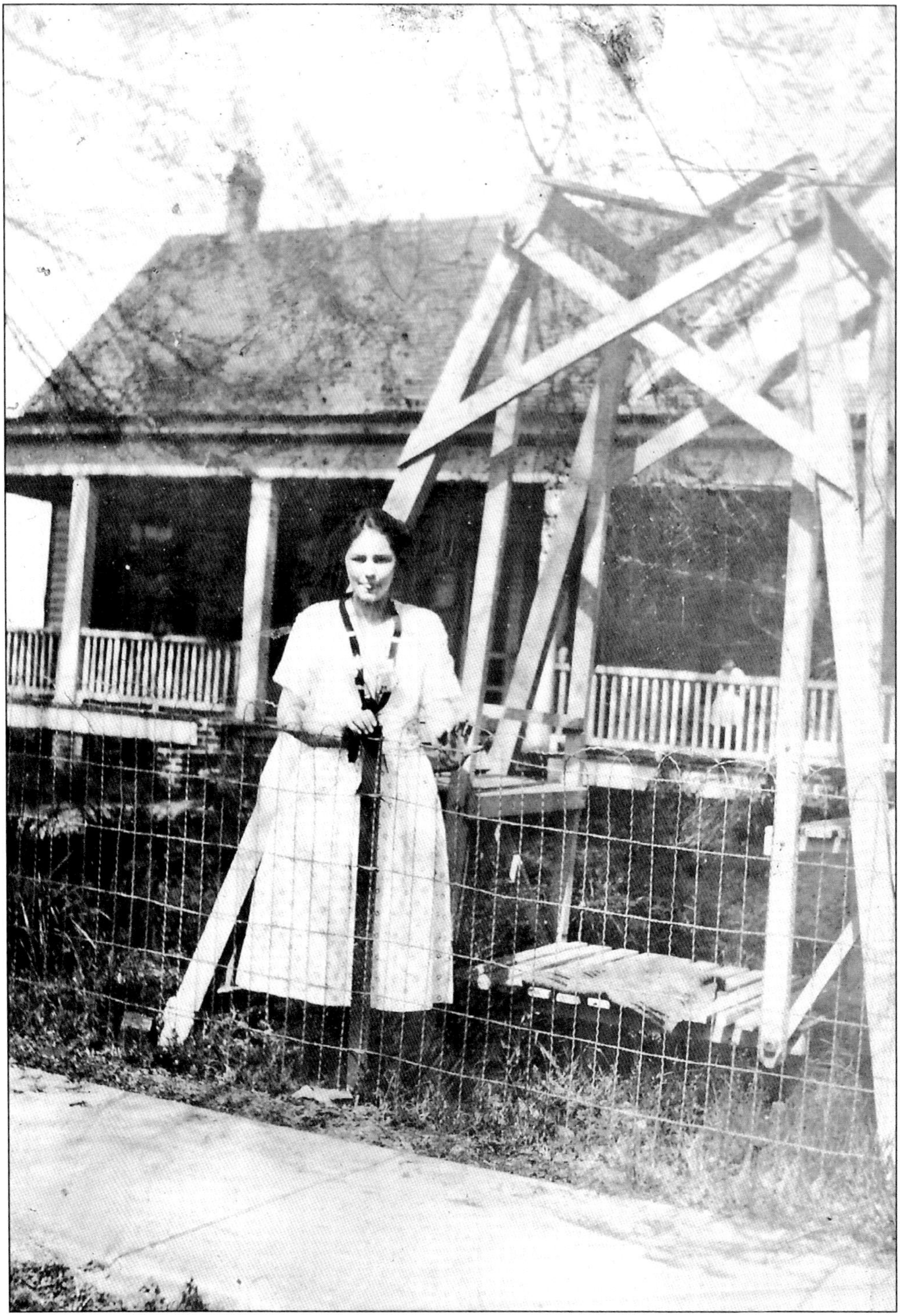

KIDD HOUSE, C. 1915. Nina Thomas is standing in front of the Luke Kidd house. She is holding some flowers and sticking out her tongue. The Kidd house was located on First Street in Childersburg. (Courtesy of Jane Limbaugh Allen.)

One

Hernando de Soto at Coosa

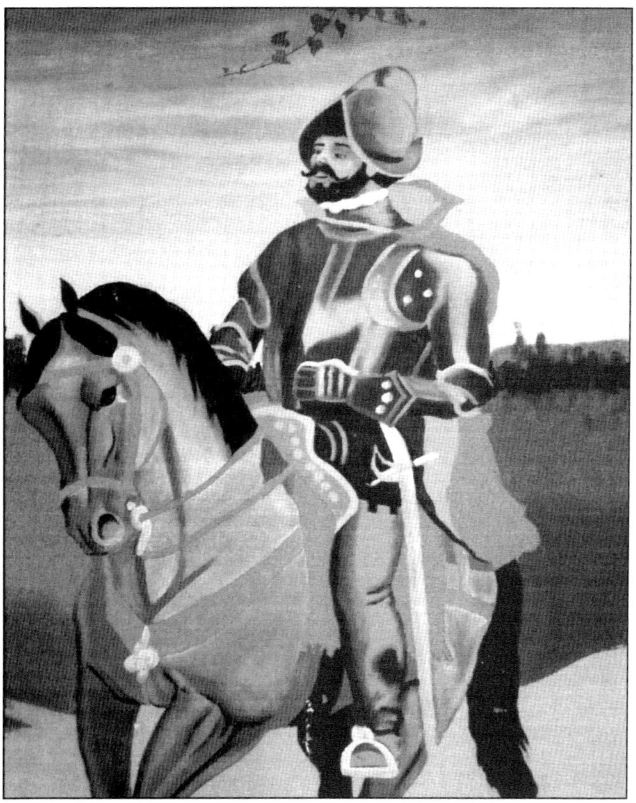

Mural of Hernando de Soto, 1993. This is part of the mural just outside the entrance to Kymulga Cave at DeSoto Caverns. It shows Hernando de Soto on horseback. It was painted by J. Kirkland and N. Phillips.

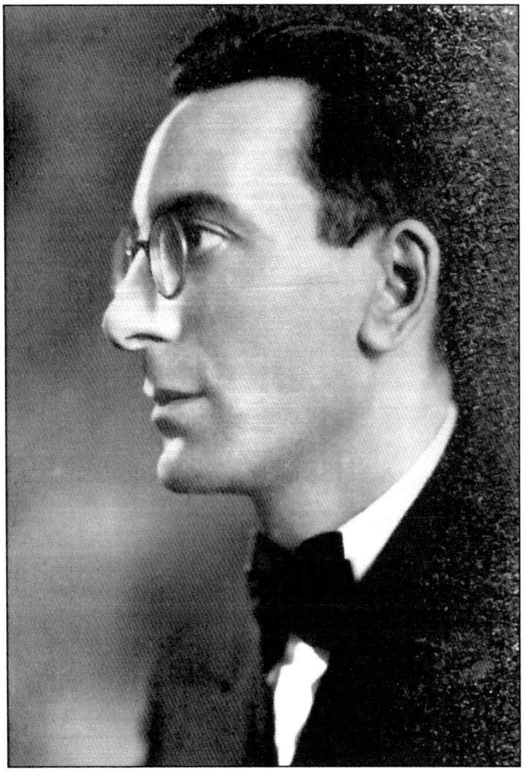

JOSHUA "GATTY" D'ASTON (1894–1960), C. 1922. Of French Canadian ancestry, Joshua had many talents—botanist, inventor, historian, photographer, and artist—and he excelled at them all. He lived in Childersburg, Alabama, but worked for the Chicago Museum of Natural History. He grew rare cactuses and took copious notes on them and many other plants. He often went out into the wilderness to observe plant life and see what he could learn. (Courtesy of Clarence Edwin "Mickey" Finn.)

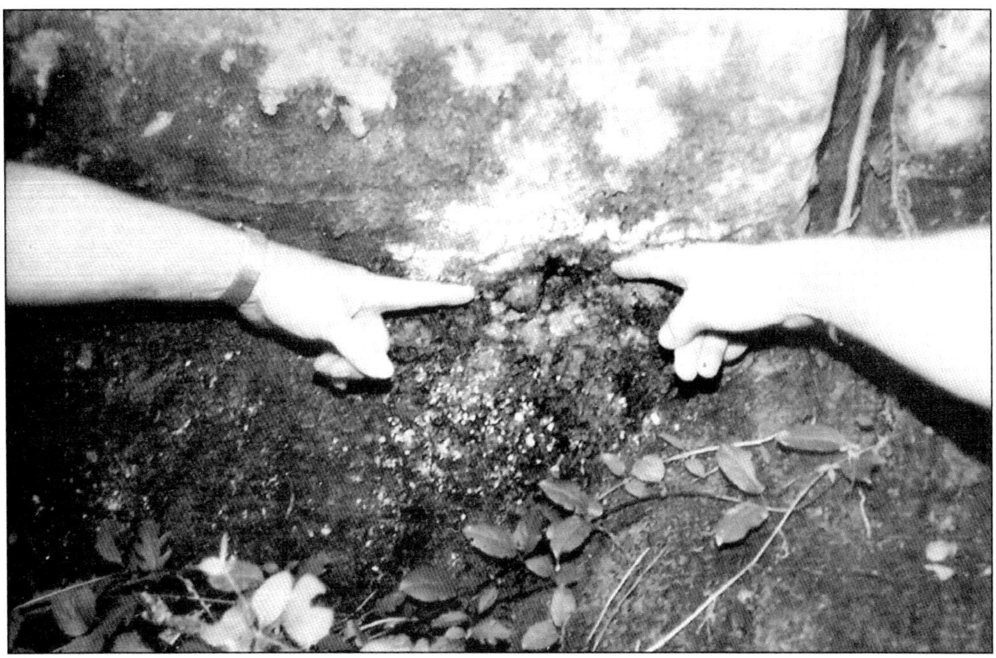

SPANISH MARKING SPIKES, C. 1980. This is a photograph of the Spanish marking spikes found by botanist Joshua "Gatty" D'Aston in Childersburg. One day, Gatty was on one of his plant observation hikes and found these Spanish marking spikes, believed to have been left here by the de Soto Expedition. (Courtesy of Billy Atkinson Sr.)

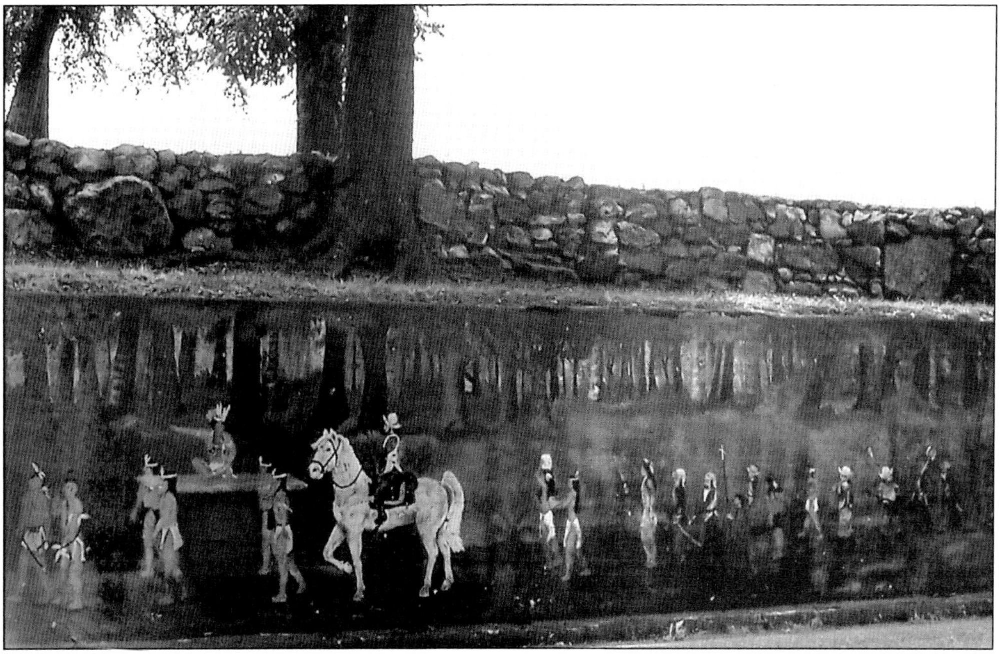

DE SOTO MURAL ON FIRST STREET. This de Soto mural was done in 1984 by Carlton Sims of Birmingham, Alabama. It is located on First Street in Childersburg on the wall below the Rainwater Museum. Months of research were done for authenticity, and it depicts the descriptions of the first meeting of de Soto and Chief Tushkalusa in 1540. (Courtesy of Marian Payant.)

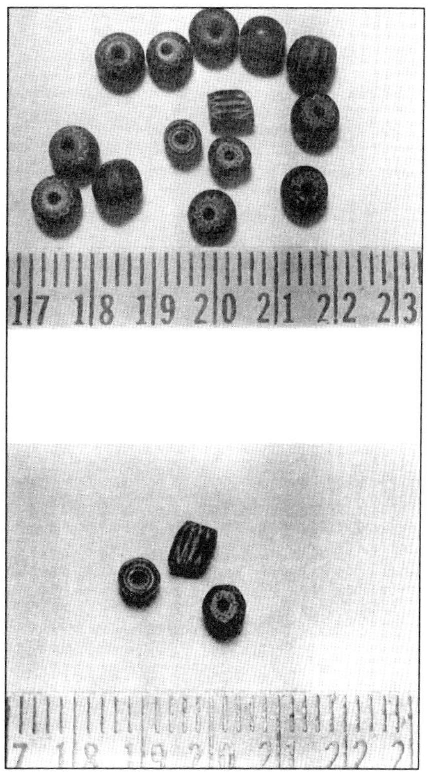

NUEVA CADIZ AND CHEVRON BEADS. This is a photograph of a Nueva Cadiz beads found at Ogletree Island on the Coosa and chevron beads found on the banks of the Coosa River near Childersburg. Just before de Soto's army arrived in Coosa in 1540, they visited an island in the Caribbean called Nueva Cadiz. The Indians on Nueva Cadiz made a bead design that was made nowhere else in the world. Nueva Cadiz was completely destroyed and sunk into oblivion by a hurricane in 1545, so the beads most likely came to rest here by means of the de Soto Expedition. (Courtesy W. C. Eubanks, *The Soto States Anthropologist*, Vol. 92 Numbers 1 and 2: January and April 1992, published under the auspices of the Point Foundation.)

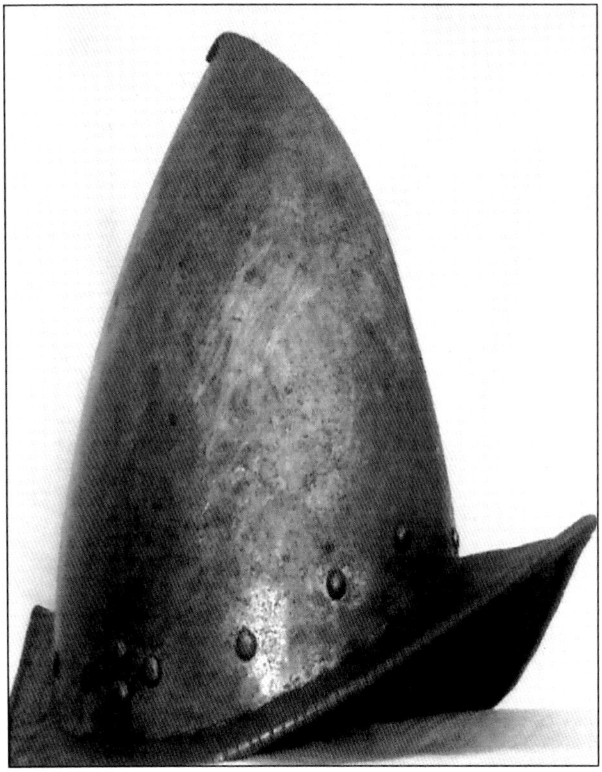

Spanish Helmet from the de Soto Expedition. A helmet similar to this one was found in Childersburg in the early 1940s during the construction of the Alabama Ordnance Works while workers were digging a basement. According to N. C. Pitts, it was given to the Talladega County Museum, which closed. Their collections were given to the University of Alabama, and it was subsequently lost. (Courtesy of Tim Burke of the Calderon Company.)

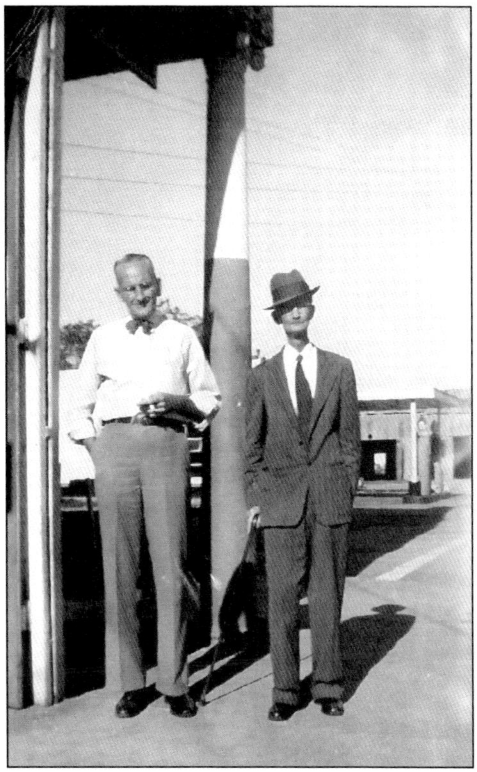

Civil Servants Benefield and Oden. The man on the left is Mr. Benefield. He always wore a bow tie. The man on the right is Mr. Dempsey "Demps" Alexander Oden (1871–1953). Both men worked for the city. They are standing outside Childersburg's first city hall building, which was in the location of the hardware store on First Street. Oden was active in the research and promotion of the history of Childersburg. He was once Childersburg's city clerk, he wrote the treatise *Childersburg (Coosa) America's Oldest City*, he wrote for *The Powdertown News*, and he was secretary of the Tallasahatchee Historical Society. Demps lived in Childersburg all his life. His grandfather Joshua Oden was one of the first settlers in Childersburg. Demps hoped that some day Childersburg would change its name back to Coosa. (Courtesy of Clarence Edwin "Mickey" Finn.)

Two

DESOTO CAVERNS

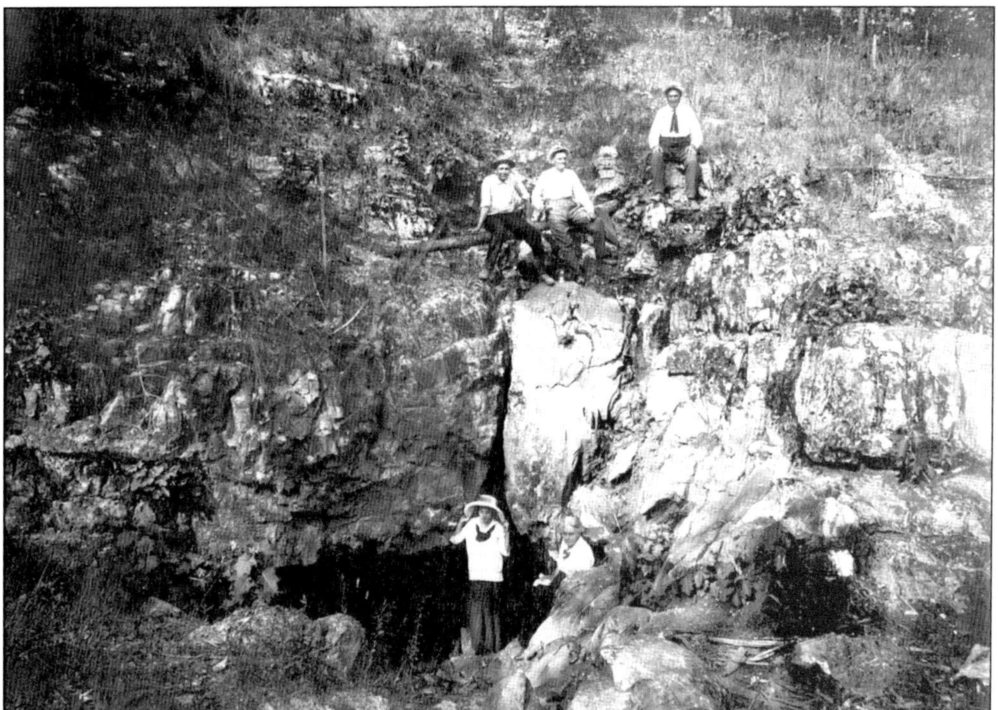

KYMULGA CAVE ENTRANCE, 1920. Allen W. Mathis Sr. is sitting on the log to the far left in this picture. The lady on the right of the cave entrance, Ida Mathis, along with some investors, purchased the cave property in 1912. They hoped to mine the onyx in the caverns as decorative stone. After some research, they found that the business would not be as lucrative as they first believed, and so the cave was never mined. Ida bought out the other parties' interest in the cave, and it has passed down through the generations of her family since. It is currently owned and operated by the fourth generation—Allen W. Mathis III and his wife, Danielle. Today, DeSoto Caverns Park generates 80,000 to 100,000 tourists per year. (Courtesy of Allen W. Mathis III.)

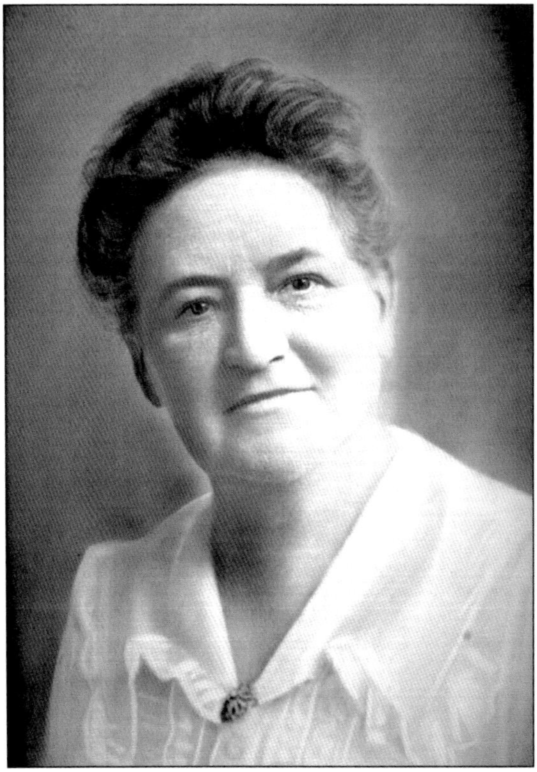

IDA MATHIS. Ida Mathis purchased the caverns back in 1912. She is honored in the Alabama Woman's Hall of Fame for her contribution to the growth of agriculture in the United States. She was a pioneer in crop rotation and spoke all over the United States on the subject. (Courtesy of Allen W. Mathis III.)

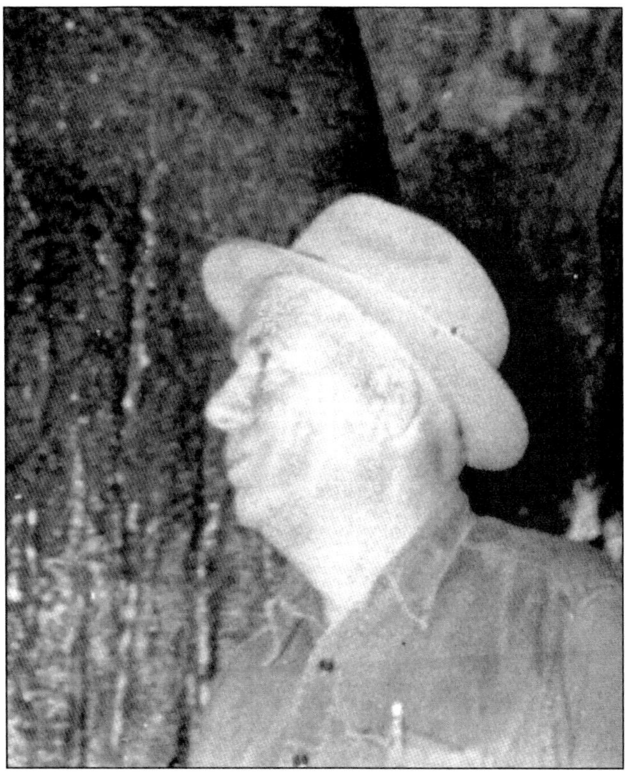

MR. FRED LAYTON INSIDE KYMULGA CAVE. From 1965 to 1975, Fred Layton developed and opened Kymulga Onyx Cave as a show cave on the strength of the "Florida Short Route" traffic that passed on Highway 21. In 1965, I-75 opened going through Atlanta to Florida and the traffic disappeared from Highway 21. Layton didn't realize this problem until it was too late and decided to open the cave for tours anyway. Unfortunately, without the nearby tourist traffic to support the show cave, it was not a successful business venture, but he continued to give tours through the cave for all 10 years of his lease. (Courtesy of Allen W. Mathis III.)

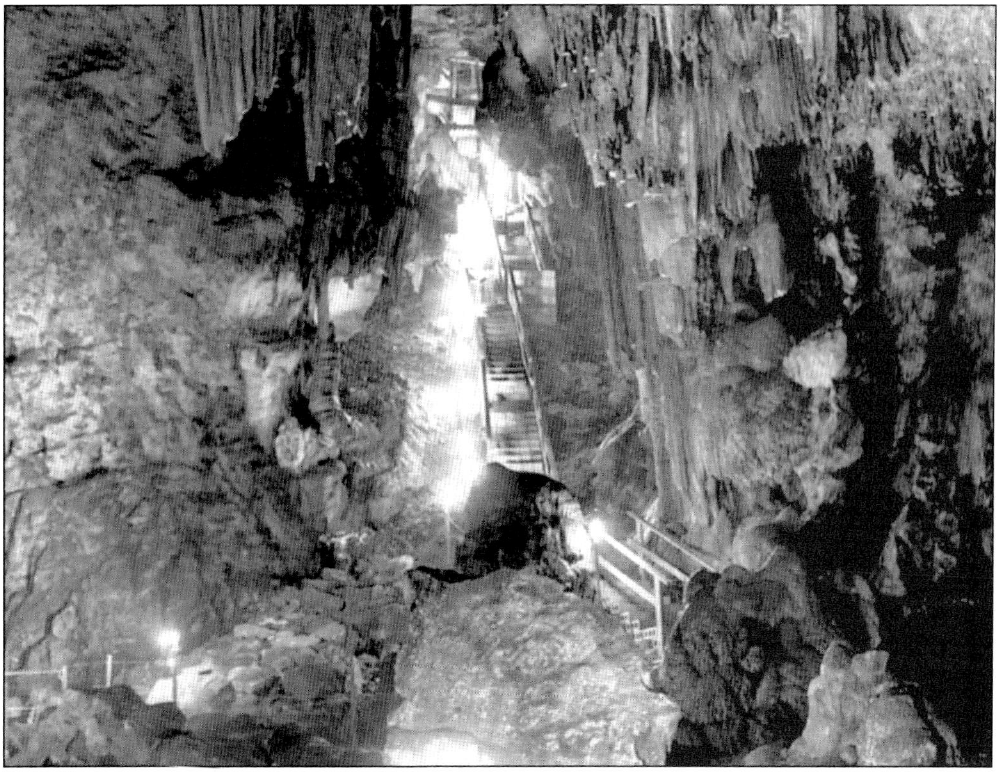

FIRST STEPS BUILT INSIDE KYMULGA CAVE. These are the first steps built inside Kymulga Cave. They were constructed in the cave by Fred Layton. Layton was the first official developer of Kymulga Cave. In 1965, he leased the cave from the owner, Allen W. Mathis Sr., and put the first steps and electric lights in the cave. This picture was taken around 1970. (Courtesy of Allen W. Mathis III.)

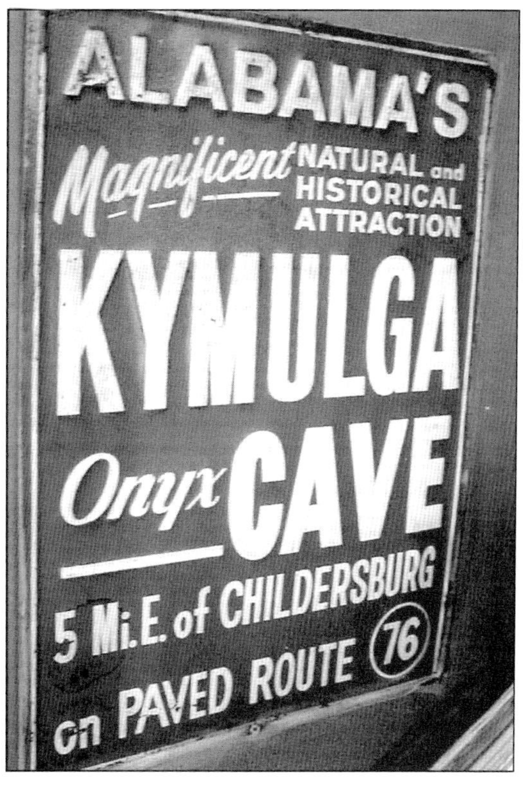

OLD CAVE SIGN, C. 2002. These signs were everywhere back in 1970. Hunters would get lost in the woods and then they would come upon one of these signs. This is a picture that was taken in China in 2002. (Courtesy of Allen W. Mathis III.)

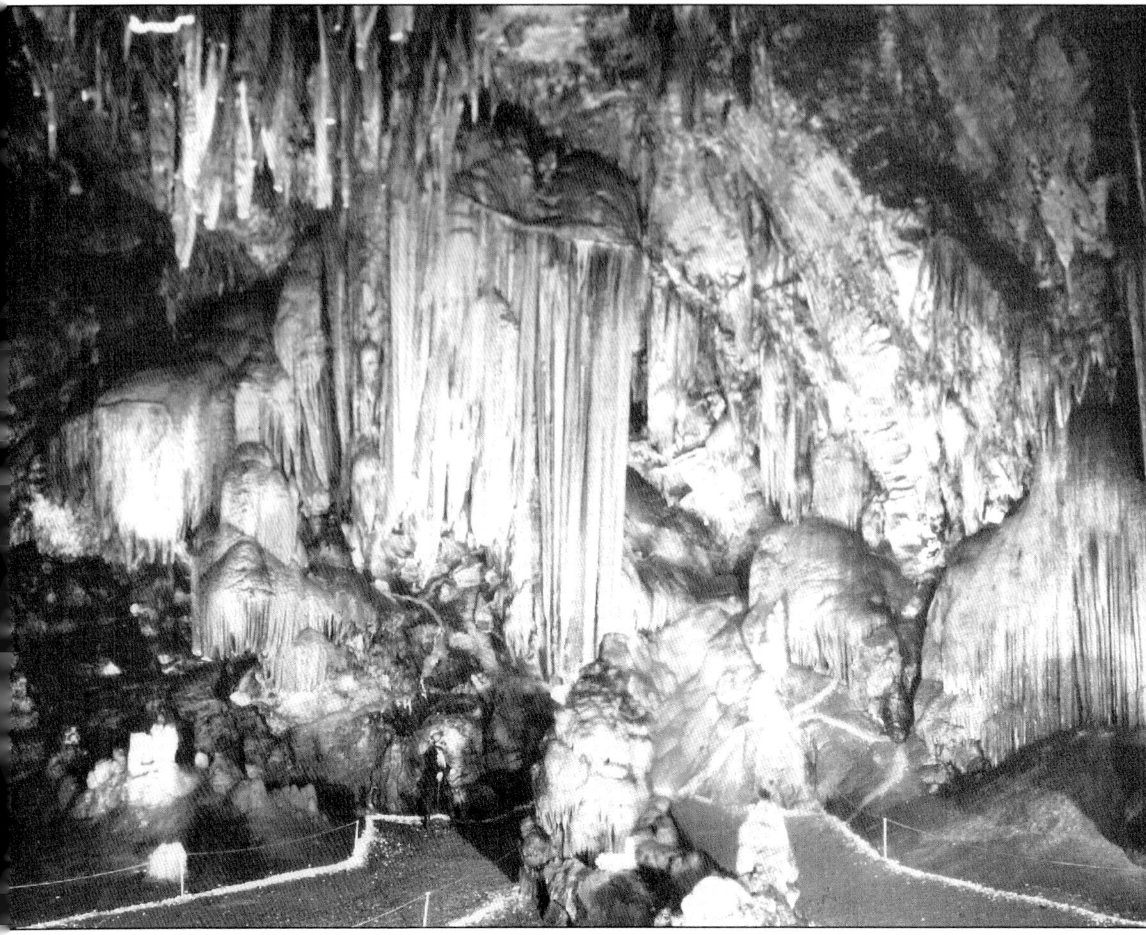

ROCK FORMATIONS INSIDE KYMULGA CAVE, C. 1972. Notice the natural perfection of the curtain formations. Kymulga Cave is the first cave of record in the United States. It was recorded by one of George Washington's Native American scouts back in 1796. This cave is one of the foremost Native American burial caves in the Southeast, with burials dating back 2,000 years. It was mined for gunpowder by Confederate soldiers during the Civil War. The Creek Indian Nation knows it as their ancestral cave. They believe that their spirits evolved out of this cave, creating their people. A few years ago, when a construction company was digging the tunnel that leads to the entrance to the cave (it replaced 83 steps), workers found a mastodon bone, which is a species from the prehistoric elephant family. In 2005, a movie crew moved into the cave for a short period of time while filming parts of the box-office movie *The Cave*. (Courtesy of the Earle A. Rainwater Memorial Library.)

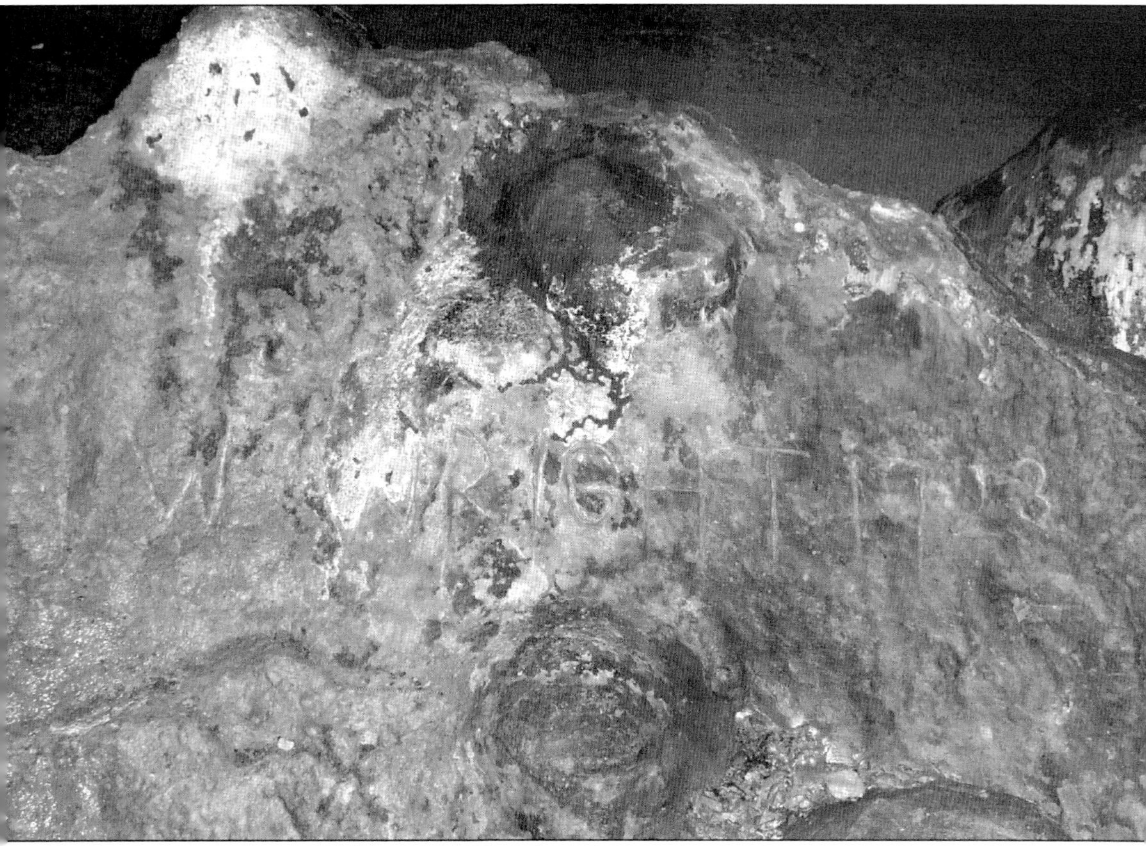

OLDEST GRAFFITI. In the late 17th and early 18th centuries, traders came to trade with the American Indians, and some married into the tribe and made Coosa their home. The Charleston-Chickasaw Trail was the route they took, which directly passed Kymulga Cave. Some of these traders only succeeded in calling on the wrath of the American Indians. I. W. Wright (Grace Jemison's *Historic Tales of Talladega* says J. W. Wright or Joseph Wright), a well-known trader from South Carolina, used this trail. He engraved his name on a rock inside Kymulga cave and dated it 1723. However, he was never seen again. It has been an oral tradition that the American Indians who lived here did not appreciate what they construed as him marking his territory on their property, so they killed him. George Stiggins (1788–1845) wrote in his *Creek Indian History* that the Abeka Indians living in the valley of Talladega were descended from the people visited by de Soto. He states, "Near one of their towns in the Valley, not very far from Soto's fortification, there is a cavern. . . . A half century ago they found human bones in the first room and right beside them carved into a rock, 'I. W. Wright, 1723.' "

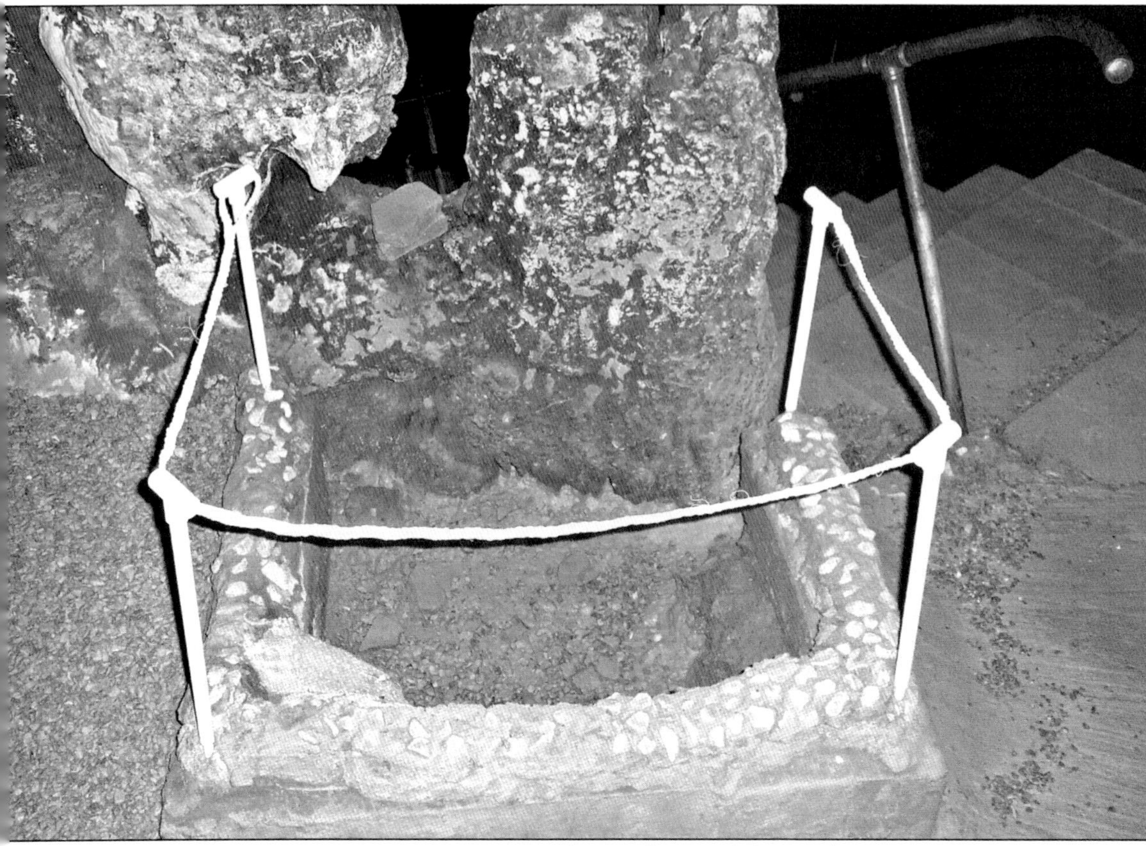

The Pulpit as It Looks Today. Notice the small size of the tomb. The Woodland-period American Indians would leave the bodies of their dead out for wild animals to feast on in order to clean the bones. Once the bones were stripped and sufficiently dried in the sun, they were taken into the cave and buried. The cave soil preserved the bones.

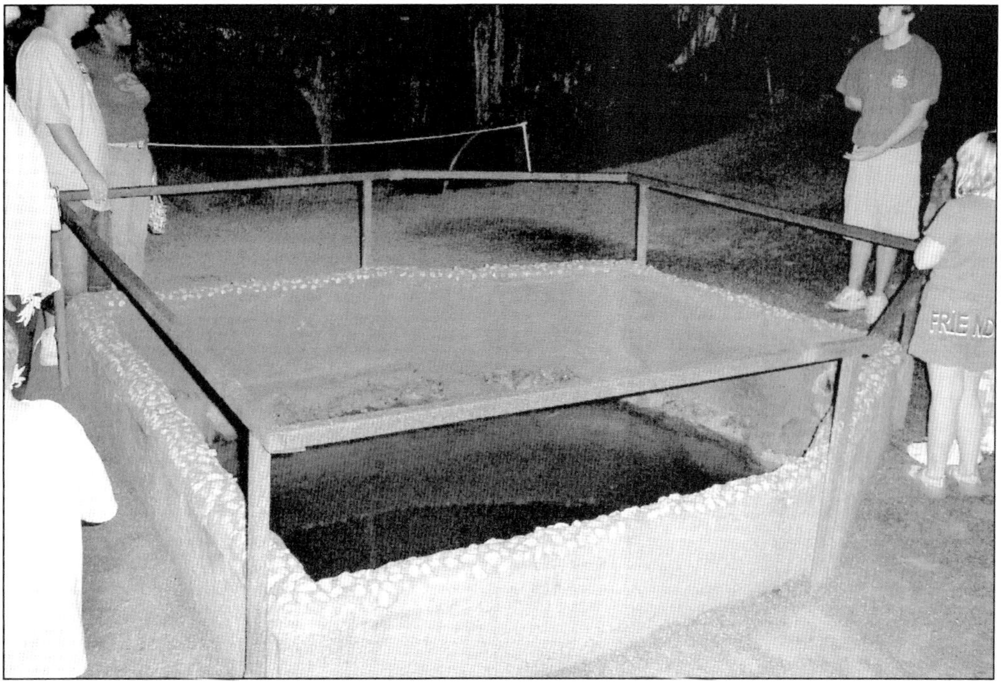

WELL DUG INSIDE CAVE BY CONFEDERATE SOLDIERS. This well was dug inside Kymulga Cave by Confederate soldiers. The cave entrance was steep and muddy. This well kept them from having to haul water down that entrance. Rebel soldiers mined this cave for saltpeter, used to make gunpowder.

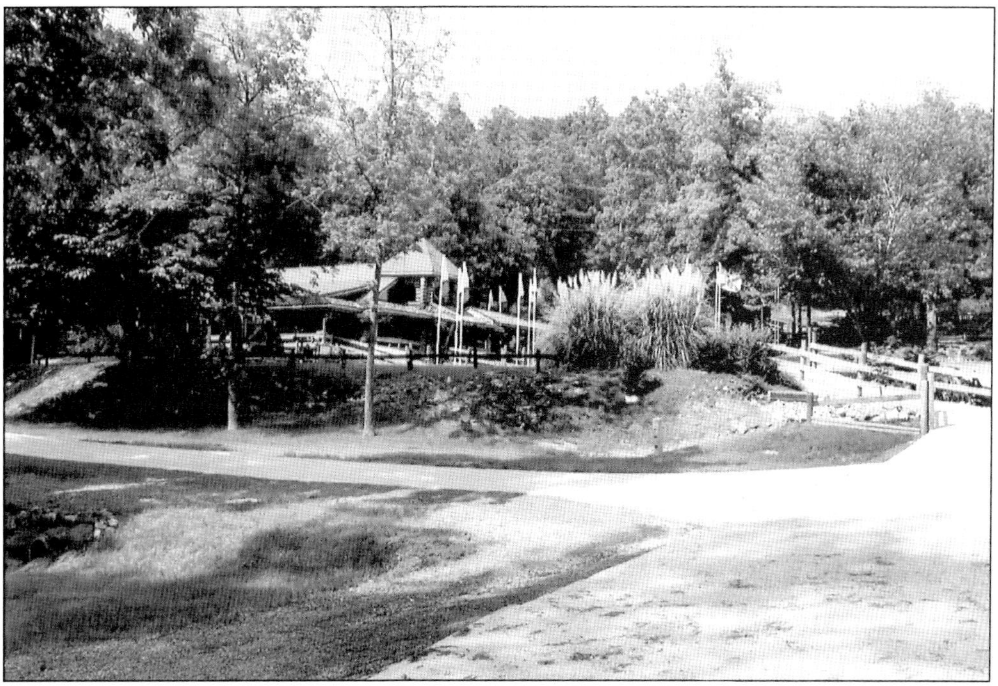

PARK ENTRANCE AT DESOTO CAVERNS PARK. This is the entrance to DeSoto Caverns Park from the parking lot. (Taken by Rodney Powell; courtesy of the Rocket City Relic Hunters.)

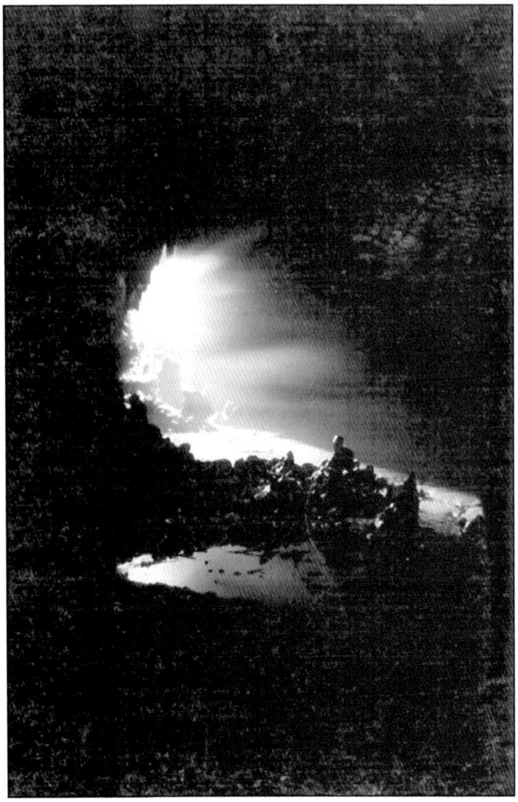

CAVE ENTRANCE FROM INSIDE CAVE, 1939. This photograph of the cave entrance was taken from inside the Kymulga Cave on August 8, 1939. (Courtesy of Clarence Edwin "Mickey" Finn.)

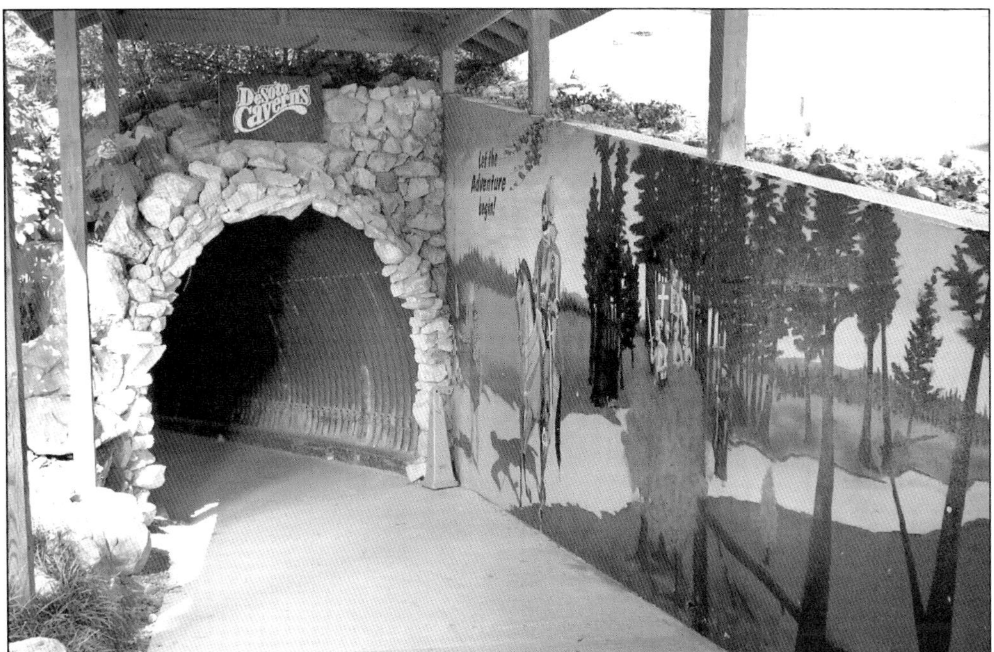

CAVE ENTRANCE FROM OUTSIDE CAVE TODAY. Notice the beautiful mural of de Soto's visit to Coosa. This is the mural done in 1993 by J. Kirkland and N. Phillips.

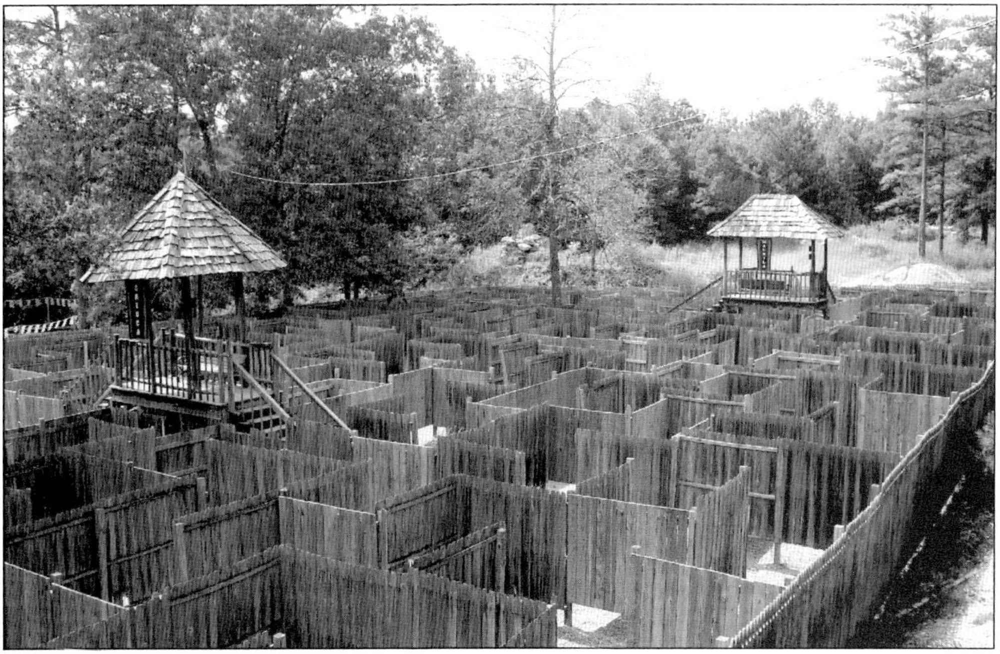

MAZE AT DESOTO CAVERNS. This maze is as big as a football field. Today there are many unique and interactive attractions at DeSoto Caverns Park for children, such as mining for jewels and fossils, a cave wall climb, water-balloon battle forts, water golf, and putt-putt golf, as well as some unique rides.

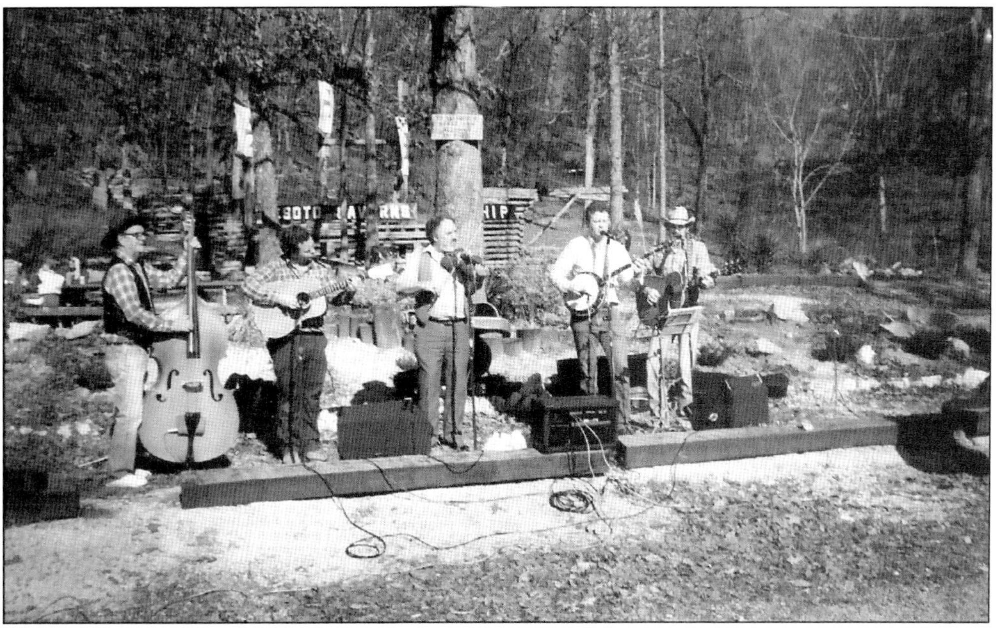

BAND PLAYING AT THE AMPHITHEATER, C. 1986. This is a photograph of the Mountain Fever Bluegrass Band playing at DeSoto Caverns. On bass is Al Whitstone, the acoustic guitar at left is Gerald Smitherman, Paul Wallace is playing the fiddle, Buddy McKinnon is on the banjo, and the acoustic guitar at right is Joe Lett of Childersburg. (Courtesy of Wanda McKinnon and Betty Lett.)

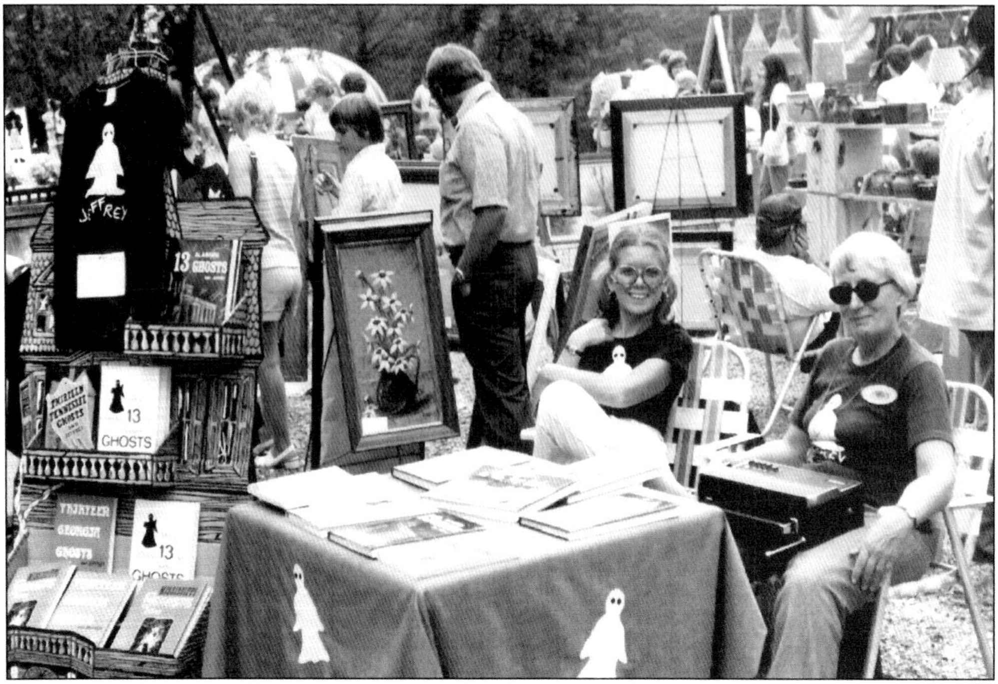

FAMILIAR FACES. Kathryn Tucker Windham wrote *Thirteen Alabama Ghosts and Jeffrey*. Her Alabama, Mississippi, and Georgia ghost books were in libraries and bookstores all over the country. In this photograph, she was doing an appearance at DeSoto Caverns in the 1970s. (Courtesy of the Earle A. Rainwater Memorial Library.)

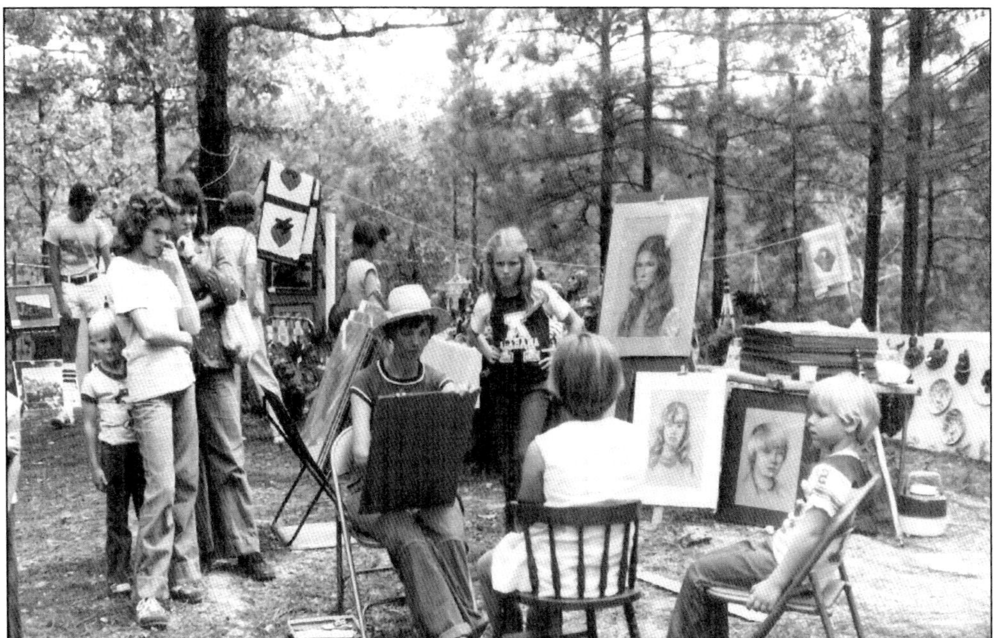

ARTISTS AND CRAFTSMEN, C. 1978. Many artists and craftsmen can't wait to display and sell their wares at the festivals at DeSoto Caverns. This artist is painting portraits at the fall festival. (Courtesy of the Earle A. Rainwater Memorial Library.)

Three

Businesses

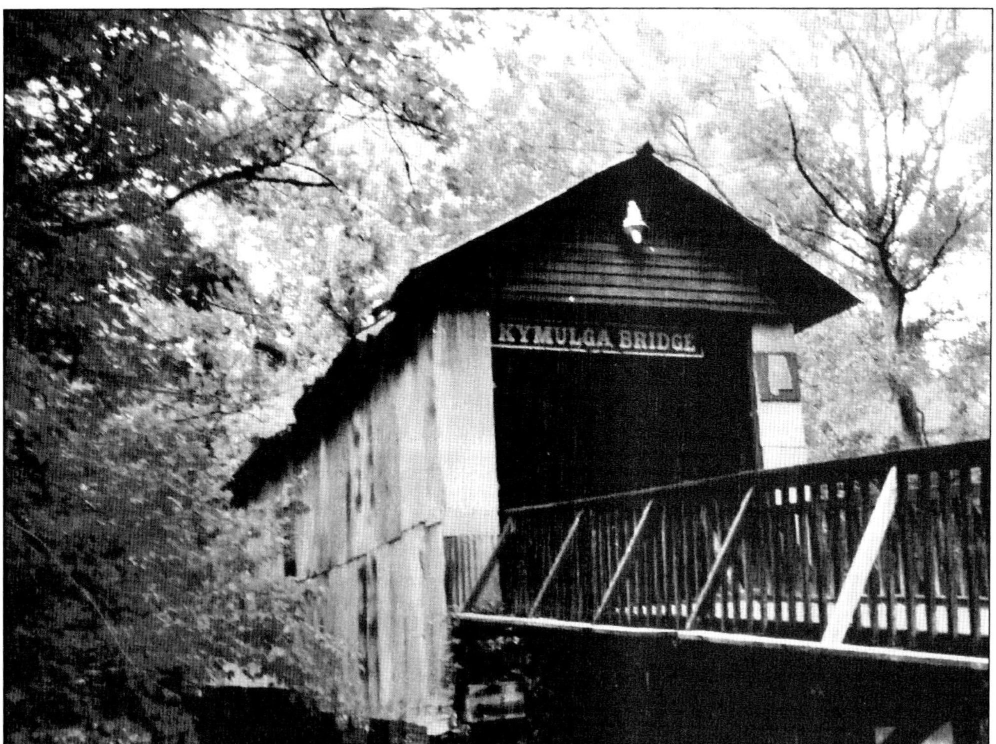

Kymulga Covered Bridge. Built just before the Civil War, Kymulga Covered Bridge crosses beautiful Talladega Creek. It is 105 feet long. This covered bridge is adjacent to the Kymulga Grist Mill. (Courtesy of Michael Giddens.)

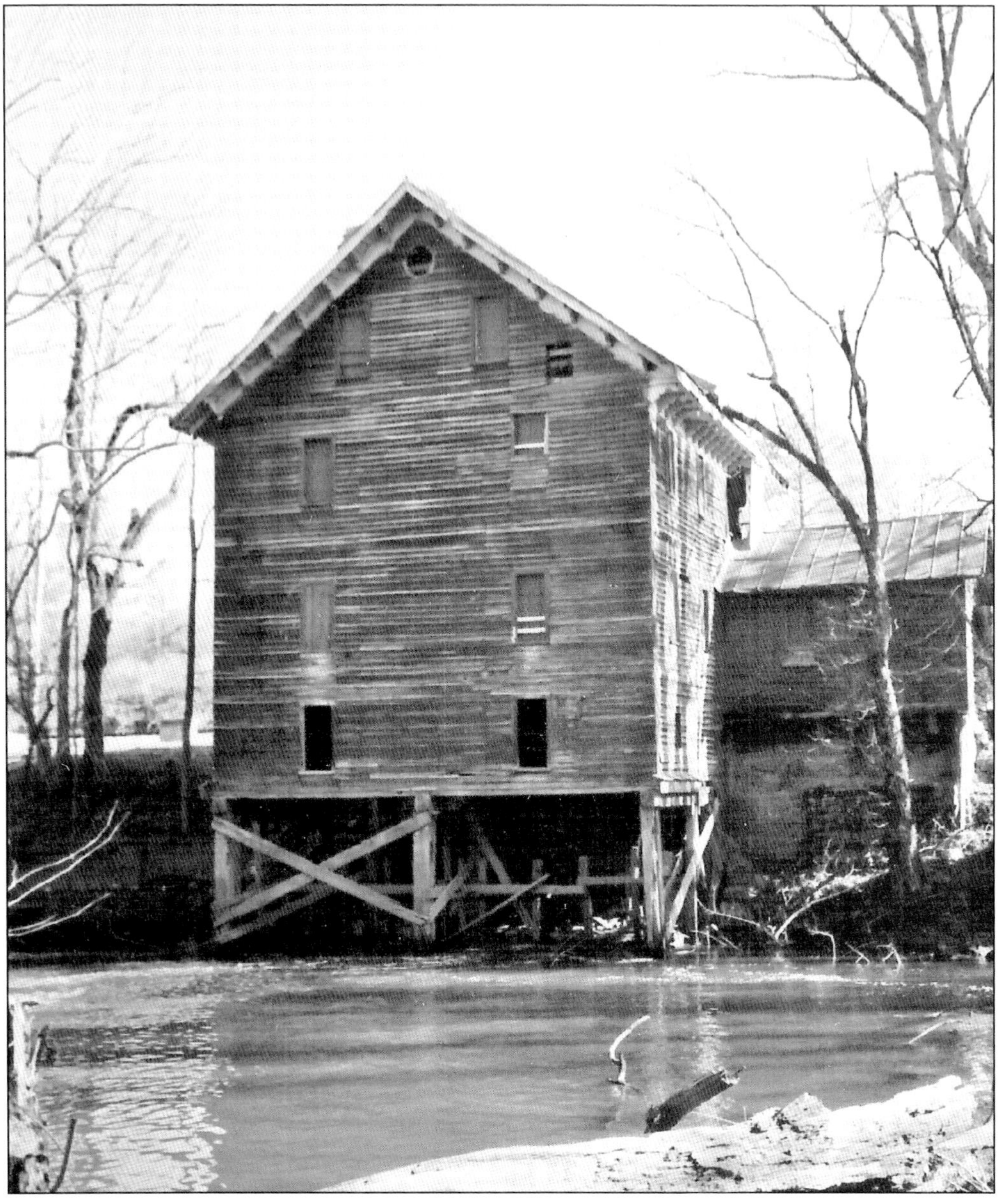

KYMULGA GRIST MILL. Built just before the Civil War, this gristmill has five sets of grinding rocks, with two sets coming from France. A slave drove two yokes of oxen to Mobile to haul them back to the mill. These stones are called French Buhrs and are believed to be the hardest rock in the world. One old set of rocks in the mill was used in an old mill that was across the creek before this one was built. The Kymulga mill was run by three underwater turbines and was contracted to be built by Confederate army captain Forney. Forney died before completion, and his wife allowed the contractor to complete the mill. The contractor was a German from South Carolina by the name of G. E. Morris. Morris was building three other mills at the same time. Union soldiers burned those mills but missed this one. The lumber and timbers were cut from the mountains across the creek, and the big timbers were hewn out in the local woods. All lumber was cut using waterpower. The mill is still in operation, and you can still purchase cornmeal ground by the original stones. (Courtesy of the Childersburg Chamber of Commerce.)

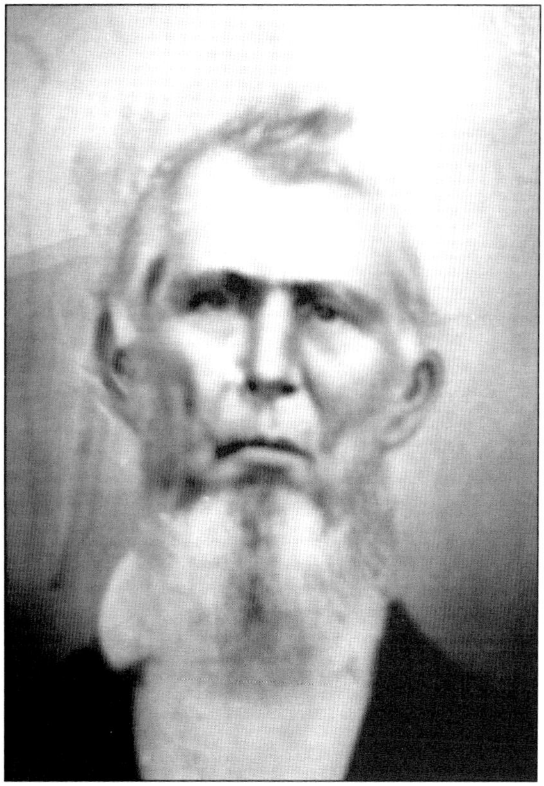

WILLIAMS CHANCELLOR (1816–1907), C. 1890. Williams Chancellor started Chancellor's Ferry around 1860, just before the Civil War. Chancellor's Ferry was the way the people of Childersburg crossed the Coosa River into Shelby County. (Courtesy of Mary Farr Stone Hamby and Mike Hamby.)

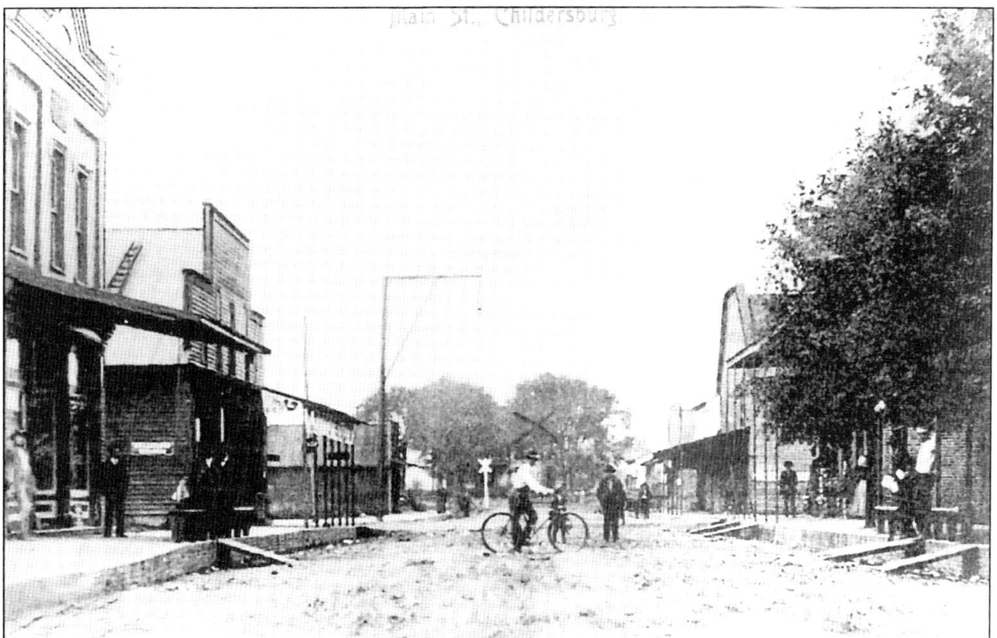

DOWNTOWN CHILDERSBURG, C. 1900. Unfortunately the person on the bicycle is unidentified. This is one of the oldest photographs of downtown Childersburg. Notice the dirt roads and the plank sidewalks. (Courtesy of the Earle A. Rainwater Memorial Library.)

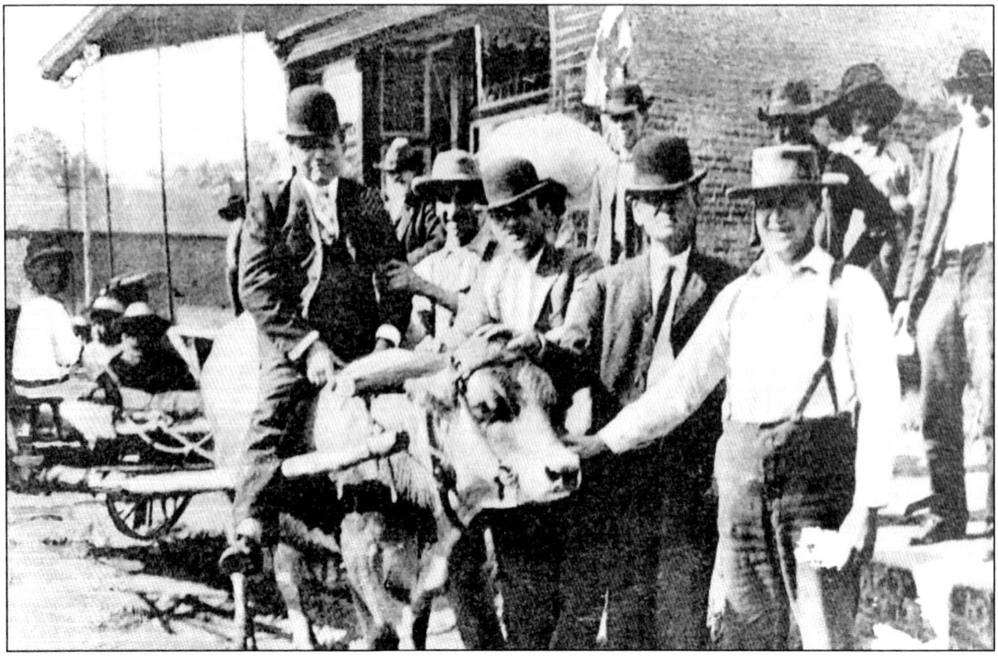

Reeves Men, c. 1920. These early residents of Childersburg have been identified as Reeves men. The five men on the curb are unidentified. Trion Reeves's son is mounted on what appears to be an ox yoked to a wagon. The other men are, from left to right, unidentified, Trion Reeves (born 1880), Marion Reeves (born 1870), and Francis John Thompson "Thomps" Reeves (born 1873). Notice the style of the hats. (Courtesy of the Earle A. Rainwater Memorial Library.)

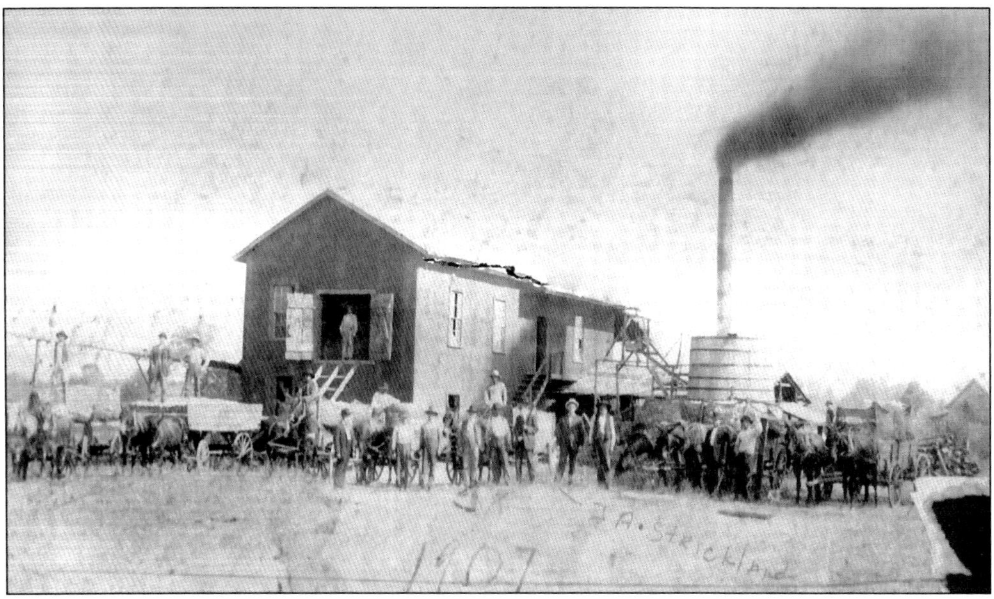

Earliest Photograph of Cliett's Gin, 1907. Notice the man standing in the loft area. Someone has written on the original photograph "1907" as well as "J. A. Strickland" with a line pointing into the crowd. Jerry A. Strickland became mayor pro tempore for the city of Childersburg during the population boom of World War II. (Courtesy of Patricia Teague Wesley Godfrey.)

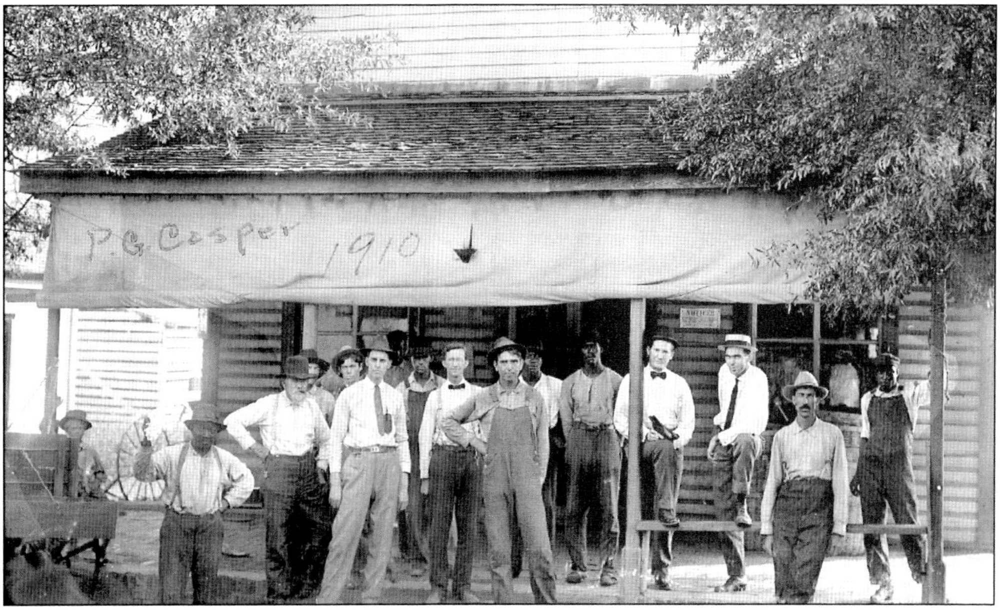

General Mercantile, 1910. This store is believed to have been located on Eighth Avenue. Shown here are, from left to right, Elbert Davis, unidentified, Demps Oden Sr., unidentified, Elbert Conville, Alvin Hobbs, unidentified, Leonard Heath, Sim Cosper, Boling Cosper, two unidentified, an unnamed shoe salesman, P. G. Cosper, and Leo Henderson. (Courtesy of Jane Limbaugh Allen.)

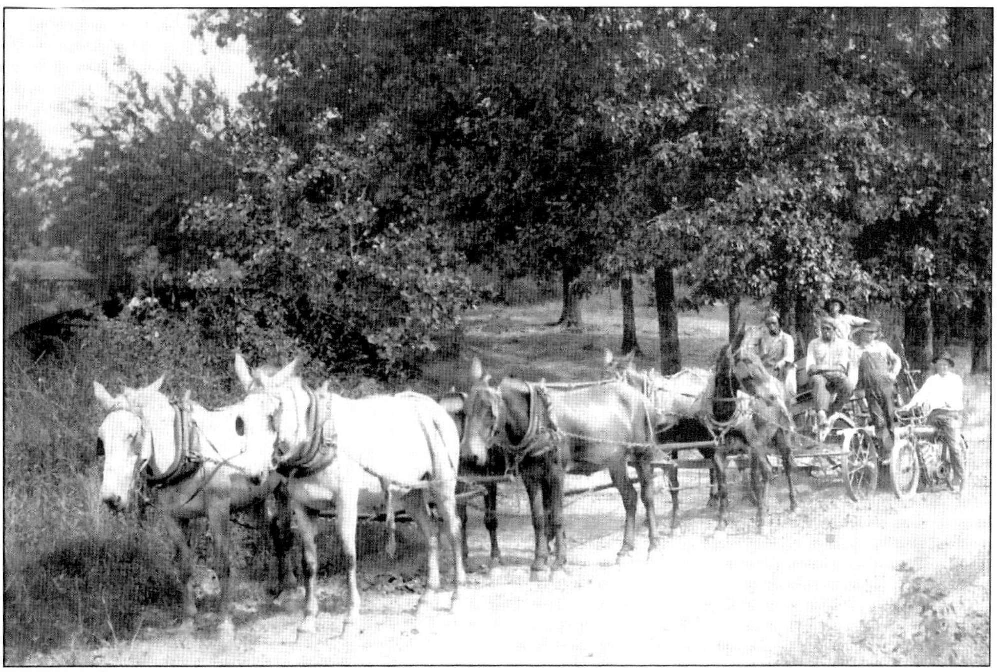

Talladega County Road Crew, c. 1910. E. V. Ogletree (1883–1957) is the supervisor on the roadster. He was working for Talladega County. Their job was to scrape the dirt roads with this horse-and-wagon contraption. His crew is unidentified at this time. (Courtesy of Howard "Bucky" Riddle.)

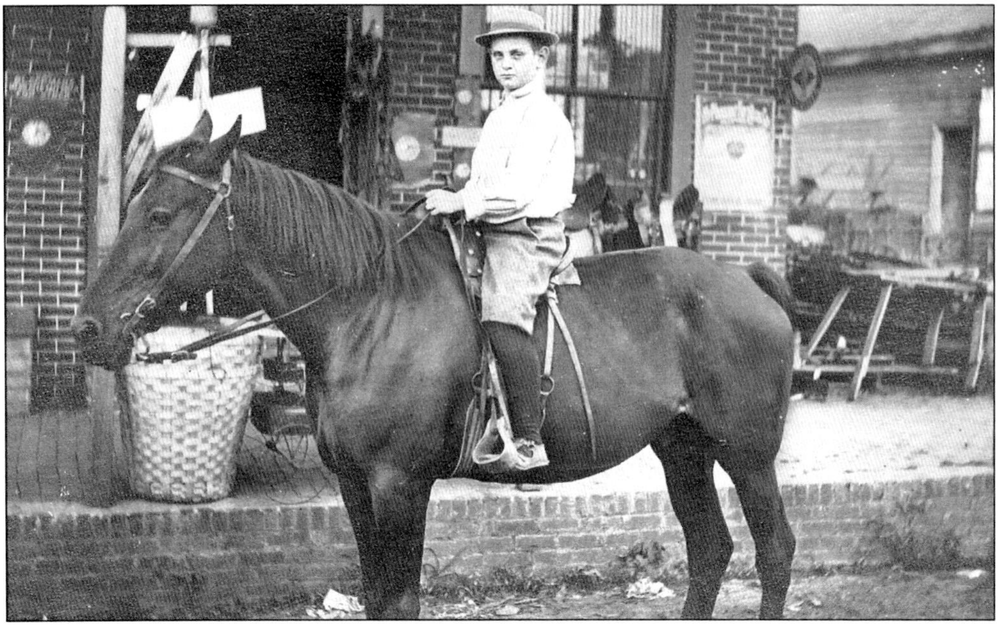

WILLIAM HENRY CLIETT, 1911. This photograph was taken outside Cliett's Hardware. Henry is about 10 years old and riding his horse. William Henry Cliett served two terms as mayor for Childersburg and several years on the city council. He attended local schools as well as Vanderbilt University. He was a farmer and a merchant for over 45 years. His father's store, Cliett Hardware, was among the oldest businesses in Childersburg. Cliett was director of the First National Bank of Childersburg, which he helped create. He served on the board of directors of the National Securities Insurance Company of Elba and was director of the National Skeet Association. (Courtesy of Frances Hudson.)

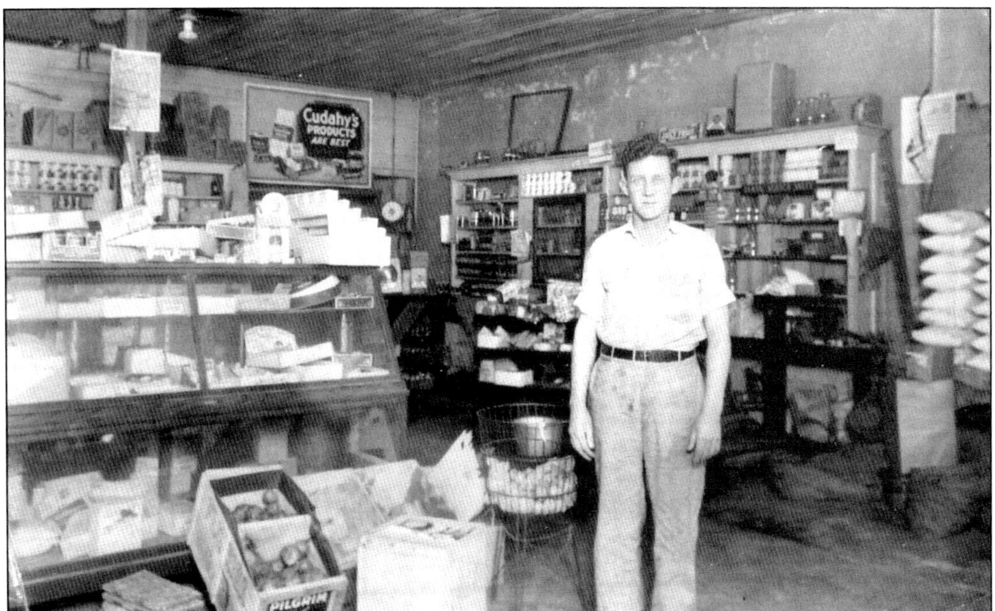

VEAZEY'S GROCERY, C. 1931. Veazey's Grocery was located in downtown Childersburg. The man in the photograph is the owner, Wallace H. Veazey. (Courtesy of Kim Veazey Knight.)

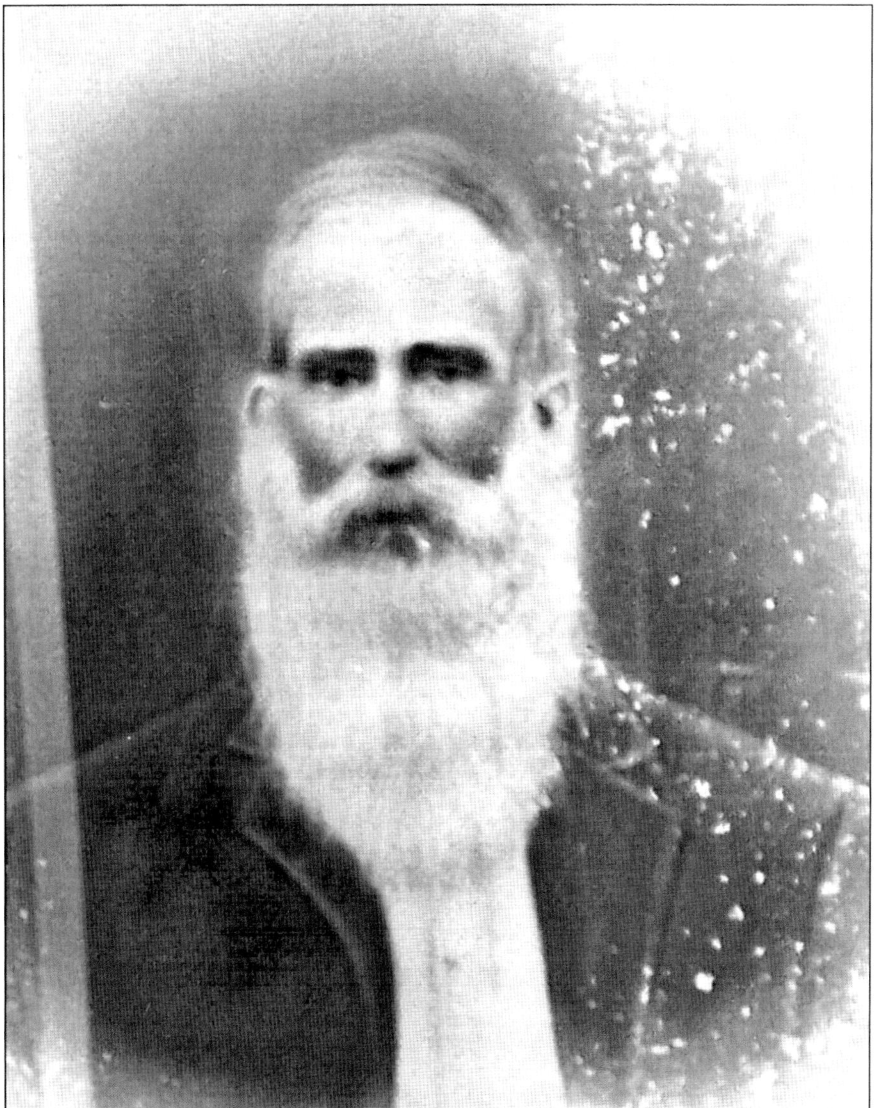

JAMES ALONZA FINN I, C. 1915. James Alonza Finn I was born in Childersburg on December 10, 1853. He married Virginia Hulley Hughes. James and Virginia owned the first Finn Hotel across the street from the Southern Depot and the Finn Saloon on Ninth Avenue and Southern Street. One night, a Yankee got off the train and checked into the Finn Hotel. He came into the saloon and ordered a whiskey. The locals made fun of the way he talked and kept trying to pick a fight with him. James asked the local ruffians to leave because this "Yankee" was his paying customer. The locals waited for the Yankee outside the pub. As the man walked outside, they all attacked him. James went out to help the Yankee fight them off, but, to his surprise, he noticed the man didn't need any help at all. They all knew they had seen that man before . . . in the newspaper! He was John L. Sullivan, passing through on the train coming from Richburg, Mississippi, from his last fight, where he had won the World Heavyweight Championship from Jake Kilrain on July 8, 1889. For some time, Childersburg was abuzz with the news about the prizefighter who came in on the train and whipped all of the hooligans. (Courtesy of Timmy and Lisa Finn.)

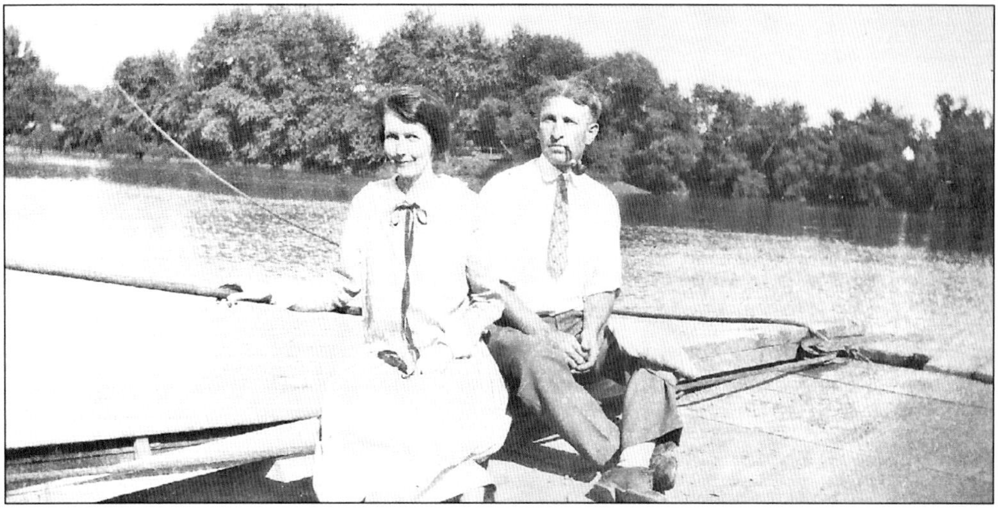

RARE PHOTOGRAPH OF CHANCELLOR'S FERRY, C. 1915. Lena Chancellor Stone and her husband, Ike Stone, are the passengers. The people of Childersburg depended on this ferry to cross the Coosa River into Shelby County. Chancellor's Ferry was started around 1860 by Williams Chancellor. He passed it on to his son, Ike Chancellor, who passed it on to his sons, Forrest, Lee, and Walter Chancellor. Mary Farr Stone Hamby, granddaughter of Ike Chancellor, remembers the charge to cross being 25¢. (Courtesy of Mary Farr Stone Hamby and Mike Hamby.)

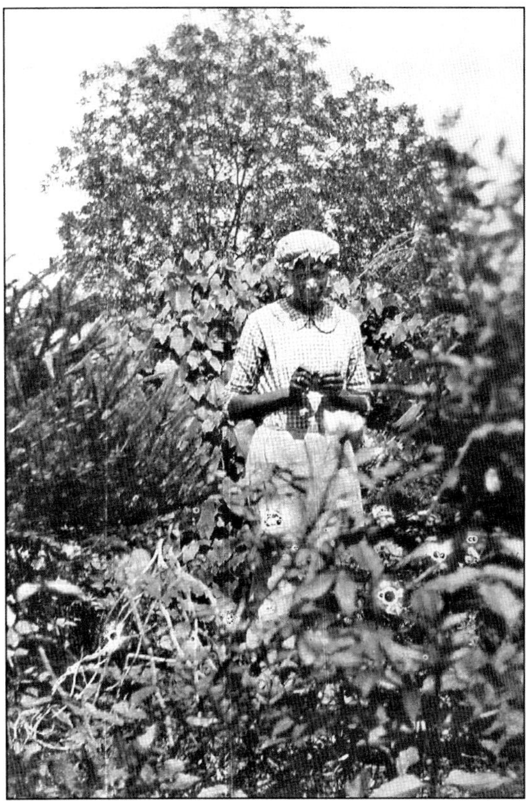

GIRL IN THE FIELDS. Unfortunately, the girl is unidentified and the date uncertain, but the dates of the other photographs in this collection are in the 1920s. (Courtesy of Joyce Smith Caldwell Norris.)

Janie Finn at New South Finn Hotel, c. 1920. At this time, Janie's father, Daniel E. Finn, was proprietor; his father, Jeremiah James Alonza Finn, had passed it on to him. Daniel did renovations, reopened, and moved his family into the hotel around the turn of the century. (Courtesy of Joyce Smith Caldwell Norris.)

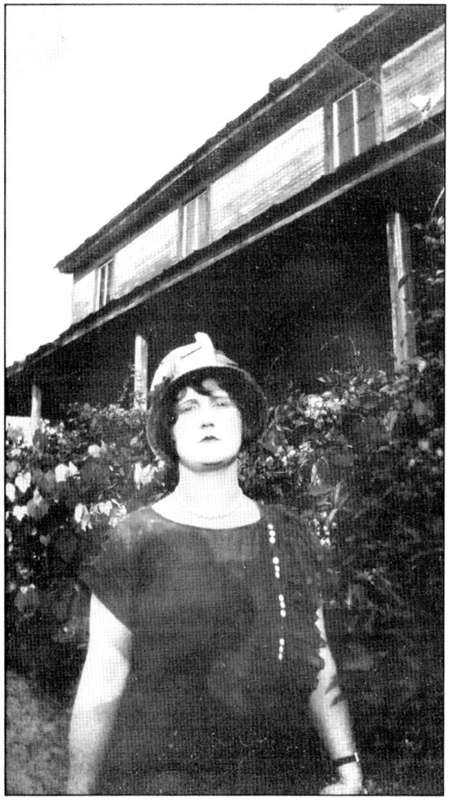

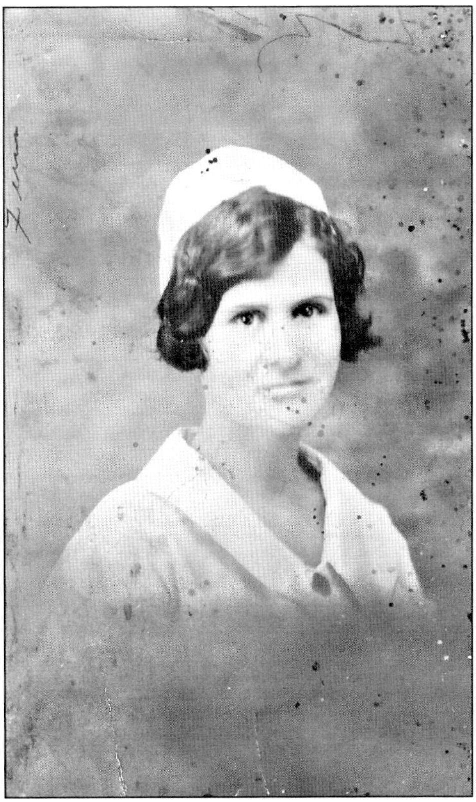

Nurse Edna Giddens, c. 1920. Born in 1895, Edna was the daughter of Madison Whitfield "Babe" Giddens and Annie Hammett. Edna never married. (Courtesy of Ralph and Dolly Finn.)

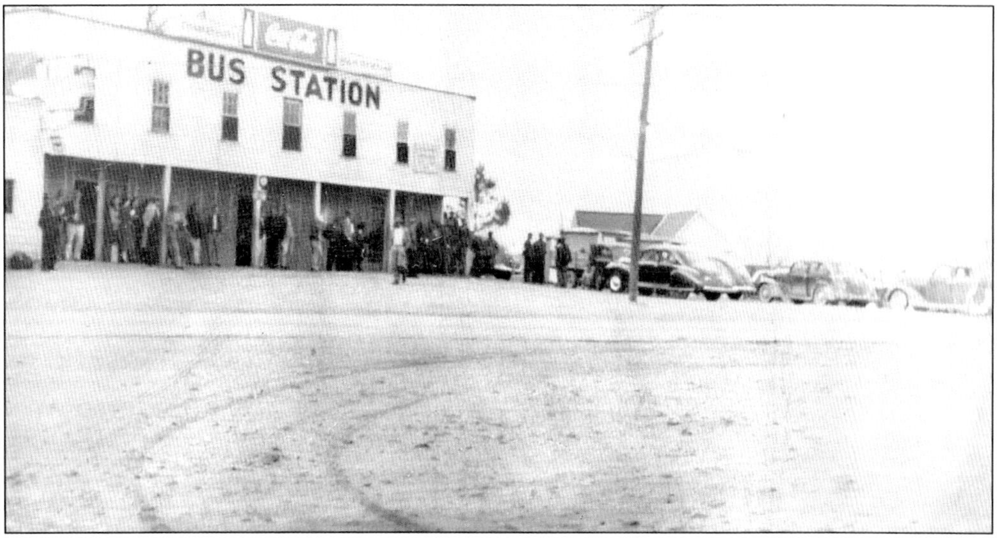

CHILDERSBURG BUS STATION, EARLY 1930S. The bus station stood in the spot where the De Soto Monument stands today at the intersection of Highways 280 and 76. It was built and owned by Constantine "Gus" Frangopoulos, an immigrant from Greece. His descendants still live in Childersburg and the surrounding areas. (Photograph by and courtesy of Katherine Frangopoulos Commander Blackerby.)

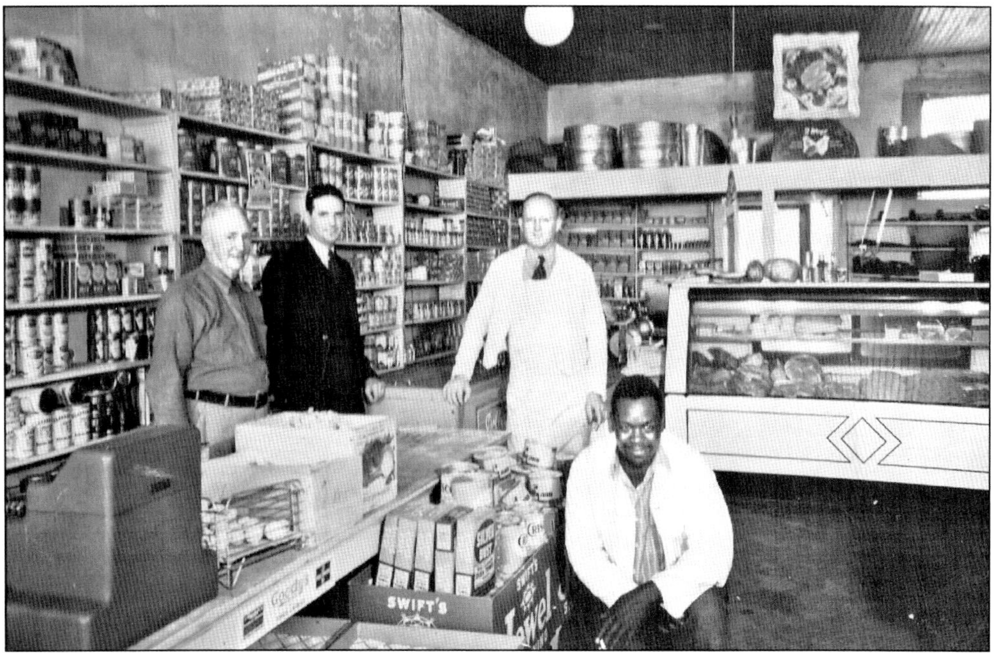

SECOND MOODY BROTHERS GROCERY STORE, C. 1937. Established in 1934 and located on Eighth Avenue, this store was owned by Henry and his brother Chuggy Moody. Pictured from left to right are George W. Moody, sons Henry Moody and Jack Moody, and John Perkins. Henry Moody served 20 years on the city council for Childersburg, was vice chairman of the Talladega County Democratic Committee, was chamber of commerce president, and was appointed in 1959 by Gov. John Patterson to serve on the Talladega County Jury Commission. (Courtesy of Dr. Marcus "Dee" Moody.)

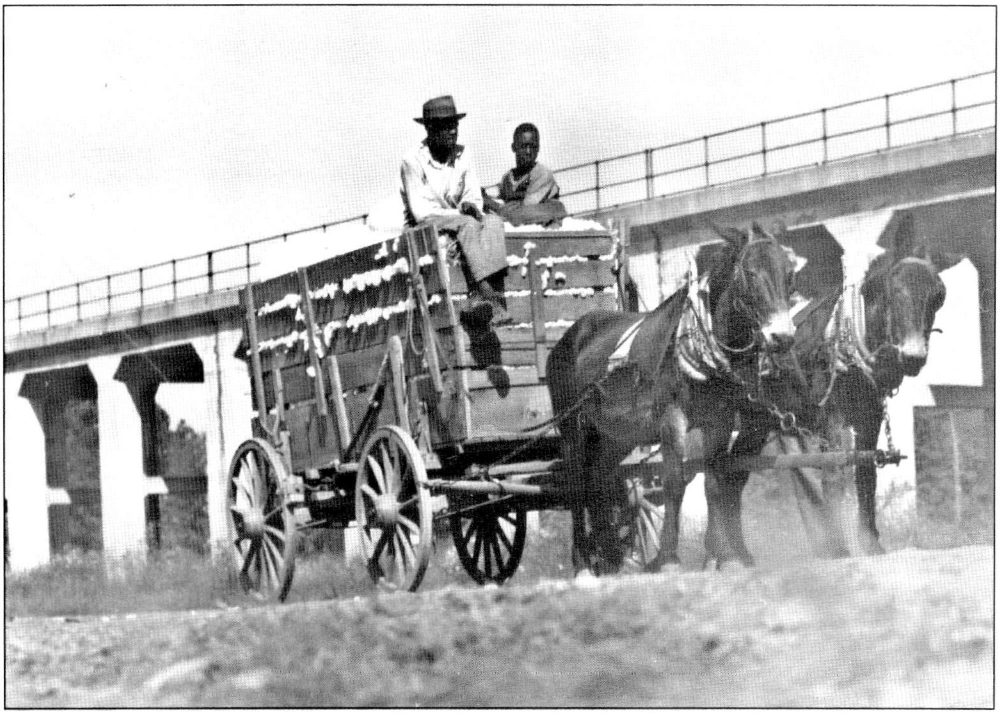

COTTON GINNING TIME. This photograph was made in the 1930s, when Childersburg was still a center for cotton ginning. This man and boy are headed to Cliett's cotton gin with their wagon full of cotton. (Courtesy of the Earle A. Rainwater Memorial Library.)

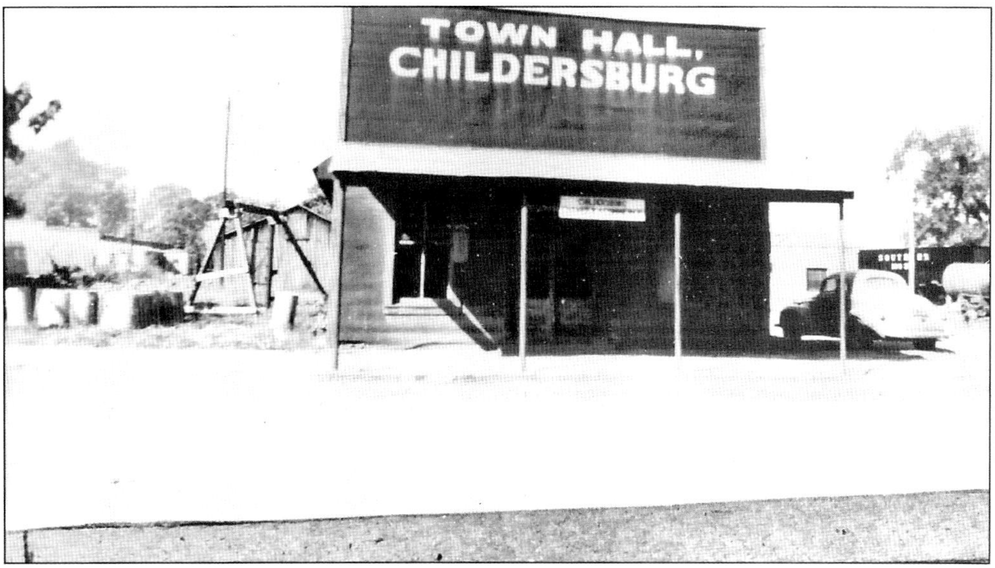

SECOND CITY HALL BUILDING, 1930S. This building was also used as the chamber of commerce in the boom period of World War II and later as the library beginning in 1946. (Photograph by and courtesy of Katherine Frangopoulos Commander Blackerby.)

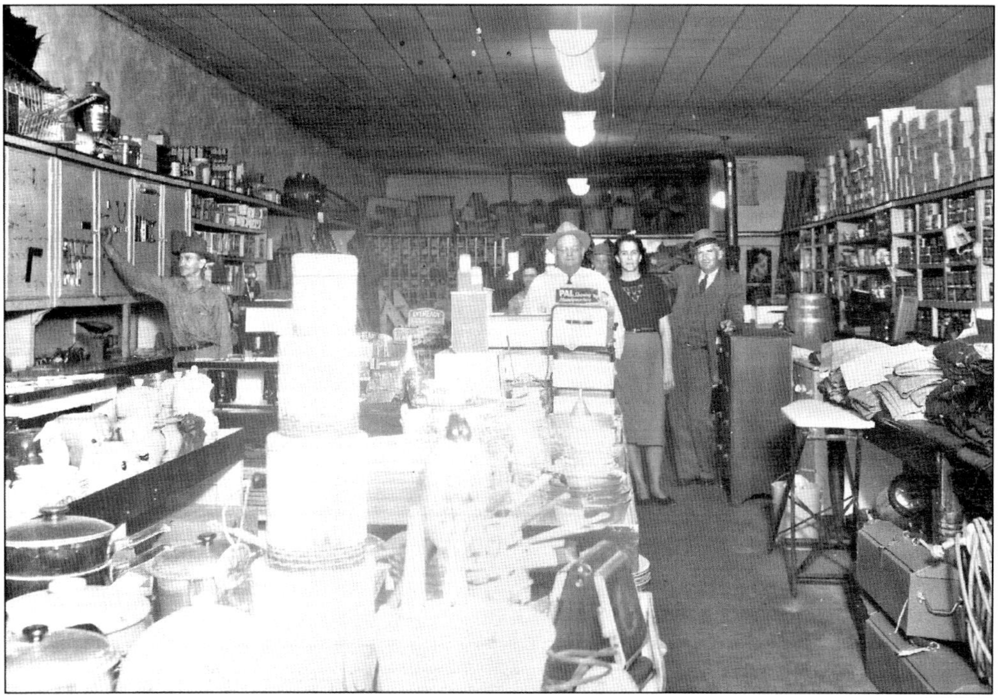

CLIETT'S HARDWARE, C. 1930S. The two people in the back are unidentified. From left to right are Leon Lemuel Smith, Henry Cliett (owner), Ethel Cosper (clerk), and John Robinson (sheriff of Talladega County). (Courtesy of the Earle A. Rainwater Memorial Library.)

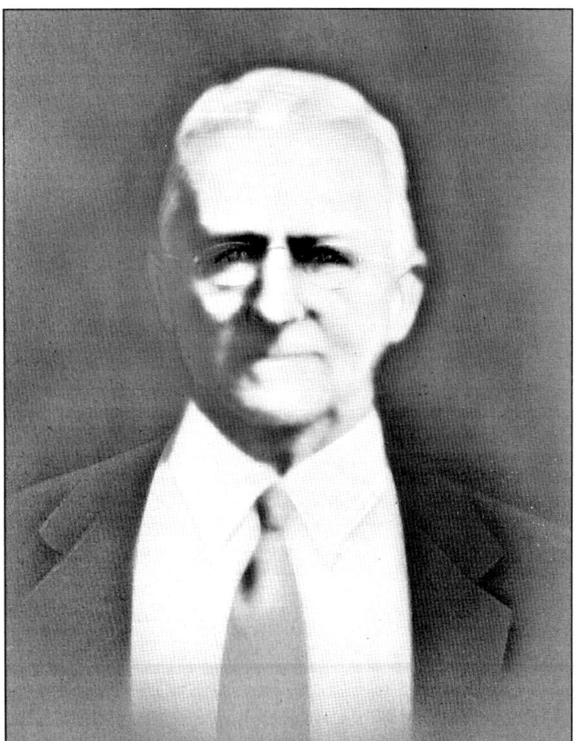

GEORGE WASHINGTON MOODY, C. 1930. George moved to Talladega County from Russell County, where he was born on September 3, 1876. He married Fannie A. Giddens in 1897. They opened a general mercantile store in Childersburg around 1900 that prospered until 1916. As was the custom of the day, George furnished credit to the local families, and when harvest was over in the fall, the farmers would come in and settle up. In 1916, Childersburg suffered unusually heavy rains. The Coosa River and Tallasahatchee and Talladega Creeks flooded, and crops were wiped out. The farmers could not pay, and the store was forced to close. (Courtesy of Dr. Marcus "Dee" Moody.)

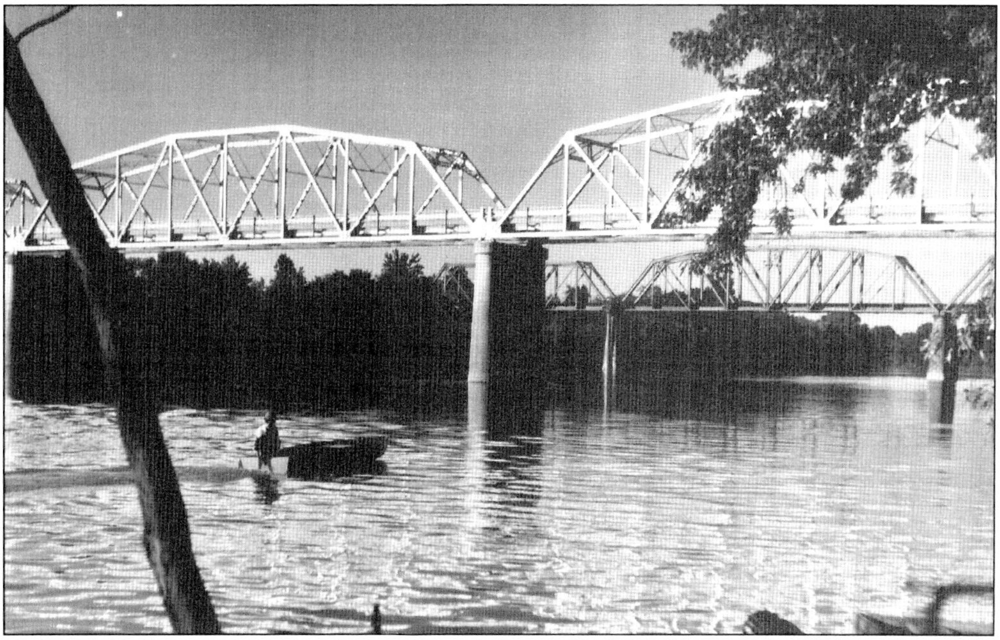

MORGAN'S BRIDGE, C. 1932. This is a rare photograph of the first bridge built for automobiles across the Coosa River between Childersburg and Harpersville. It was built as a toll bridge. Around 1936, it became a free bridge. Later it was believed that the river would be navigated, so the bridge was torn down and a higher one was built so that cargo and tugboats could pass under. (Photograph by and courtesy of Katherine Frangopoulos Commander Blackerby.)

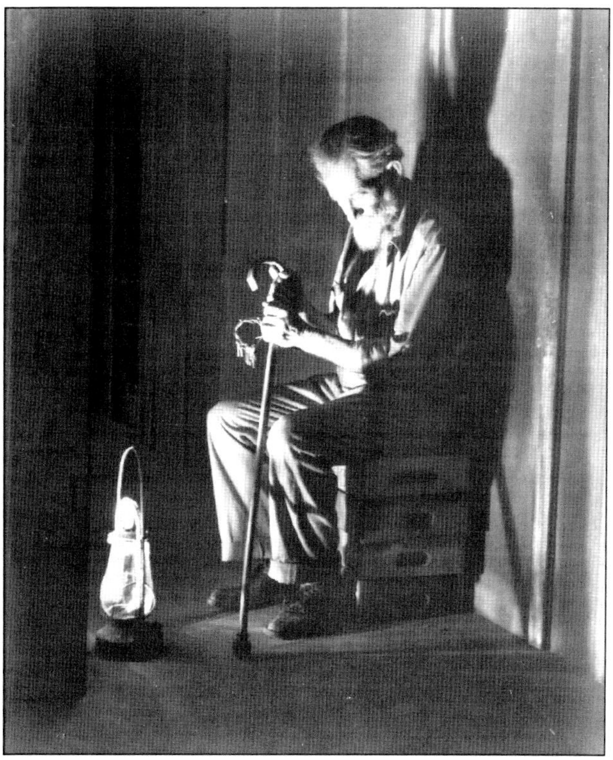

THE NIGHT WATCHMAN, C. 1935. Fred Palmer, also known as "Kilroy," was the night watchman at the Childersburg Bus Station. Katherine Frangopoulos Blackerby took this photograph of him while he was working. Notice how she managed to capture his essence, from the keys and cane in his hands to the lantern and the crates on which he is sitting. His expression is solemn and humbling. Many of Katherine's photographs, including this one, won awards. (Photograph by and courtesy of Katherine Frangopoulos Commander Blackerby.)

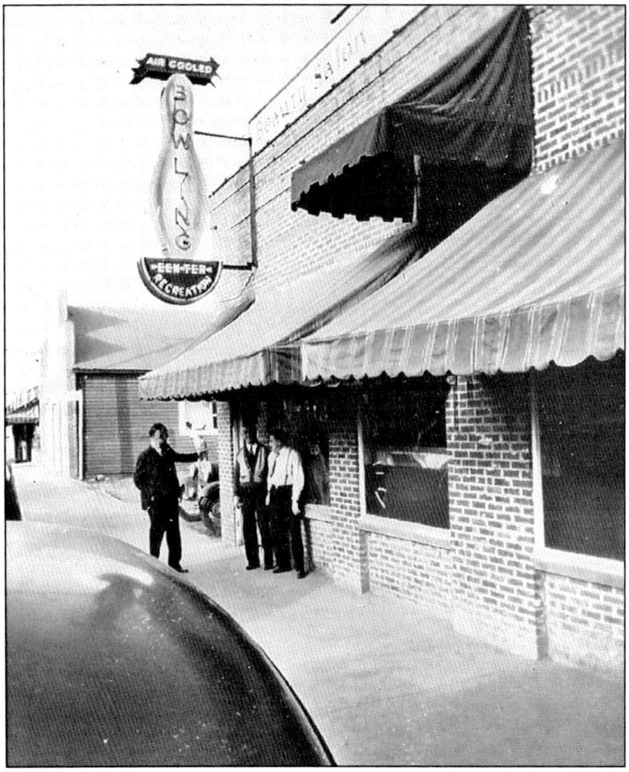

BOWLING ALLEY, C. 1941. This bowling alley was located on Eighth Avenue. It went out of business after World War II, and Moody's Grocery moved into the property. (Courtesy of Clarence Edwin "Mickey" Finn.)

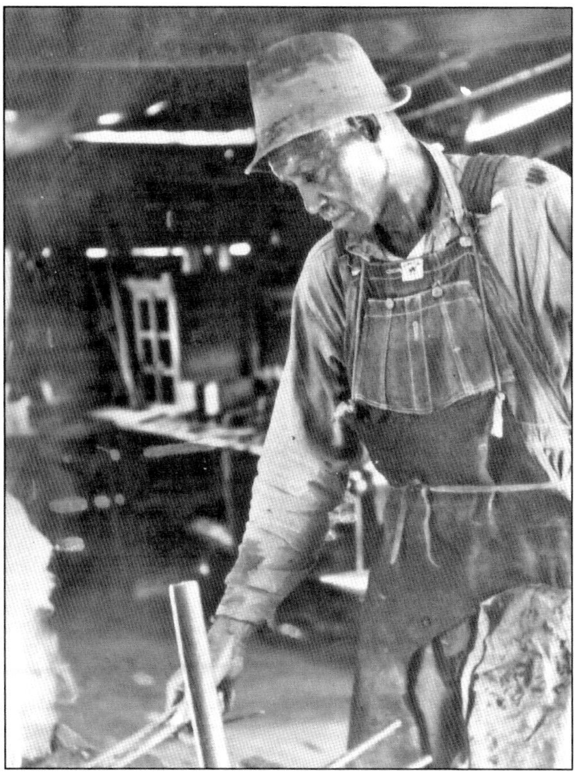

THE BLACKSMITH, C. 1942. John Templeton was a Childersburg blacksmith in the area now known as Pleasant Valley. This is a prize-winning photograph of him working his craft. (Photograph by and courtesy of Katherine Frangopoulos Commander Blackerby.)

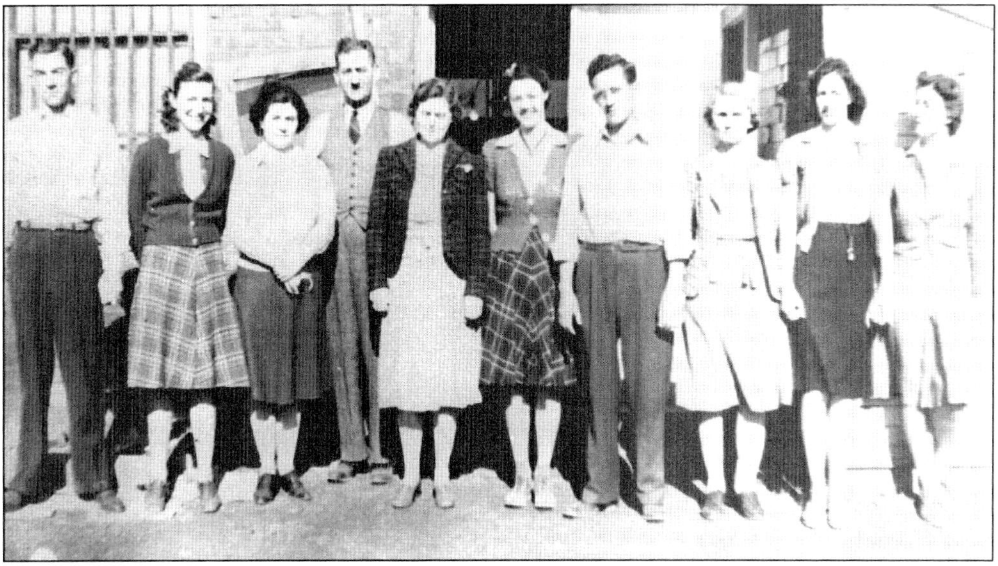

CHILDERSBURG POST OFFICE WORKERS, 1942. Childersburg's post office was established on February 2, 1855. These workers are, from left to right, Dan Spivey, Sarah Anderson, Irene Giddens, unidentified, Annie Louise Ryder-Bush, Mildred Strickland, Wallace Veazey, Annie L. Gardner, Wanda Fuller, and Leona Jones Nichols McCallum. These workers were all very outgoing in their community. Annie Louise Ryder-Bush wrote *Memoirs of Childersburg*, which has been a treasure for the history of the town. She writes of her memories as well as stories about Childersburg told to her by her parents and grandparents. (Courtesy of Jane Limbaugh Allen.)

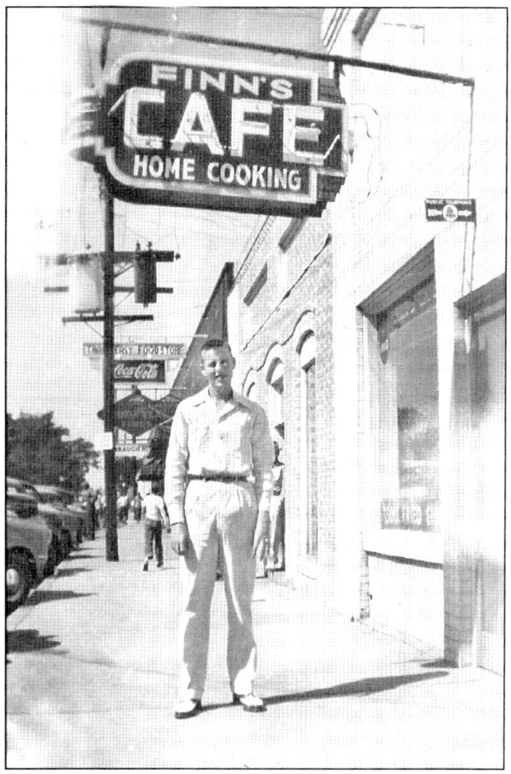

FINN'S CAFÉ, C. 1943. The man in the photograph is unidentified at this time. Finn's Café was owned and operated by William "Bill" Finn during the population boom in Childersburg. (Courtesy of Clarence Edwin "Mickey" Finn.)

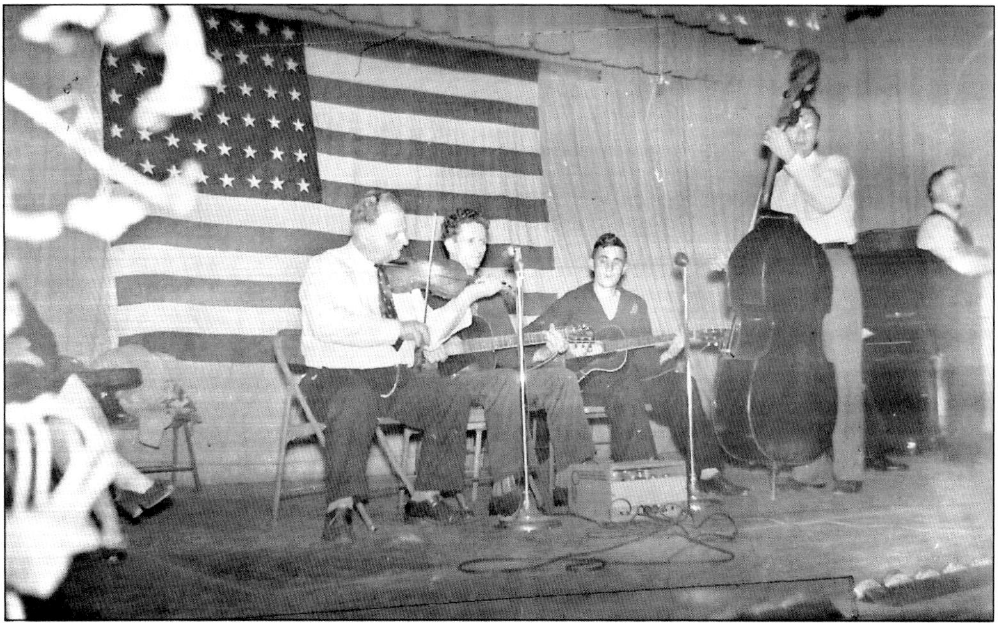

BAND PLAYING AT USO, C. 1943. This photograph was found in the collections of the late Evelyn Conville. The USO was located across the street from the old Childersburg Hospital on the corner of Sixth Avenue and Seventh Street, SW. (Courtesy of Jane Limbaugh Allen.)

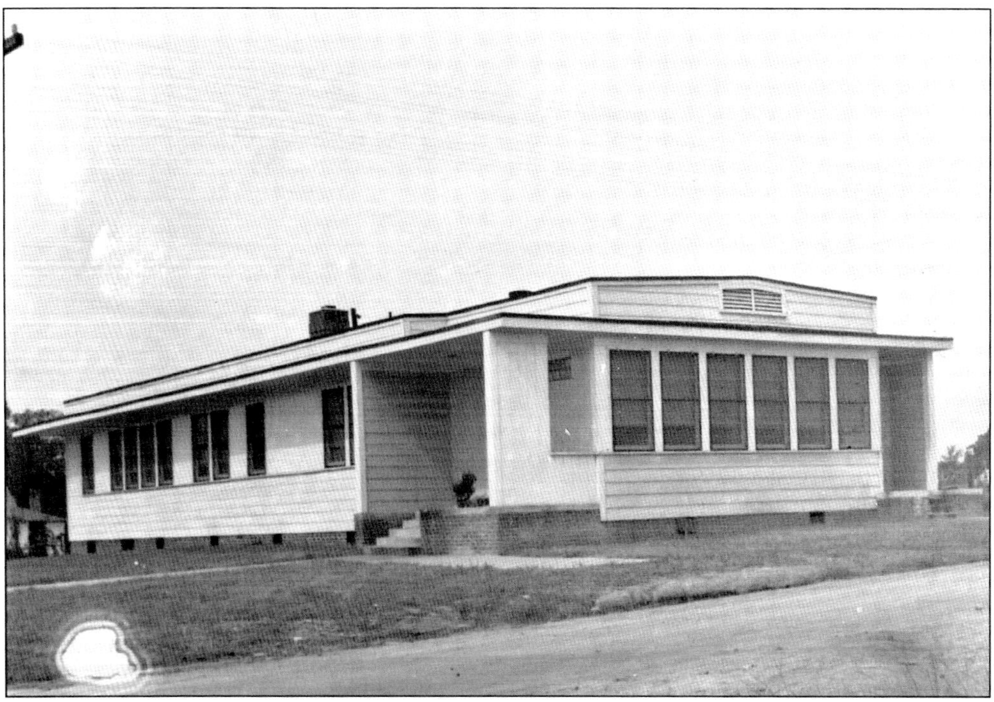

CHILDERSBURG HOSPITAL, C. 1943. The hospital was located on Seventh Street, SW. It was run by Dr. Robert P. Stock and his staff. (Courtesy of the Earle A. Rainwater Memorial Library.)

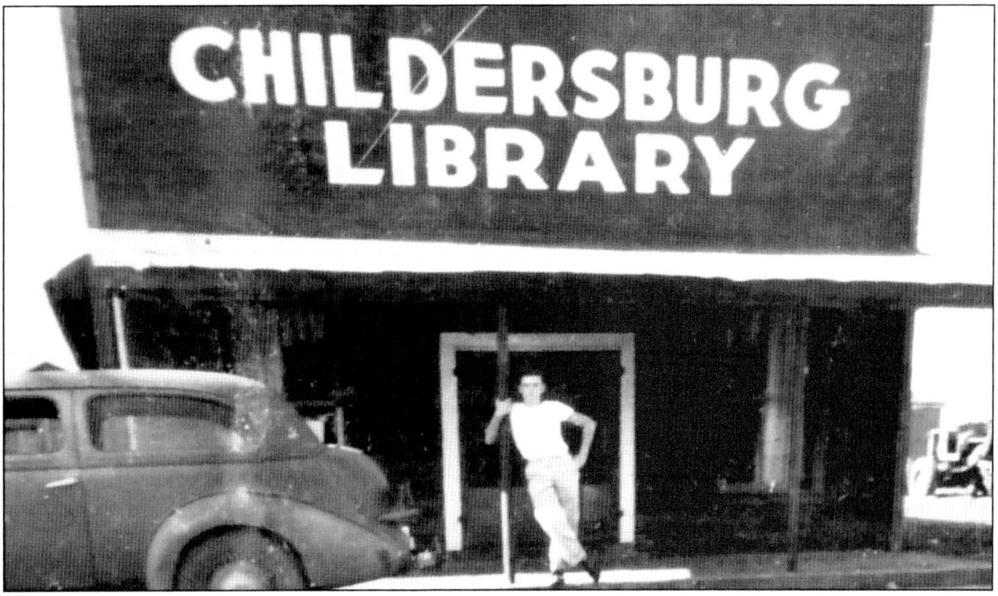

CHILDERSBURG'S FIRST LIBRARY, C. 1946. The man pictured here has been identified as Calvin Spates. Childersburg's first library began with the Ladies Book Club. Their first meeting was on October 10, 1906, at the home of Mollie Oden. Instead of money for dues, each member gave a book that was censored by a committee. The number of books multiplied so quickly that a new librarian was elected every two years to oversee them in her home. In 1946, when the Alabama Ordnance Works closed, the USO donated several hundred books. The old city hall building was used to house these books and opened as the Childersburg Library on March 18, 1946. The Ladies Book Club is still going strong. (Courtesy of the Earle A. Rainwater Memorial Library.)

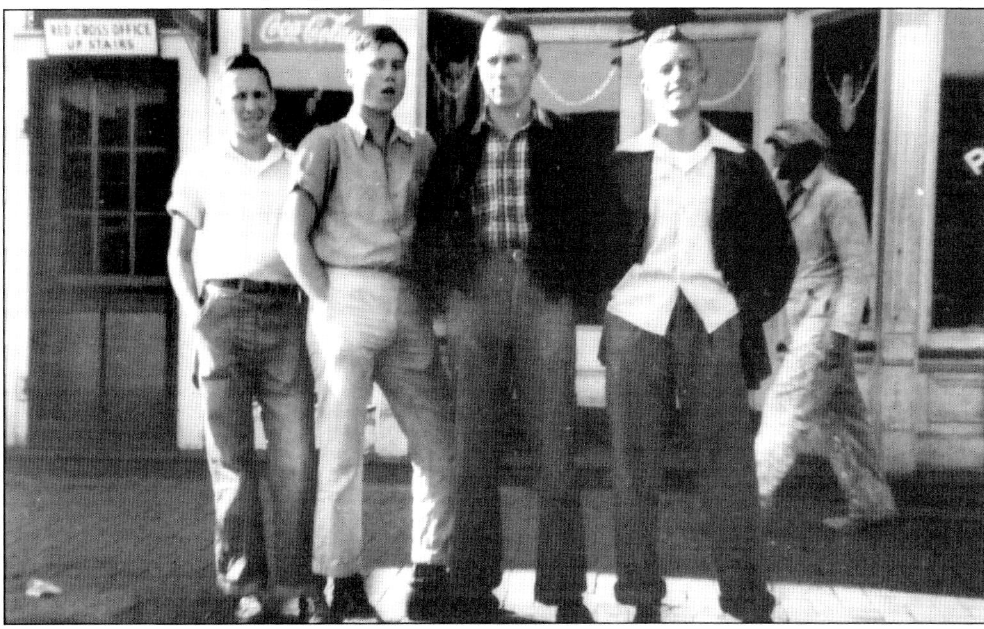

TEENAGERS AT POWELL DRUGS, 1946. Jackie Thomas, Lewis Allen, Doyle Holliday, and Jack Ray are pictured here from left to right. Doyle is the brother of Childersburg native and Hollywood actress Polly Holliday. (Courtesy of Jane Limbaugh Allen.)

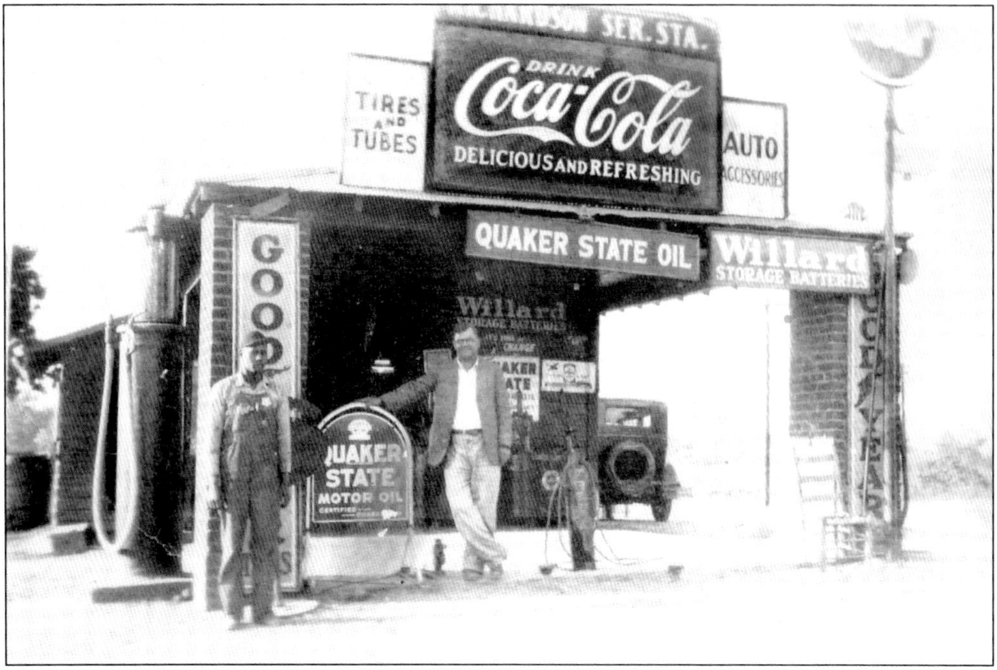

RICHARDSON'S SERVICE STATION. The man on the left is unidentified, and the man on the right is Elbert R. Conville. (Courtesy of Jane Limbaugh Allen, Evelyn Conville Collection.)

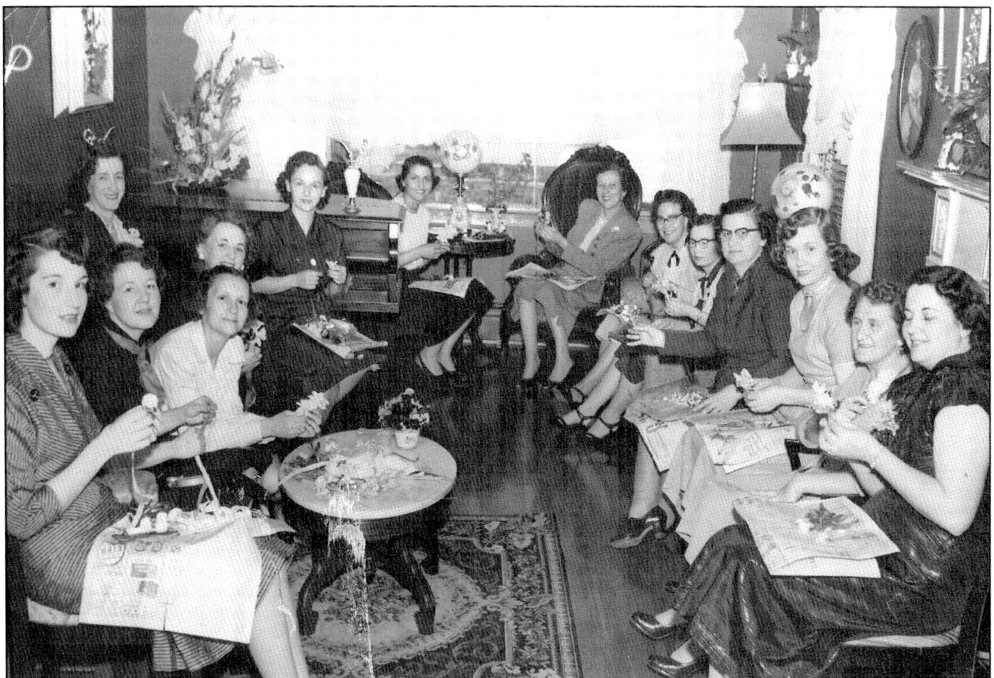

COOSA GARDEN CLUB, C. 1952–1953. From left to right are unidentified, Jackie Daffron, Betty Fitzgerald, Leona McCallum, Grace Peterson, Hilda Campbell, Ollie Limbaugh, Fern Green, Violet Phillips, Helen Duke, Evelyn Conville, Doris Richardson, Dorothy Merrill, and Paula Jones. (Courtesy of Jane Limbaugh Allen.)

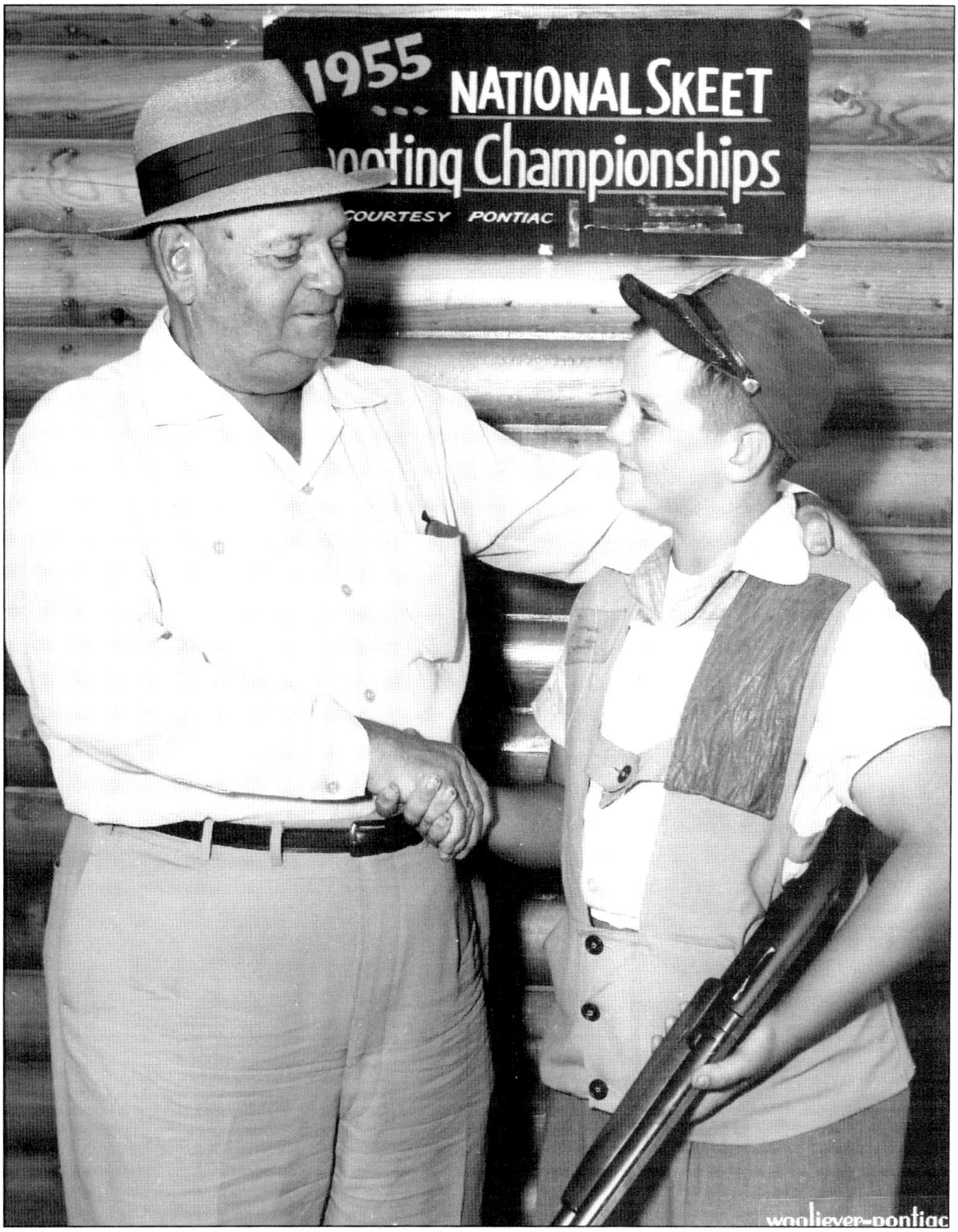

Henry and Miner Cliett, 1955. This is a photograph of Henry and Miner (1944–1992) after winning the National Skeet Shoot Championship. Miner was 11 years old at this time. At one time, Miner Cliett held 18 world titles in skeet shooting. Miner was a member of the U.S. Shooting Team selected to shoot in the World Skeet Shoot Championship held in Oslo, Norway, in 1961 (he was 17 years old), in which he won the gold medal. He was written about in too many publications to mention, including *Sports Illustrated*, *Field and Stream*, *Southern Outdoors*, and the *United States Congressional Record* in July 1958. He also appeared on the nationally syndicated *Arthur Godfrey Show* at the age of 14. (Courtesy of the Earle A. Rainwater Memorial Library.)

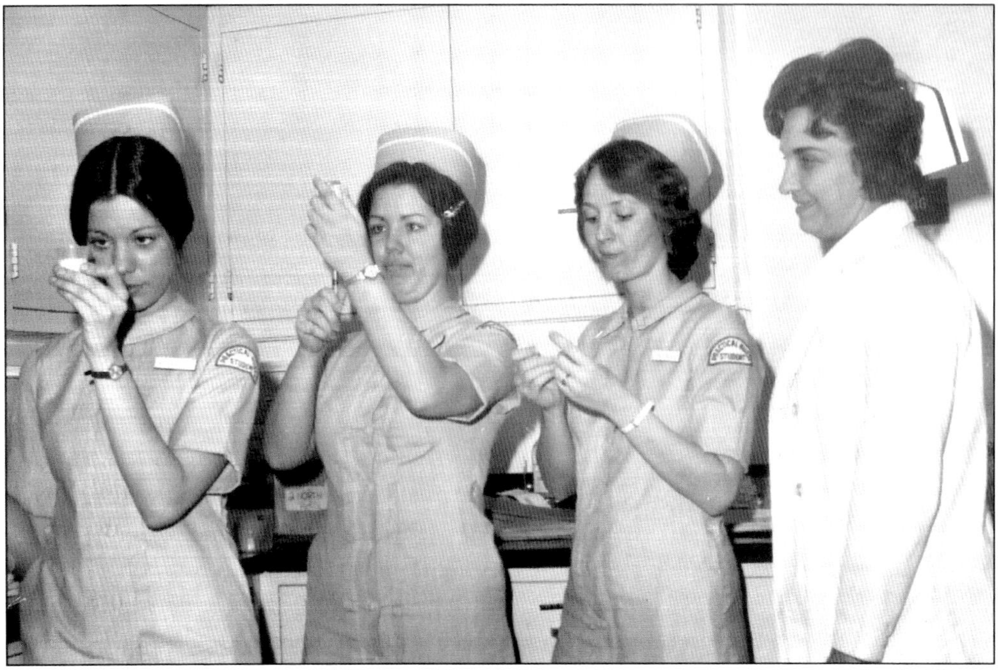

NUNNELLEY NURSING, C. 1966. Pictured from left to right are nursing students Belinda Moore, unidentified, and Janelle Poe with June Ward Bacon, a nursing instructor at N. F. Nunnelley State Technical College in Childersburg. (Courtesy of the Earle A. Rainwater Memorial Library.)

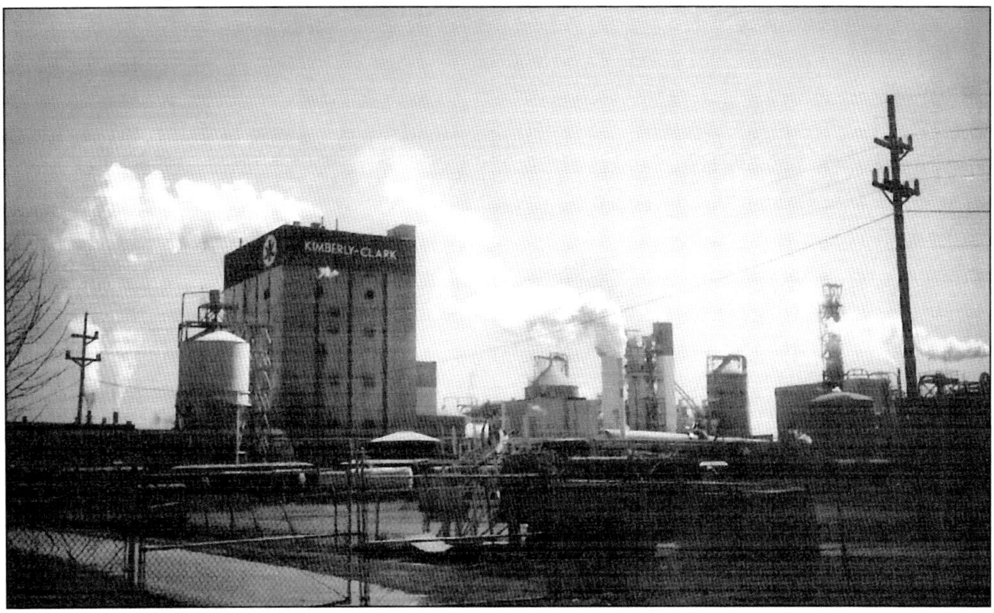

KIMBERLY CLARKE CORPORATION, C. 1972. Kimberly Clarke was a descendant of the old sawmills in Childersburg. It provided the largest number of good jobs for the community. It was purchased from Coosa River Newsprint, who began after the Alabama Ordnance Works closed after World War II. Kimberly Clark sold to U.S. Alliance, and U.S. Alliance sold to Bowater Newsprint. Bowater still provides the largest number of good jobs to the community. (Courtesy of the Earle A. Rainwater Memorial Library.)

Four

CHURCHES

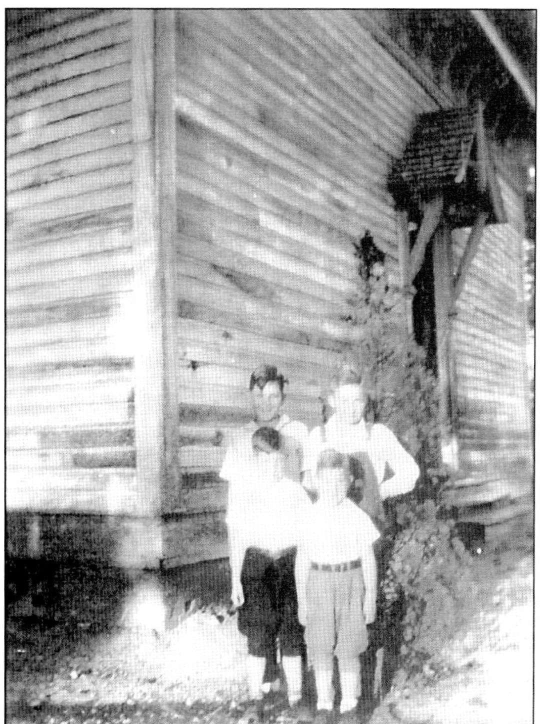

CHILDREN AT THE OLD METHODIST CHURCH, C. 1930. From left to right are (first row) Lewis Finn and unidentified; (second row) Johnny Blocker (or possibly Hagan Limbaugh) and Mickey Finn. (Courtesy of Clarence Edwin "Mickey" Finn.)

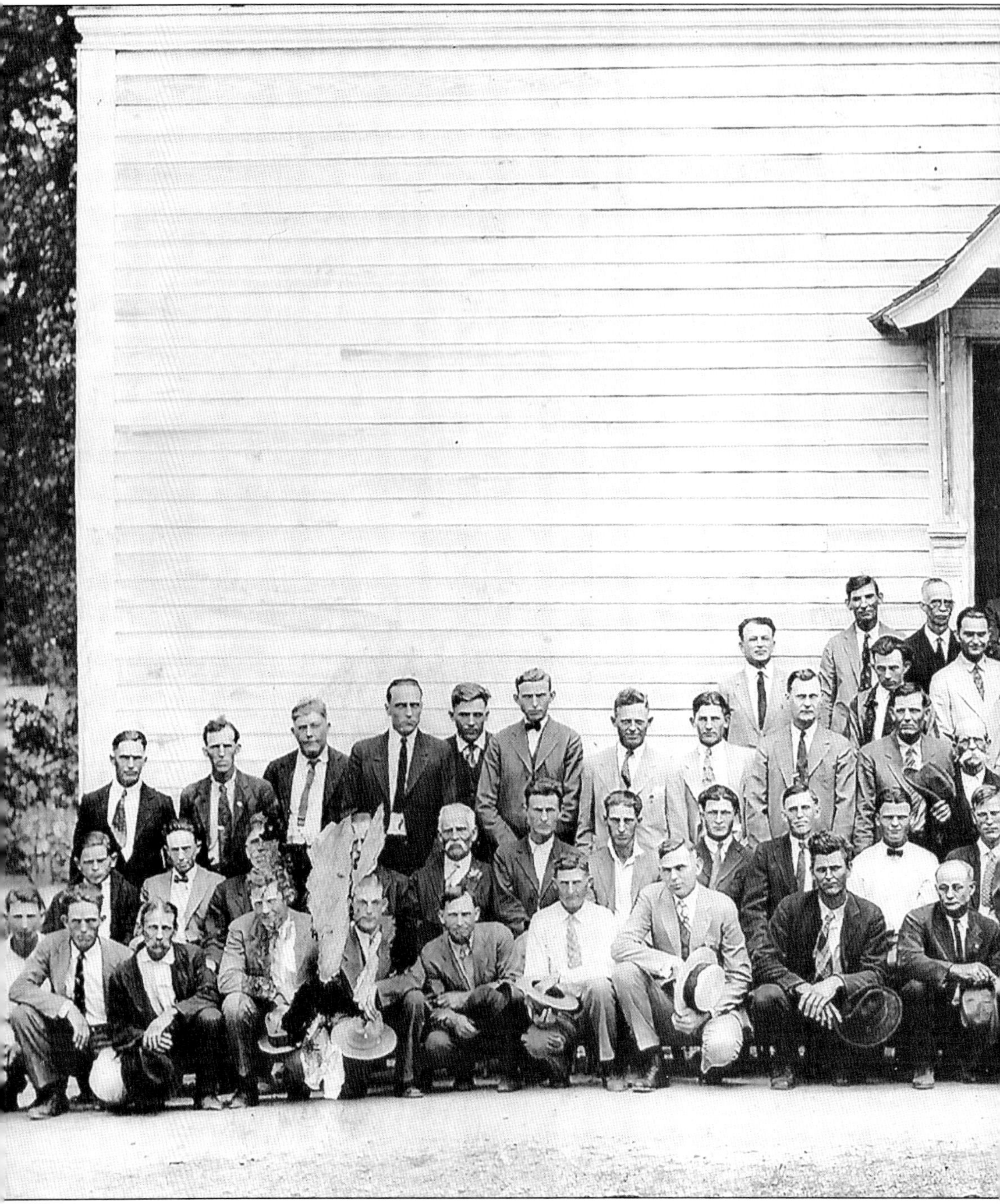

THE METHODIST MEN'S SUNDAY SCHOOL IN 1926. This photograph was taken in front of the original Methodist church. Shown here are (first row) two unidentified men, ? Burton, four unidentified men, P. G. Cosper, ? Horton, Malley Limbaugh, John Haywood, Will Anderson, George Strain, France Rowland, Bruce McDowell, Offord Cull, two unidentified men, and Jeremiah James Alonza Finn; (second row) 20 unidentified men, with possibly W. Jesse Limbaugh at far right; (third row) unidentified, Albert Burton, Arthur Riley, Luke Kidd,

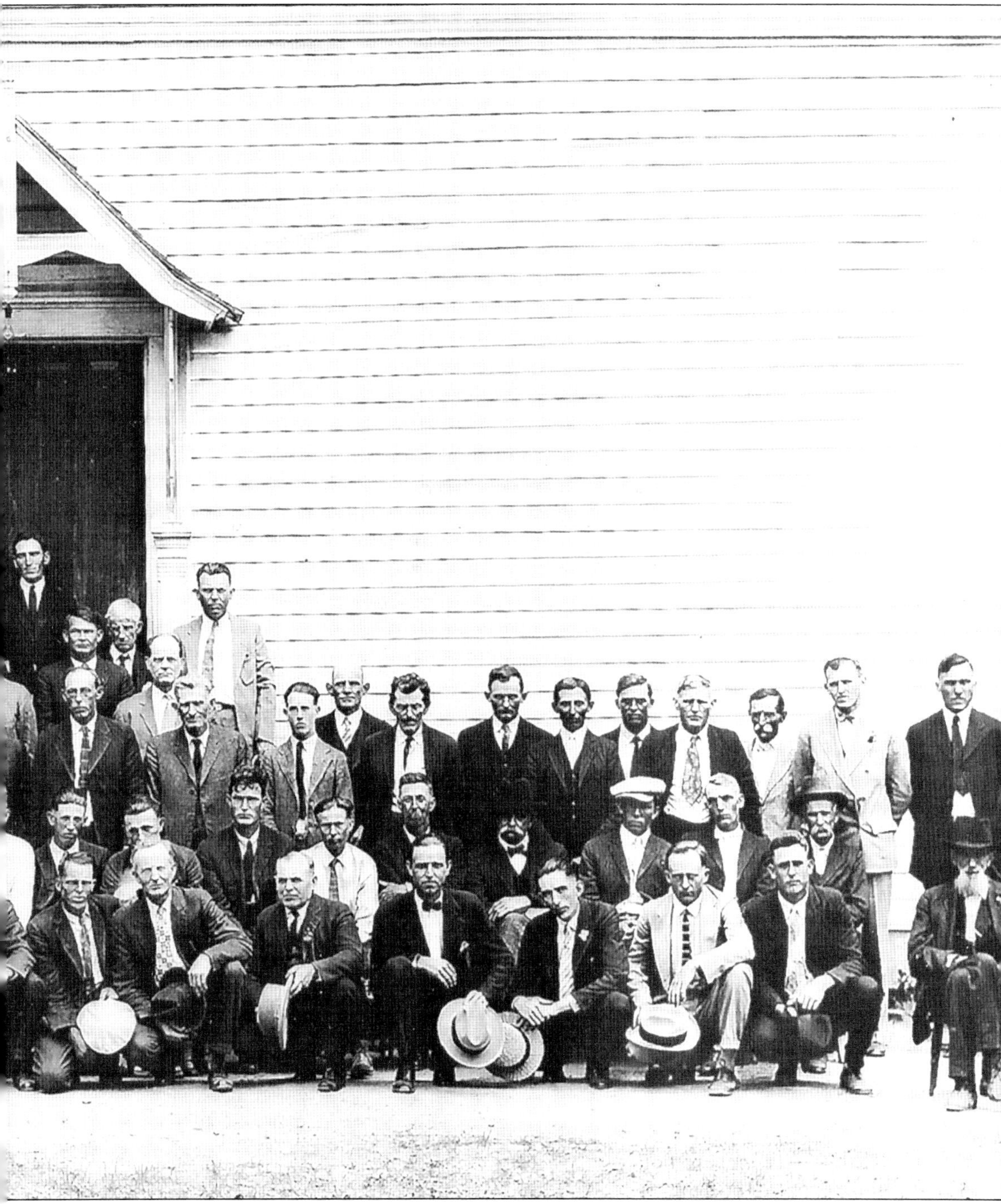

unidentified, Graham Cosper, two unidentified men, ? Tinklepaw, three unidentified men, ? Horton, six unidentified men, ? Burton, G. Hagan, and three unidentified men; (fourth row) Horace Wilson, unidentified, Coleman Pricket, Forest Chandler, and Jerry Strickland; (fifth row) unidentified, W. B. Tate, R. T. Jones, an unidentified preacher, Demps Bussey Oden, and unidentified. (Courtesy of Jane Limbaugh Allen.)

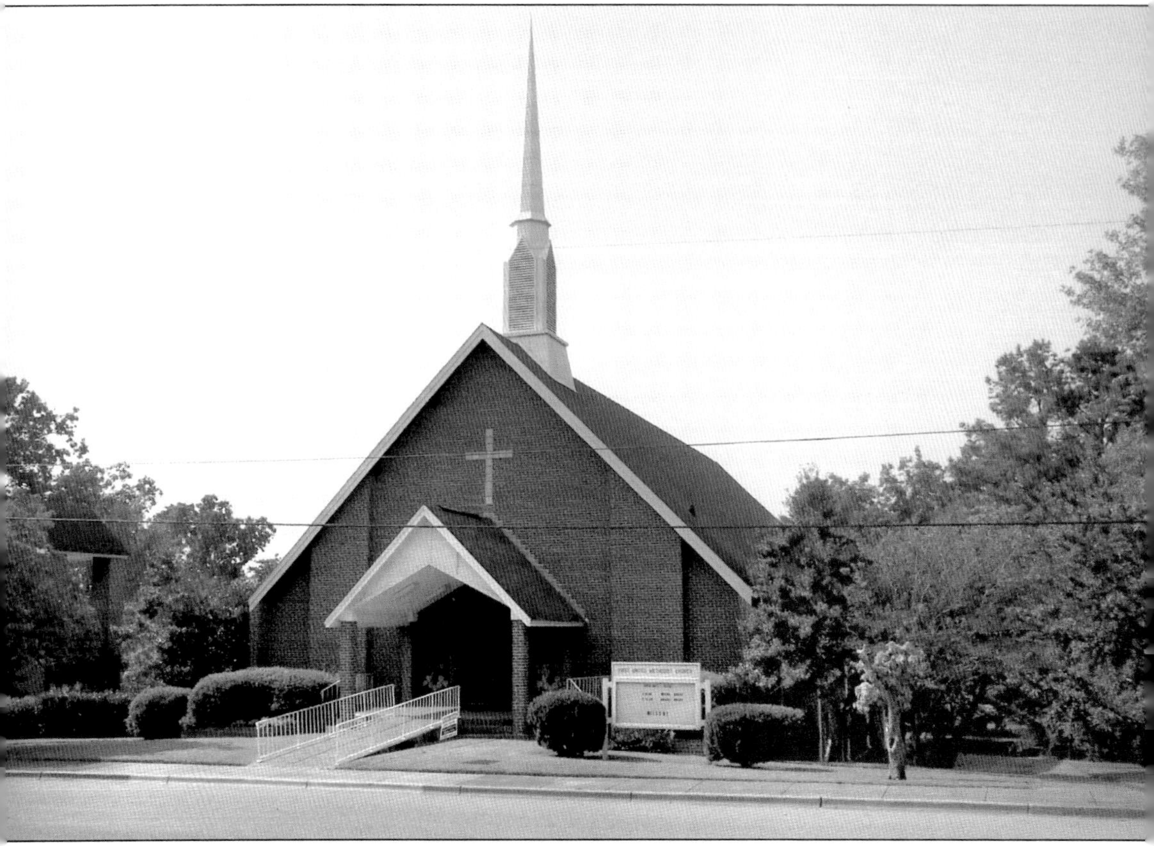

FIRST UNITED METHODIST CHURCH. In 1832 at the Methodist Conference, the Talladega Mission was established. About 1846, the Fayetteville circuit was formed and Fourmile Church was organized. Childersburg Methodists had to travel four miles to church. Mrs. William Henry Keith and Dempsey B. Oden decided in 1870 that they would build a church in Childersburg. The lot was donated by Capt. John Piney Oden. He also donated the land for the Childersburg Cemetery. Augustus Carlisle, a Baptist, was given the building contract. The church was built in 1871 under a brush arbor near the old Childersburg Cemetery. The church was served by the circuit riders, a group of traveling preachers. By 1895, the membership had moved closer into the town of Childersburg, leaving the church "off center." The contract was given to Bill Stewart, and Charlie Butler donated new land. A five-member board of deacons decided to move the church closer to town. The church was put on huge logs and pulled with chains down Sixth Avenue to its current location. It took all summer to move the church. On Sundays, they stopped wherever they were and had church services.

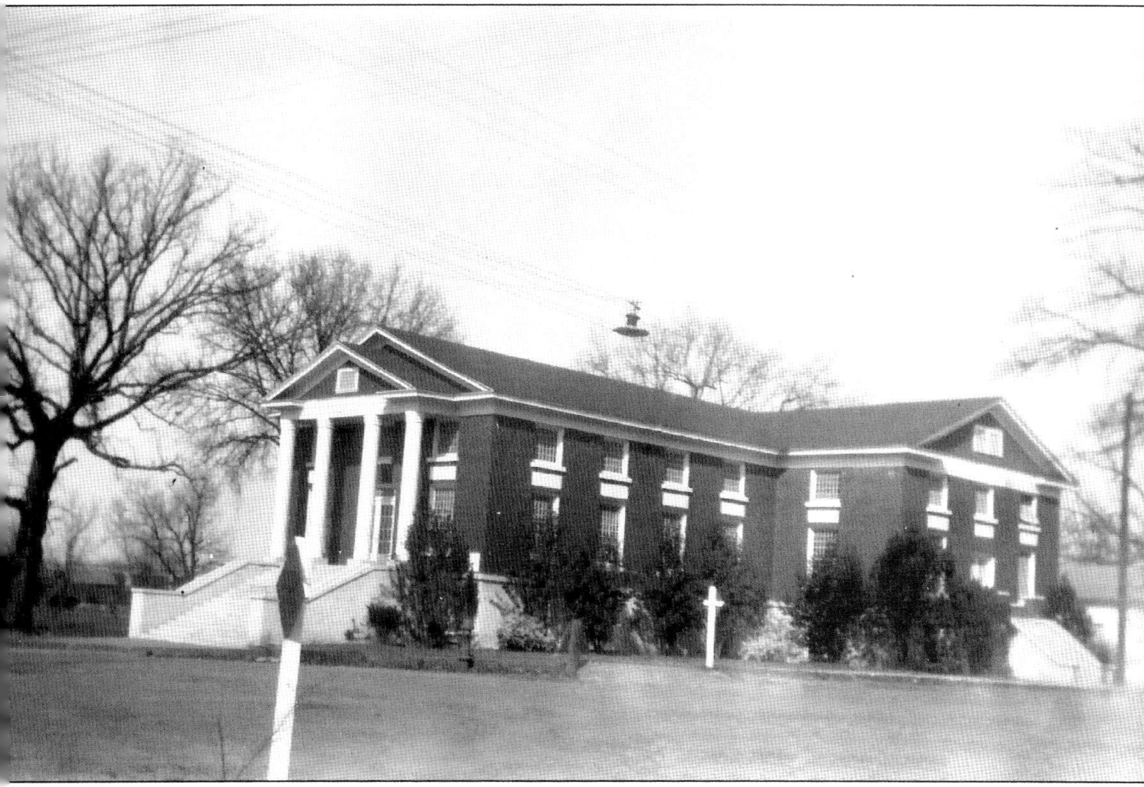

FIRST BAPTIST CHURCH, 1942. The first Baptist church in Childersburg was built in 1871 and established in 1872. The Baptist and Methodist churches were fund-raising and building simultaneously. The Methodist church was built by a Baptist, and the Baptist church was built by a Methodist. There was a general feeling of goodwill and helpfulness between the two churches. Capt. J. P. Oden and his brother Demps B. Oden, both Methodists, donated the lumber to the Baptists for their church. George Butler donated the lot. There was a great deal of donated labor and material as well. The first pastor was Dr. Washington Wilkes, who served until 1875. In 1927, a major building expansion took place. In addition, a new auditorium was erected and the remaining part of the original church was converted into Sunday school rooms. (Courtesy of Clarence Edwin "Mickey" Finn.)

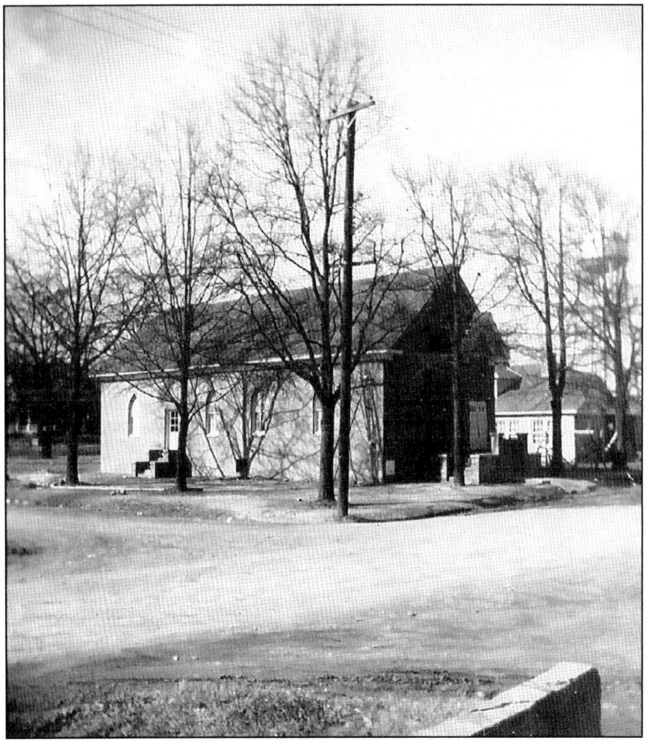

FIRST CHURCH OF CHRIST. The Church of Christ was first located on Eighth Avenue. This church was started by Willie Pauline Montgomery Cliett, J. M. Barnes, and John T. Lewis. The congregation began meeting in 1907 in the home of Mrs. Cliett. There were 17 people at the first meeting. In 1909, they began meeting in the second floor of the city hall building on First Street. A lot was purchased on the corner of Third Street and Eighth Avenue, and this building was erected in 1911 and later bricked. The land for the present Church of Christ on the plant road (Coosa Pines Drive) was donated by B. C. Goodpasture, and the building was dedicated in 1962. (Courtesy of Clarence Edwin "Mickey" Finn.)

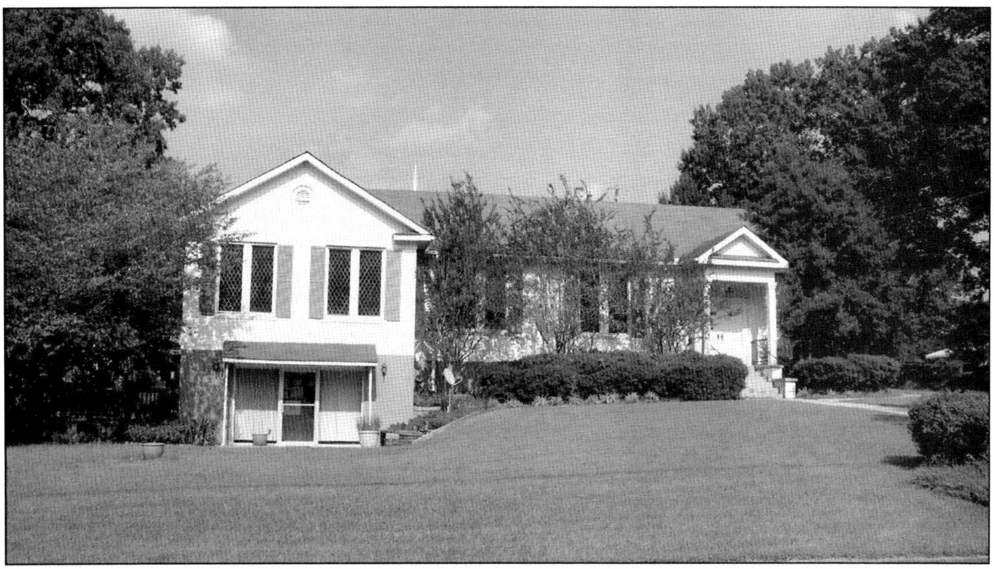

PRESBYTERIAN CHURCH. This is the home of George and Charlene Cosper. Before it was their home, it was the Presbyterian church. The church was organized in 1888 as Childersburg Presbyterian Church. Its 11 charter members were Mr. and Mrs. W. H. Huston, Laura Oden, Lenore Oden, Laura Bussey Oden, Mary Cater, Mr. and Mrs. Augustus Cater, Dr. S. M. McAlpine, and Eugenia McAlpine. This group met in an old school building until 1900, when A. H. Watwood donated $100 and suggested they build a chapel. The first church was struck by lightening in 1917 and burned. The members met at the First Methodist Church for the next 18 years.

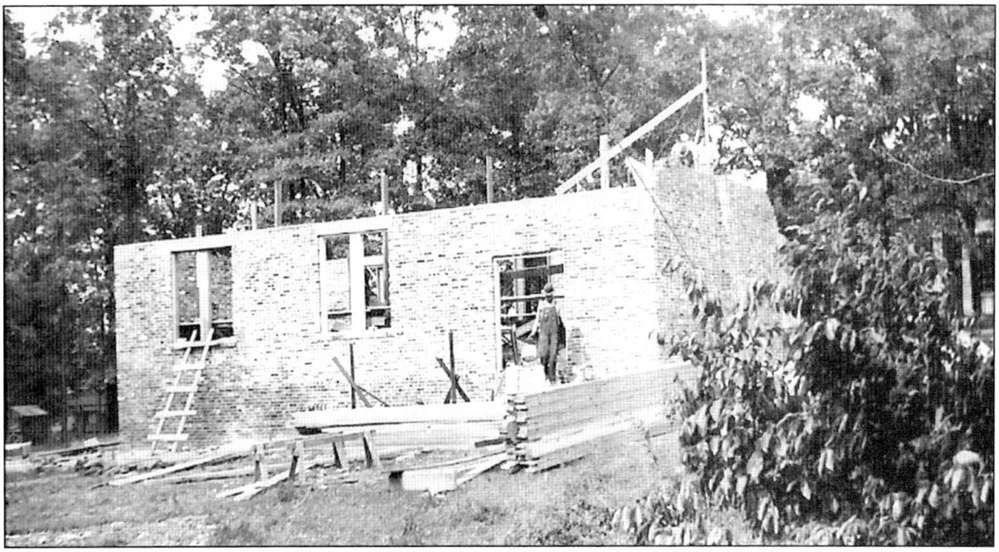

Building Presbyterian Church of Childersburg in 1935. The new church was built on the same spot as the old church by volunteer workers led by builder M. S. Anderson and his son, Malcom. Neither man would accept pay for their work. Francis and Ruby Rowland spent their honeymoon sanding and varnishing the pews made by the Andersons. (Courtesy of the Earle A. Rainwater Memorial Library.)

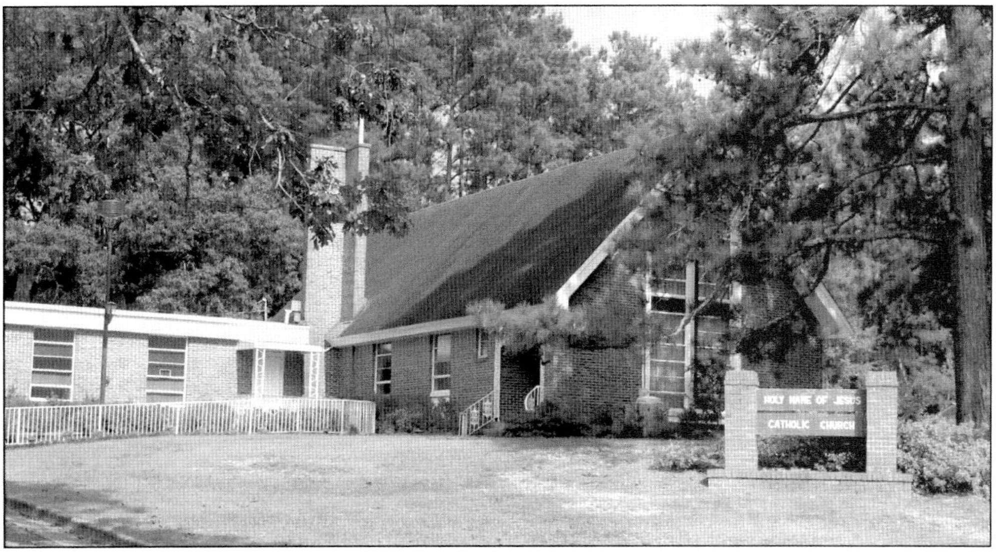

Holy Name of Jesus Catholic Church. This church, built in 1955, was founded by Fr. Mac Paul Abraham. With the population boom in Childersburg came many Catholics with nowhere to worship. At this time, the Catholic community worshipped at the Coosa Court Community Center. After the war, there were only seven Catholics left in Childersburg. Though Father Mac and his small flock were persecuted savagely at times, they persevered. No longer allowed to use the community center, they held mass anywhere they could. George Powell, a local druggist, allowed them a small area on the top floor of his business. The Holy Name Mission began a fund for the new building, and Father Mac's family made major contributions. He solicited the rest of the funds by his good works. The blessing and dedication by Archbishop Thomas J. Toolen was held on Sunday, December 11, 1955.

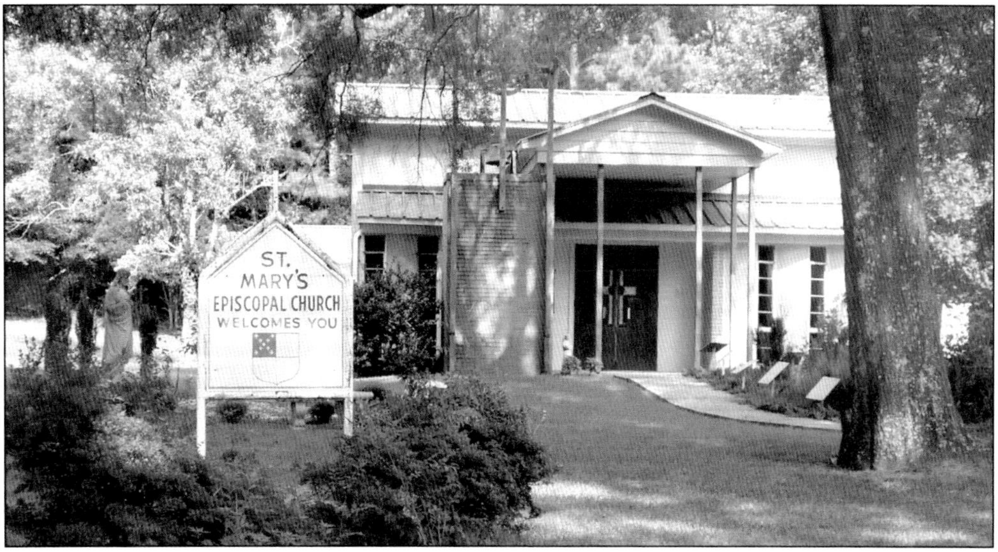

St. Mary's Episcopal Church. In 1905, their were four Episcopalians in Childersburg—Dr. J. A. Harris, Mrs. J. W. Oden, Mrs. Demps A. Oden, and Grace Martin McCloud. Later, Emmaline B. Chancellor came. Services were held in Childersburg by the minister of St. Peter's in Talladega in various places, including the Chancellor home, rooms over Powell Drugs, and the Presbyterian church. When Rev. R. Blackford came as rector of St. Peter's in Talladega, the population in Childersburg had increased drastically due to the war efforts. The Episcopal church in Childersburg was organized in the fall of 1947. The land for this church was donated by Glen Ashworth in December 1953. The church was built in 1954–1955, and the dedication service was performed on June 29, 1955.

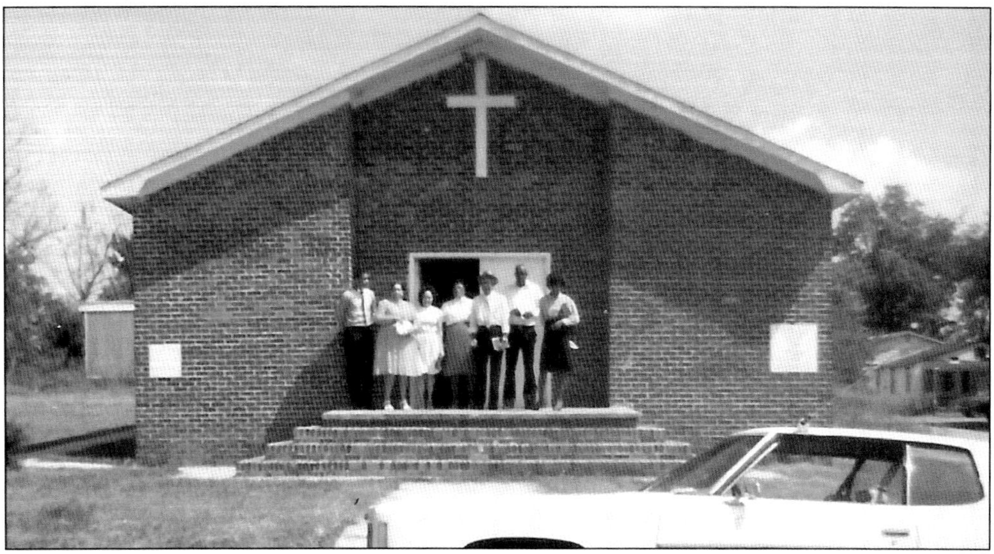

Pleasant Valley Christian Methodist Episcopal (CME) Church. This church was just a dream of Sister Lettie Moreland, who had to go all the way to Alpine to get to church in 1945. She gathered a core group, and they began having church in a small house owned by Jasper Hagan. At that time, the church was called St. James Church. They purchased the land, built the church, and named it Hagan's Chapel. In 1972, they built the church in the photograph and named it Pleasant Valley CME. The first pastor was Reverend Gibson. (Courtesy of Beasley Martin.)

Five

SCHOOLS

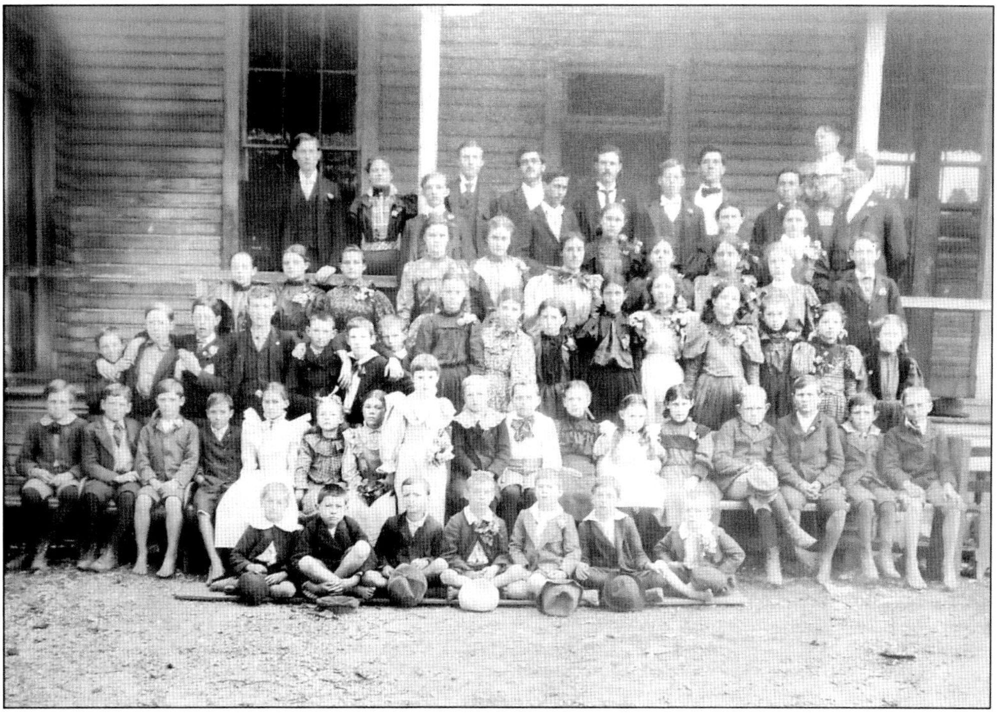

CHILDERSBURG SCHOOL STUDENT BODY, 1898. Look at the third row from the bottom on the left at the six boys with their arms around each other. The entire second row is sitting on a large bench. The two teachers on the top right appear to be giving a reprimanding stare to a guilty-looking boy in the top center. There were three early schools in Childersburg. This was probably the second school since the third one was not built until around 1904. The first one was called Sunshine Academy. According to Anne Louise Ryder-Bush, it was located inside an old sawmill just over Town Branch near the big oak, where First Baptist Church is now located. Sunshine Academy was a private school where Mrs. Ryder's mother attended. (Courtesy of the Earle A. Rainwater Memorial Library.)

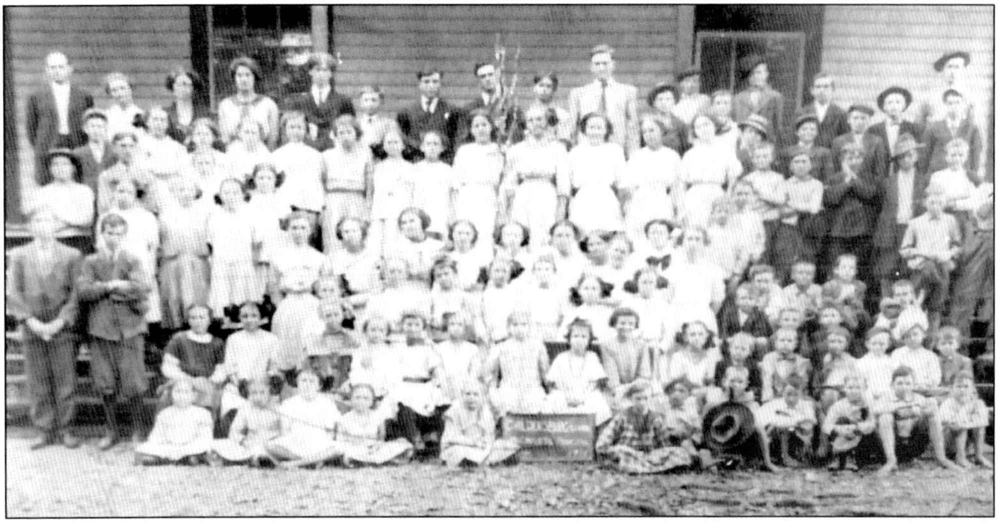

STUDENTS AND FACULTY OF CHILDERSBURG SCHOOL IN 1911. This school was located near where Holy Name of Jesus Catholic Church now stands, close to Sally West Park. It was about 300 yards from the railroad tracks. The school began around 1903–1904 according to Mrs. Ryder-Bush. The building consisted of three long rooms. The first room, used for seventh through 10th grades, went across the entire front of the building. The second room was in the middle of the school, and it was used for third through sixth grades. The last room in the back was used for the primary grades. At night, all the school and community events were held here until city hall was built. Unfortunately, the teachers cannot be identified in a photograph. The teachers were Bob Beavers, A. E. R. Hicks, and Mrs. Stella Powell, who taught primary school; Sarah Shook, who taught the intermediate grades; and Emma Barclay, who taught music. The high-school children at this school had to have two years of Latin, and teachers were not allowed to marry. (Courtesy of the Earle A. Rainwater Memorial Library.)

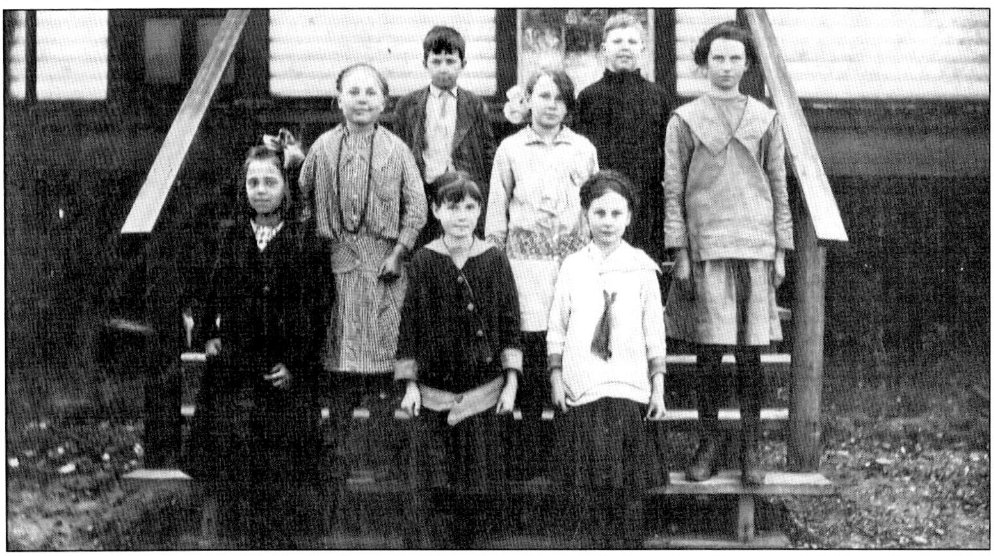

CHILDERSBURG SCHOOL, 1912. Pictured here are, from left to right, (first row) Lillian Simmons, Elizabeth Finn, and Aline Bowen; (second row) Estelle McSheridan and unidentified; (third row) Rudy Butts, Pierce Jarrett, and Powell Jones. This photograph was taken in front of Childersburg School in 1912. (Courtesy of Joyce Smith Caldwell Norris.)

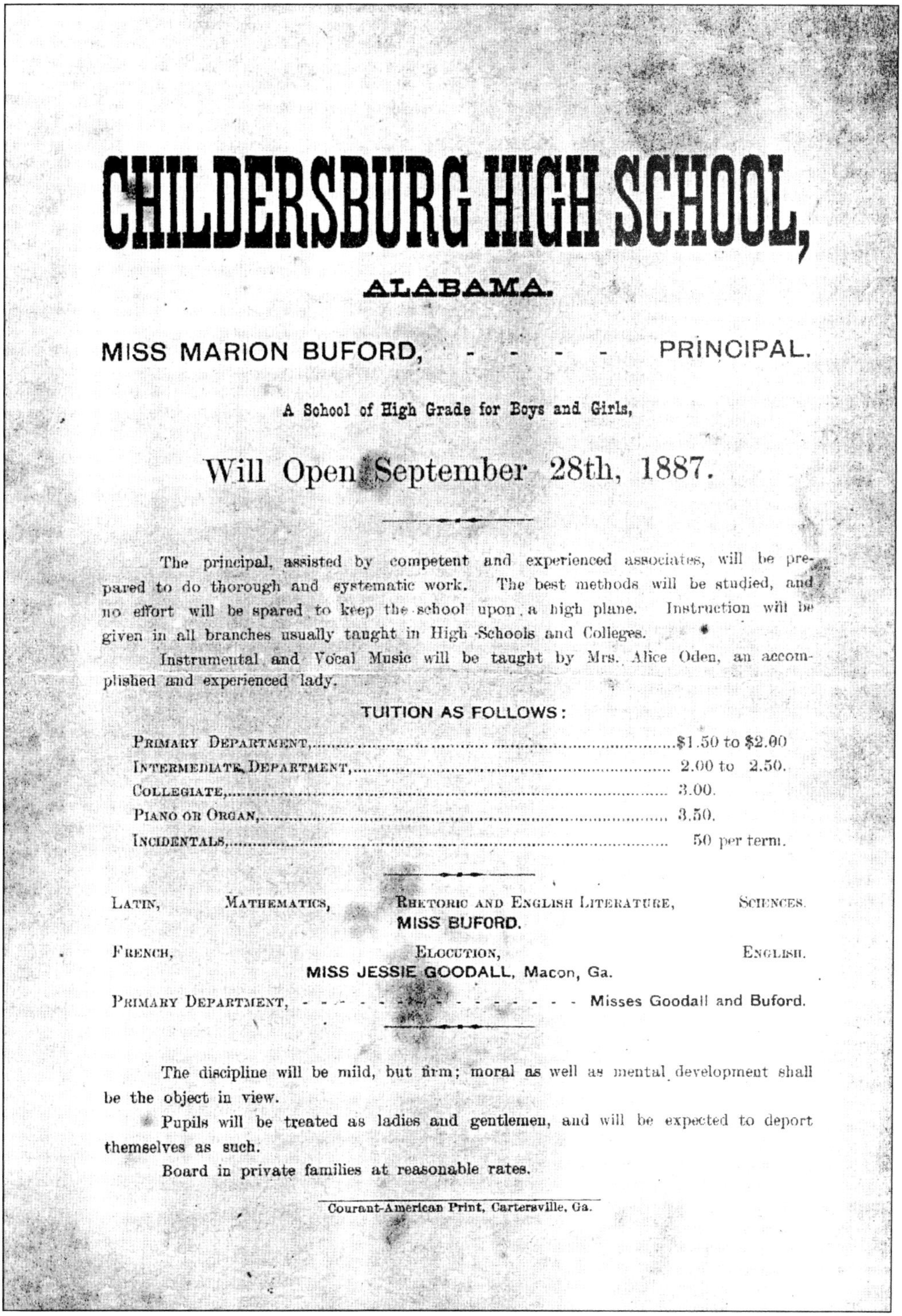

CHILDERSBURG HIGH SCHOOL,

ALABAMA.

MISS MARION BUFORD, - - - - - PRINCIPAL.

A School of High Grade for Boys and Girls,

Will Open September 28th, 1887.

The principal, assisted by competent and experienced associates, will be prepared to do thorough and systematic work. The best methods will be studied, and no effort will be spared to keep the school upon a high plane. Instruction will be given in all branches usually taught in High Schools and Colleges.

Instrumental and Vocal Music will be taught by Mrs. Alice Oden, an accomplished and experienced lady.

TUITION AS FOLLOWS:

Primary Department,	$1.50 to $2.00
Intermediate Department,	2.00 to 2.50.
Collegiate,	3.00.
Piano or Organ,	3.50.
Incidentals,	50 per term.

Latin, Mathematics, Rhetoric and English Literature, Sciences.
MISS BUFORD.

French, Elocution, English.
MISS JESSIE GOODALL, Macon, Ga.

Primary Department, - - - - - - - - - - - - - - Misses Goodall and Buford.

The discipline will be mild, but firm; moral as well as mental development shall be the object in view.

Pupils will be treated as ladies and gentlemen, and will be expected to deport themselves as such.

Board in private families at reasonable rates.

Courant-American Print, Cartersville, Ga.

CHS FLYER, 1887. This is a photocopy of a flyer printed by Courant American Print in Cartersville, Georgia, advertising: "Childersburg High School will open September 28th, 1887. Principal Miss Marion Buford." (Courtesy of Judy McSween.)

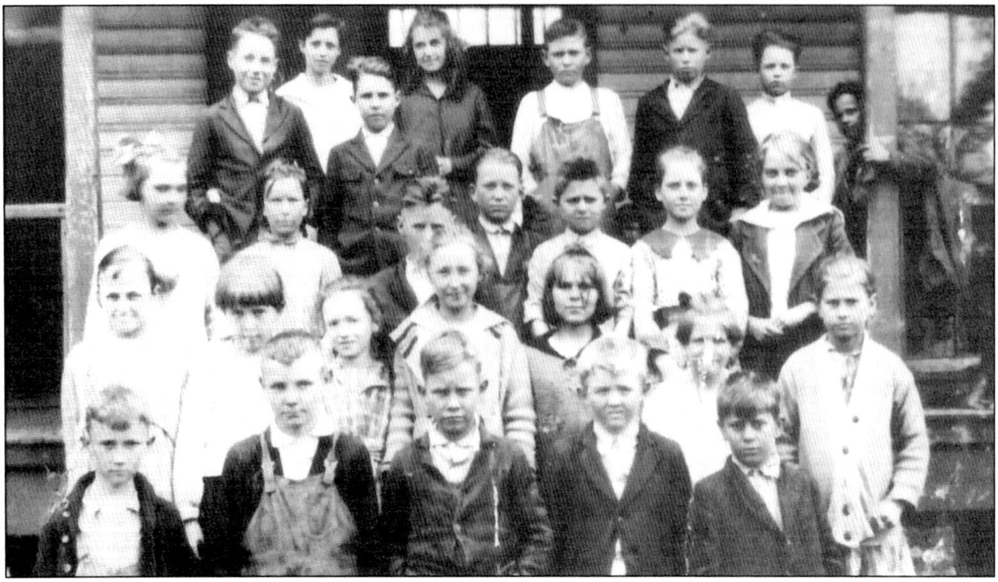

CHILDERSBURG SCHOOL 1920, THIRD THROUGH FIFTH GRADES. Pictured from left to right are (first row) Richard Finn, Dennis Finn, Alton Hobbs, Elvin Bush, and William Richardson; (second row) Myra Busby, Pauline Riley, Eddie McSheridan, Alice McSheridan, Missouri Burton, Grace Thompson, and Evelyn Richardson; (third row) Mildred Cliett, Iris Wallis, unidentified, Dewey Lightsey, Norman Thompson, Beulah H. Smith, and Fredna Hobbs; (fourth row) Leon Henderson, James Alford, Stanley Vaughn, James Pruett, and Virgil Gray; (fifth row) Aline Gray, Machell McSheridan, and Clarence Strickland (leaning on pole). (Courtesy of Jane Limbaugh Allen.)

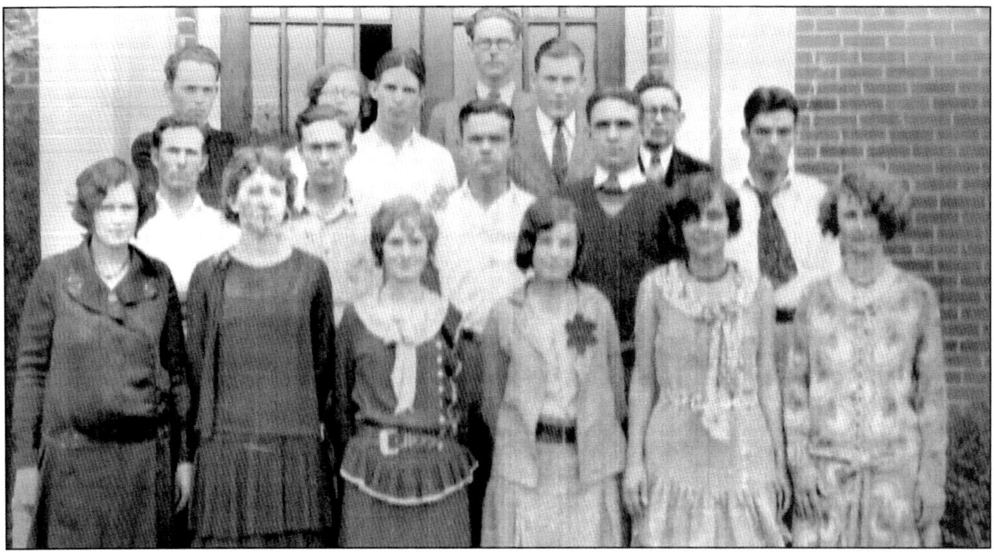

CHILDERSBURG SCHOOL CLASS OF 1929. On the back of this photograph is written, "The Lucky 13." From left to right are (first row) Levitia Sims, Evelyn Heath, Olive Gardner, Odell Washam, Dorothy Oden, and Eva Armbrester; (second row) Linwood Smith, W. A. Green, Chick Strickland, Cyril Roberts, and Hugh Ledbetter; (third row) Mr. Loudermilk, Mrs. Dillard, Henry Moody, Mr. Watwood, Clifton "Punk" Edwards, and Mr. Hammack (principal). (Courtesy of Patricia Teague Wesley Godfrey.)

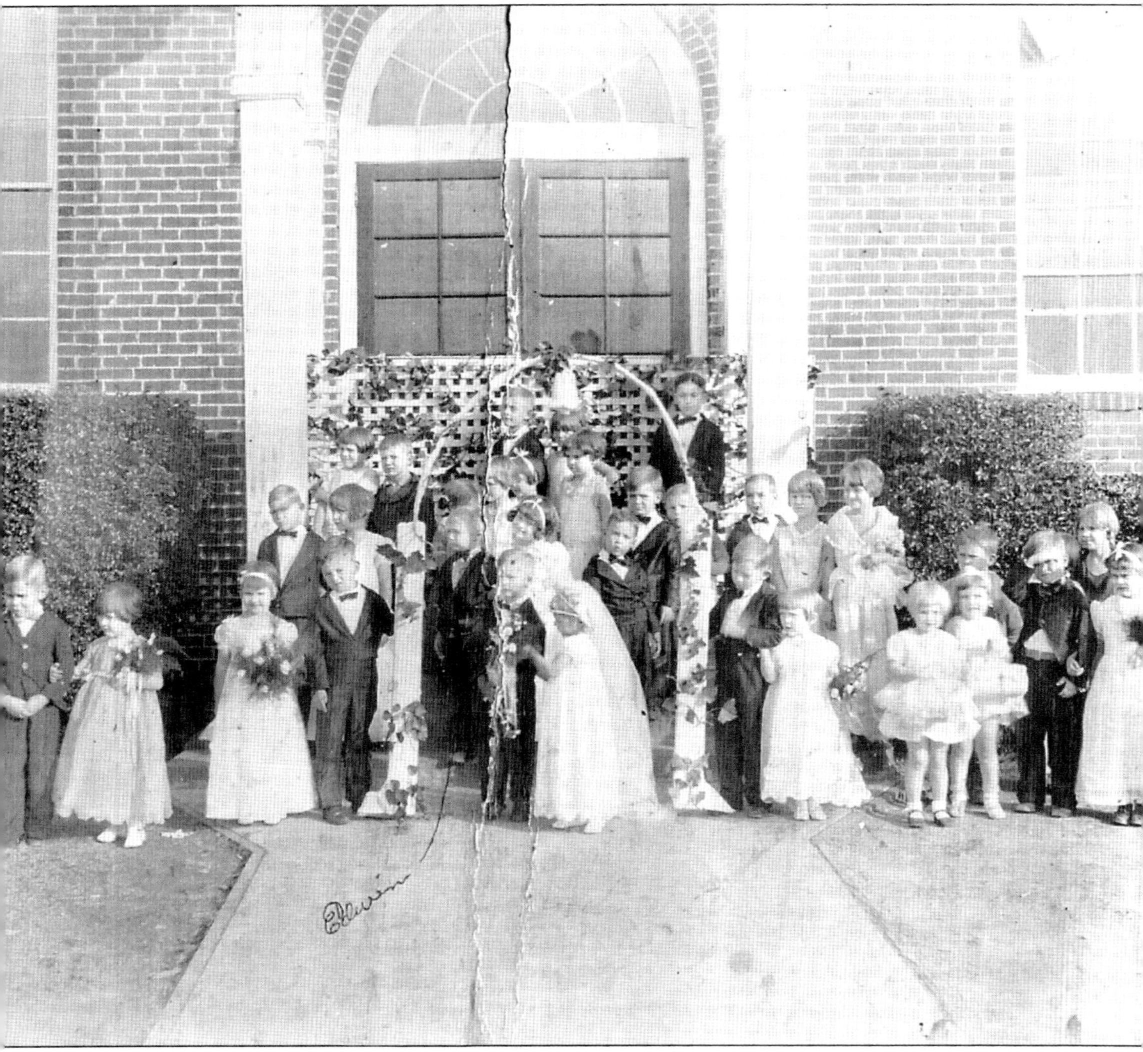

TOM THUMB WEDDING, DECEMBER 4, 1930. This play was directed by Mrs. Henry Cliett and Mrs. Horace Wilson at the Childersburg High School Auditorium. The boys do not look very happy, especially the one on the far left. The bride is Betty Jo Hammack, and the groom is Sonny Boy Wilson. Also pictured (not in order) are Grace Riddle, Rose Owens, Nada Levie, Celia Thompson, Helen James, Evelyn Vaughn, Emma Limbaugh, Dorothy Miller, Jean Wilson, Elizabeth Frangopoulos, Earl Wood, Jimmy Baker, Howard Riddle, Jimmy Lockhart, Hagan Limbaugh (the little boy on the right shading his eyes from the sun), Larson Smith, Hollis Pruett, Bruce McDowell (standing tall in the back), Jack Bush, Dorothy Wilson, Edwin "Mickey" Finn (standing just inside the arbor on the left), Ethel McSheridan, Clyde Bush, Hazel Davis, Annie Lou Matson, Clarence Morris, Johnnie Blocker, Anne Hines, Geneva Morris, Mary Jo Smith, Ernestine Brooks, Bloyce Miller, and Jack Tate. (Courtesy of the Earle A. Rainwater Memorial Library.)

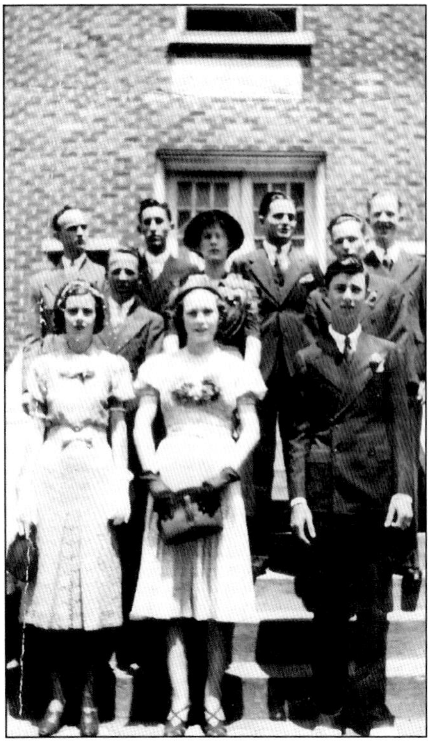

CHILDERSBURG HIGH SCHOOL CLASS OF 1938. Pictured are, from left to right, (first row) Louise Bush, Doris Richardson, and Jack Phillips; (second row) Turner Riddle, Catherine Bates, and H. P. Hines Jr.; (third row) Robert Hagan, Bruce McDowell, James Limbaugh, and Marcus "Dee" Moody. (Courtesy of Dr. Marcus "Dee" Moody.)

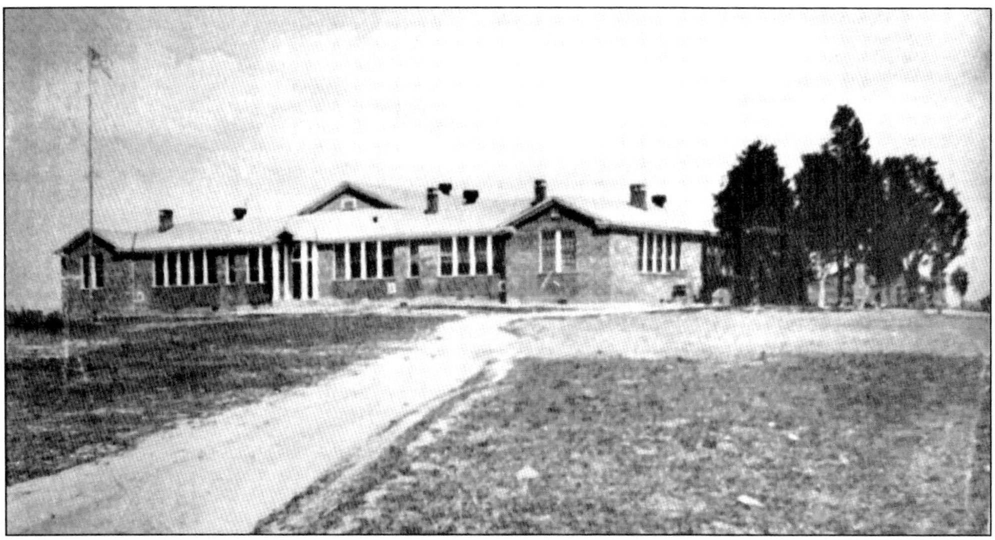

THE FIRST CONSOLIDATED CHILDERSBURG HIGH SCHOOL. This school was built in 1922. It served the community, teaching grades 1 through 12. Due to the population boom of World War II, the school had to be enlarged in 1942. An additional building was added and connected by first a driveway and then a breezeway. The new building housed the high school students, and the elementary and junior high students occupied the older building. Most of the original building burned on Sunday, December 8, 1957. Classes were moved to churches, public buildings, and the Alabama Ordnance Works. When the school was rebuilt, a new lunchroom and classrooms were added to the original 1922 building. Additions were made to a wing of the 1942 building. (Courtesy of the Earle A. Rainwater Memorial Library.)

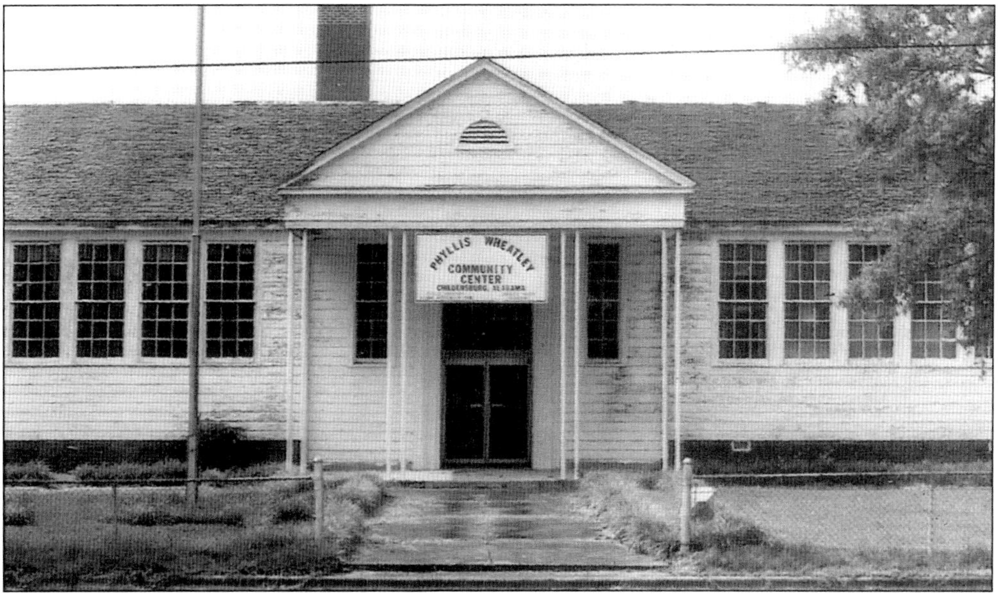

PHYLLIS WHEATLEY SCHOOL. This school is now a community center. Before integration, black children were educated in tiny schoolhouses built next to their churches. Among these were Mount Olive, Pinegrove, Enon, Tallasahatchee, Nottingham, and Cedar Creek. Eventually these schools were consolidated to form Childersburg Consolidated High School. Later it was moved to Childersburg-Fayetteville Road and renamed Phyllis Wheatley School. After the schools were totally integrated in 1970–1971, the elementary schools housed kindergarten through fourth grade, Phyllis Wheatley School had grades five through eight, and Childersburg High School had grades nine through 12. (Courtesy of Barbara "Bobbie" Anderson.)

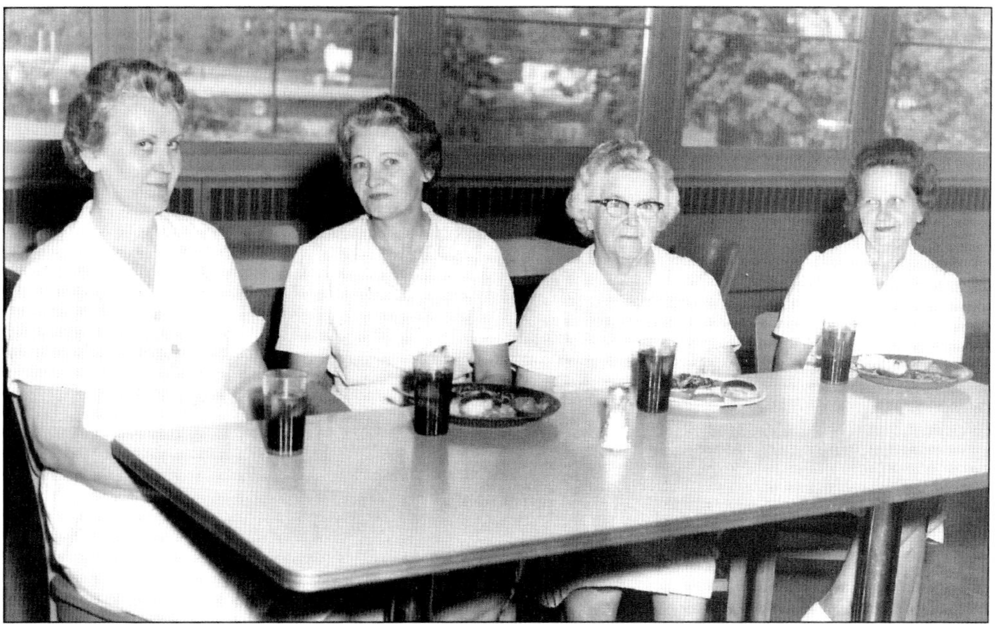

THE FIRST CHILDERSBURG HIGH SCHOOL LUNCHROOM STAFF, 1942. Pictured are, from left to right, Johnnie Haver, Mrs. Bunn, Mary Ogletree Riddle, and Maenetta Caldwell. (Courtesy of Howard "Bucky" Riddle.)

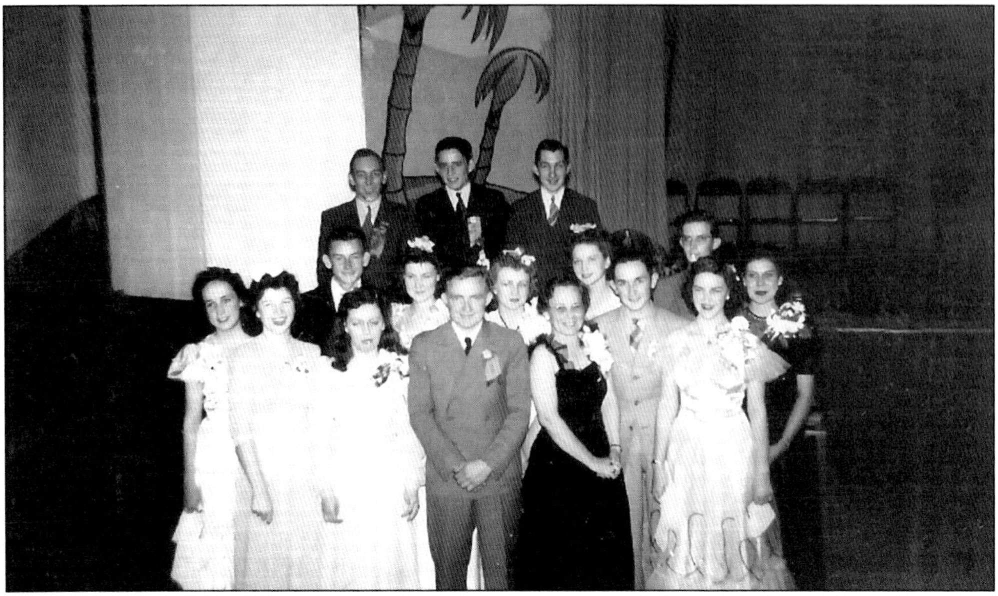

CHILDERSBURG HIGH SCHOOL CLASS OF 1943. Pictured from left to right are (first row) Frances Thompson Denmark, Jeanne Morrel Franklin, Winnie Vaughn Martin, Clarence Edwin "Mickey" Finn, Mrs. Bowen, James Hardy, and Rose Owens; (second row) Lawrence Russell, Lita Knight, Aline Wood, Sadye Mae Cook, James Campbell, and Ruth Brown McDowell; (third row) Jack Tate, Frank Limbaugh, and Thomas Pierson Jr. (Courtesy of Clarence Edwin "Mickey" Finn.)

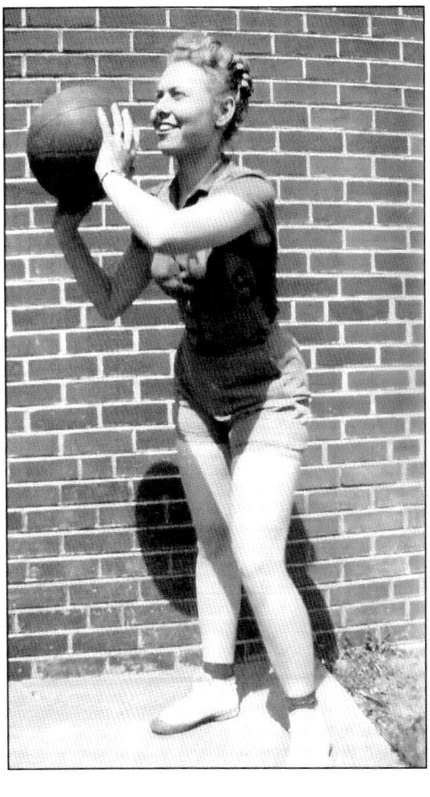

BASKETBALL DIVA, C. 1945. This beautiful girl is Eleanor Caldwell. Eleanor played basketball for Childersburg High School. Notice the CHS on her uniform. (Courtesy of Clarence Edwin "Mickey" Finn.)

BIKING BEHIND CHS, C. 1942. Mickey Finn stops for a photo opportunity on his bicycle behind Childersburg High School. (Courtesy of Clarence Edwin "Mickey" Finn.)

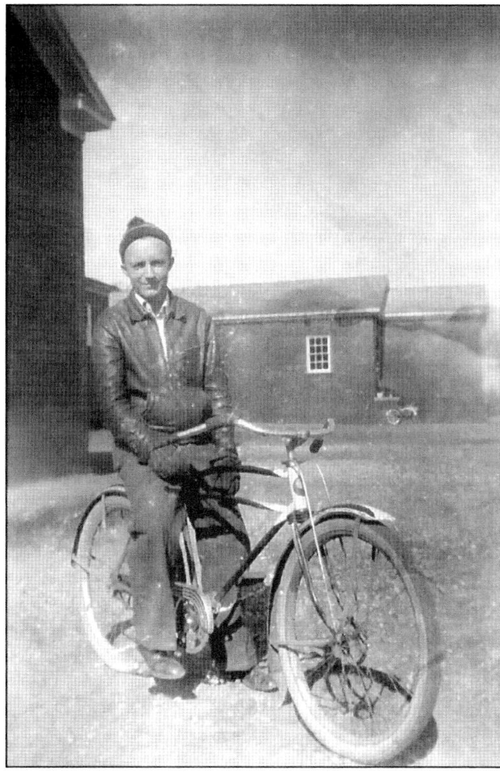

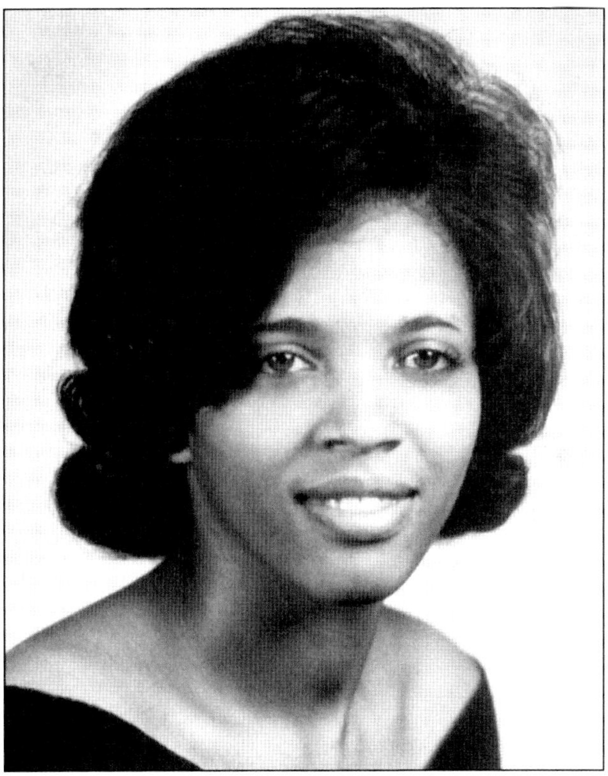

BERTHA L. SWAIN, 1967. Bertha was one of the original three black students to attend Childersburg High School under the Freedom of Choice Act. Edith Moon and Yvonne Garrett were the other two. Bertha Swain and Edith Moon graduated in 1967, the first blacks to ever graduate from Childersburg High School. Bertha lives in Jonesboro, Georgia. Edith lived in Jonesboro until her death in 2005. (Courtesy of Mrs. Beulah Garrett.)

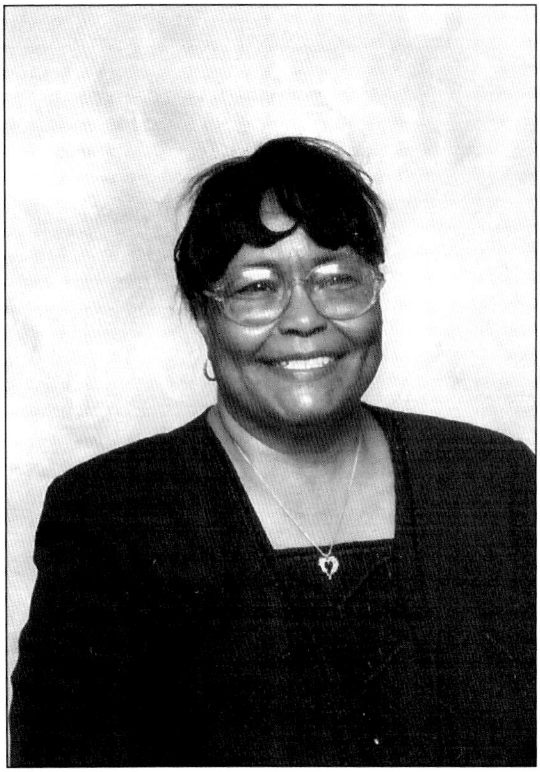

ANNIE R. EASLEY. Mrs. Easley was the first black teacher assigned to A. H. Watwood Elementary School in Childersburg. She retired in 1990 from Childersburg Middle School. The wife of John S. Easley III (deceased), she is the mother of seven children. (Courtesy of Mrs. Beulah Garrett.)

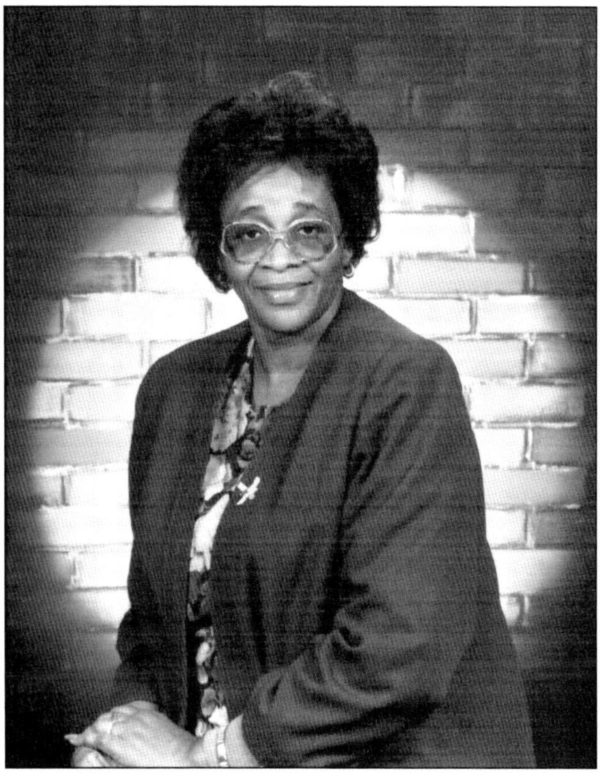

MRS. MINNIE T. COLEMAN. Mrs. Coleman was the first black teacher to teach at Childersburg Elementary School. Her daughter Angela was the first black student there. Mrs. Coleman married L. J. Coleman (deceased) and is the mother of four children: Franklin, Jennifer, Angela, and Katrina. (Courtesy of Mrs. Beulah Garrett.)

BEULAH S. GARRETT. Mrs. Garrett was the first black teacher assigned to Childersburg High School, in compliance with the 1964 Civil Rights Act. White teachers were also assigned to black schools. Mrs. Garrett transferred from Phyllis Wheatley School, where she taught Title 1 Reading, to teach seventh through 10th-grade reading. She stayed at Childersburg High School for four years until total integration, when she returned to teach at Phyllis Wheatley. (Courtesy of Mrs. Beulah Garrett.)

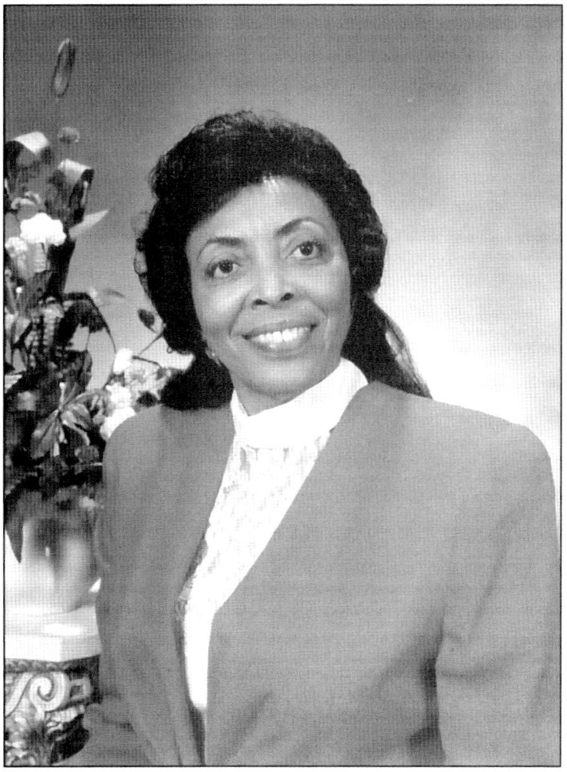

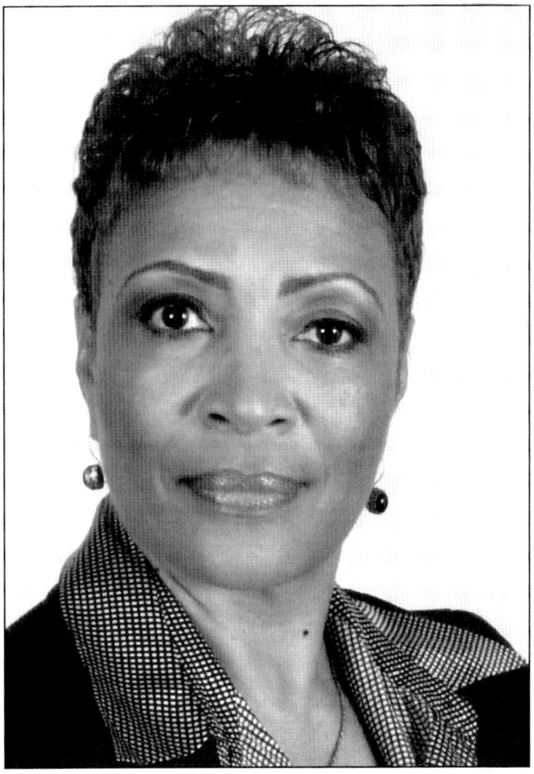

D. YVONNE GARRETT. Yvonne was one of the first three black students to attend Childersburg High School under the Freedom of Choice Act of 1965. She was also the first black tapped for the Beta Club International Honor Society. She graduated from Childersburg High School in 1970. Yvonne is the daughter of Zack F. and Beulah S. Garrett of Alpine, Alabama. (Courtesy of Mrs. Beulah Garrett.)

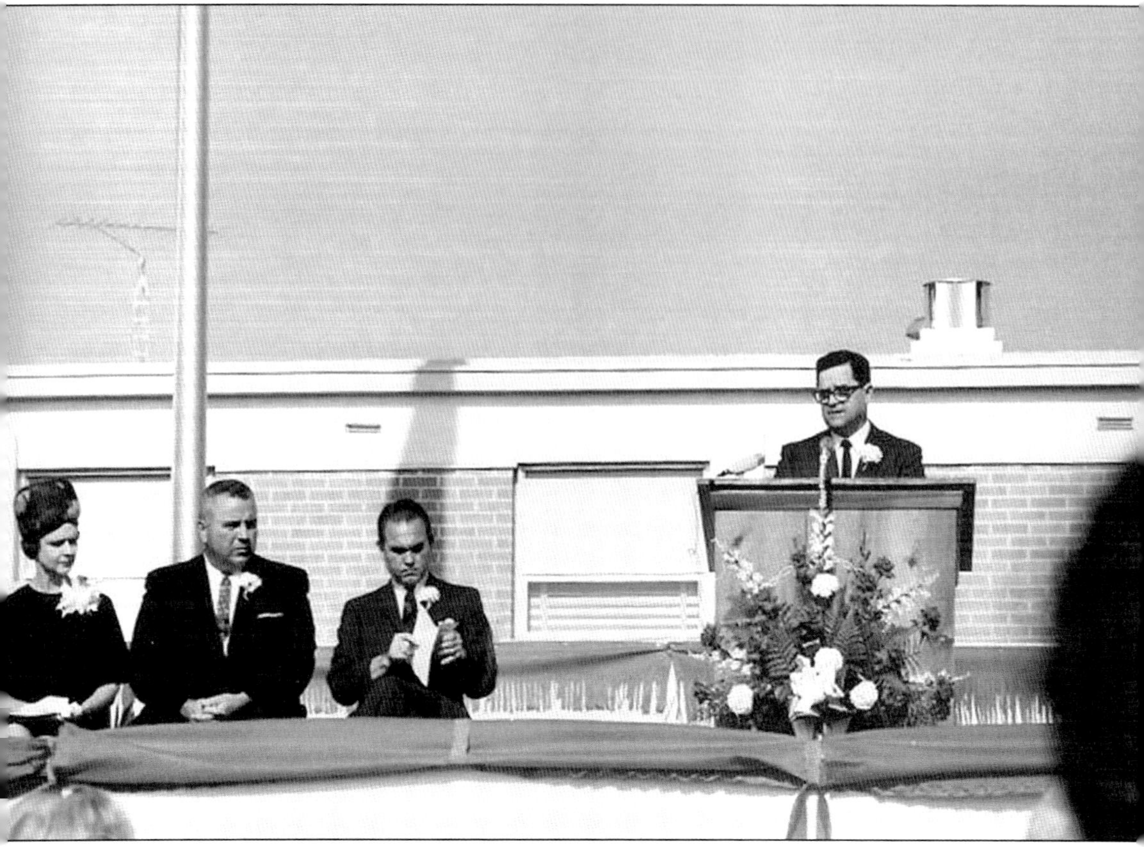

RIBBON-CUTTING CEREMONY AT N. F. NUNNELLEY STATE TECHNICAL COLLEGE. Pictured in September 1966 are, from left to right, Lurleen B. Wallace, Congressman Bill Nichols, Alabama governor George Wallace, and Childersburg mayor Robert Limbaugh. The City of Childersburg donated $24,000 to buy 25 acres on Highway 280. This acreage was donated to the state for the college site. Construction was completed in February 1966. The school officially opened on March 7, 1966, with enrollment of 35 full-time students. On September 25, 1966, Gov. George Corley Wallace delivered the dedication speech to more than 1,500. In just seven years, on December 12, 1973, Nunnelley earned Southern Association of Colleges and Schools accreditation. In 1989, Nunnelley became the Childersburg campus for Central Alabama Community College. (Courtesy of the Earle A. Rainwater Memorial Library.)

Six

Trains

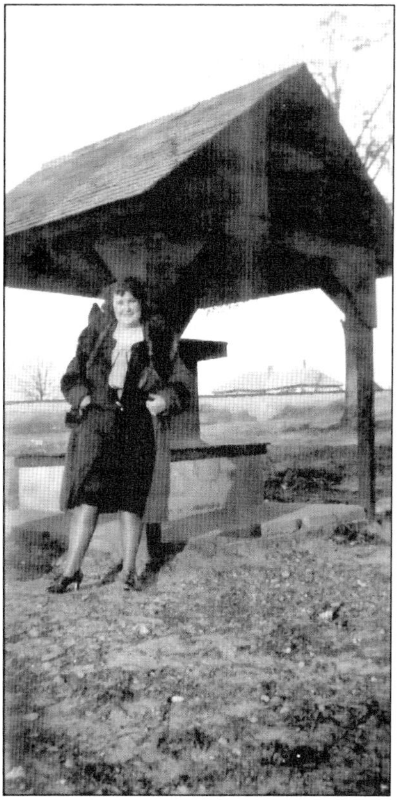

Estelle McSheridan at Southern Depot, c. 1930. Estelle (1903–1991) was the wife of Childersburg and Talladega County law officer Tim Finn and the mother of John "Bill" William and Clarence Edwin "Mickey" Finn. In this photograph, she is standing near the Southern Depot train station in Childersburg. (Courtesy of Clarence Edwin "Mickey" Finn.)

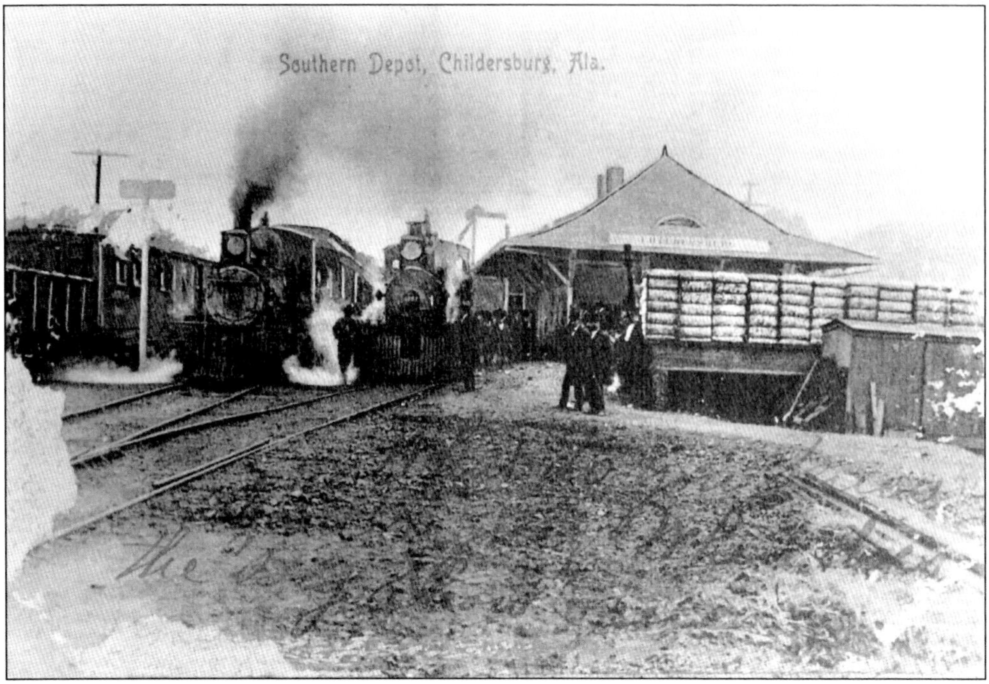

AN EARLY PHOTOGRAPH OF SOUTHERN DEPOT, C. 1908. After 1887, Childersburg was a busy railroad town. The *Dude* was the local passenger train from Childersburg to Rome, Georgia, and the *Goober* was the train between Childersburg and Columbus, Georgia. Many of the railroad workers brought their families to live in Childersburg. (Courtesy of the Earle A. Rainwater Memorial Library.)

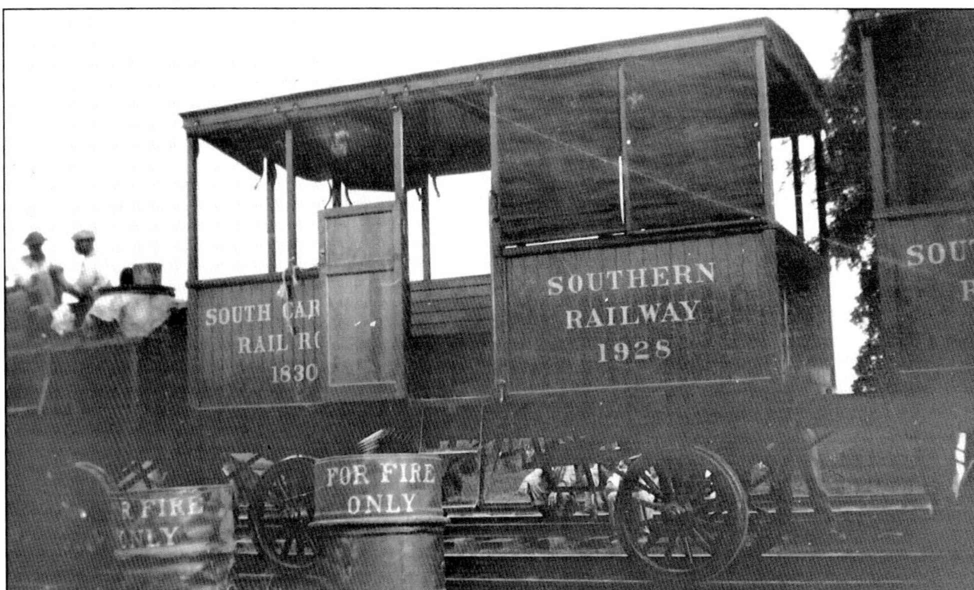

SOUTHERN RAILWAY, 1932. This photograph was taken at Southern Depot in Childersburg. This is a rare photograph of one of our early trains. Notice the barrels in front of the train that say "for fire only." (Courtesy of Howard "Bucky" Riddle.)

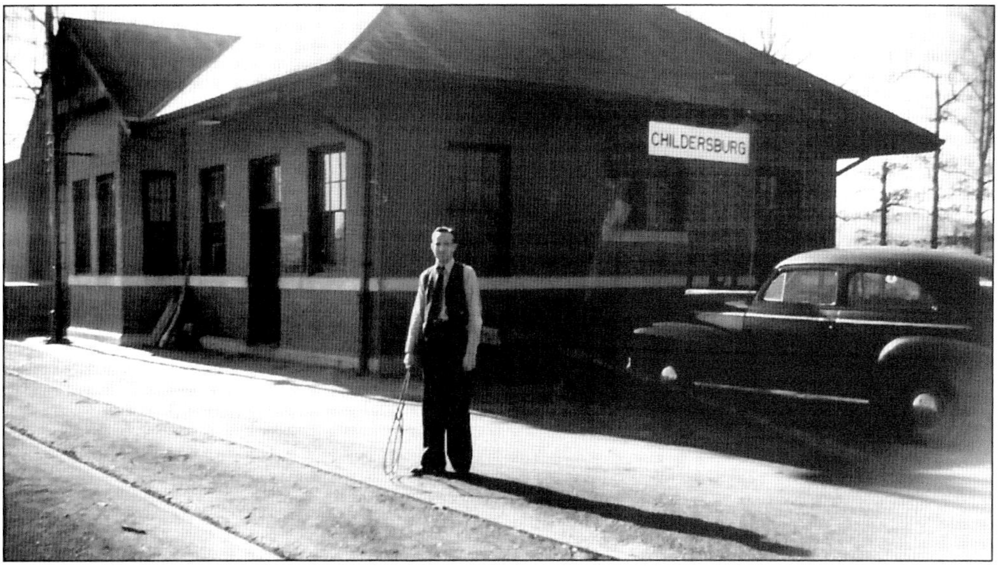

SOUTHERN DEPOT, 1943. Southern Depot was located behind where the Holy Name of Jesus Catholic Church now stands. This photograph was taken on March 2, 1943. The man in this photograph is believed to be a Mr. Lee who worked at the depot. (Courtesy of Myrtle Leach McDowell in memory of her husband, Bruce W. McDowell Jr.)

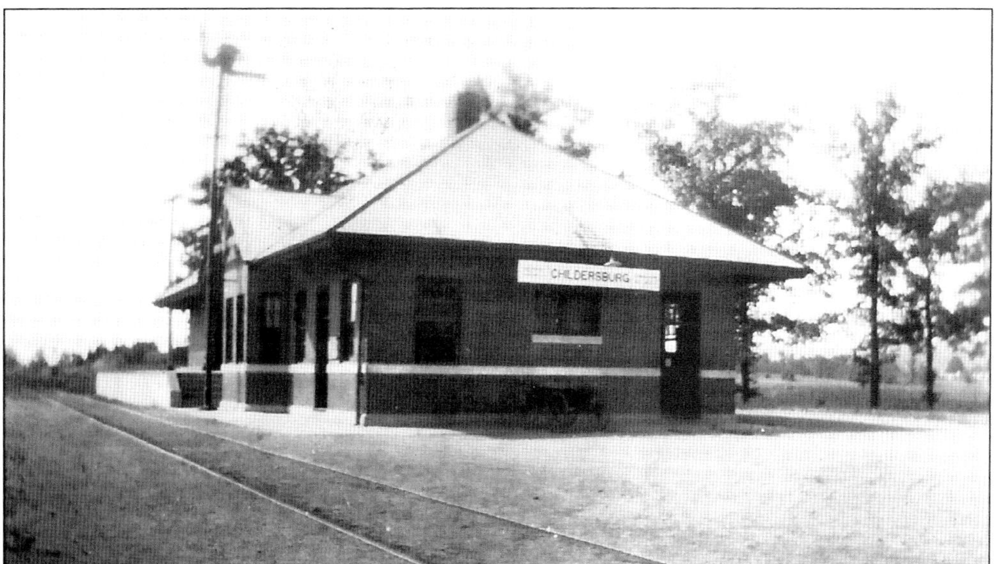

SOUTHERN DEPOT, CHILDERSBURG. It is unknown when this photograph of Southern Depot was taken. (Courtesy of Myrtle Leach McDowell in memory of her husband, Bruce W. McDowell Jr.)

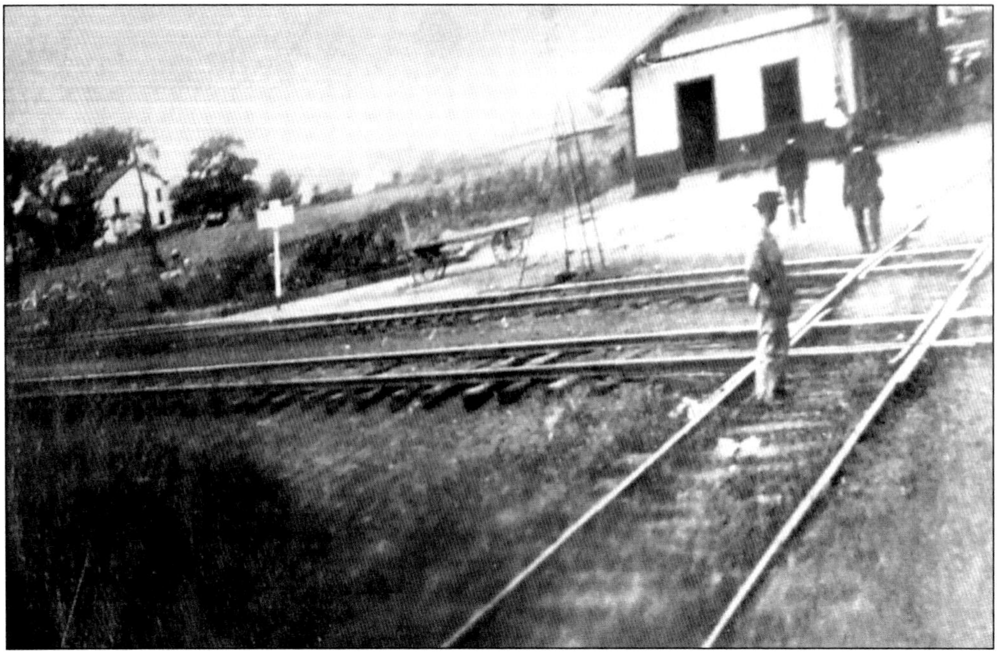

RAILROAD TRACKS, C. 1910. Before the viaduct was built, this was a dangerous crossing of the railroad tracks. (Courtesy of the Earle A. Rainwater Memorial Library.)

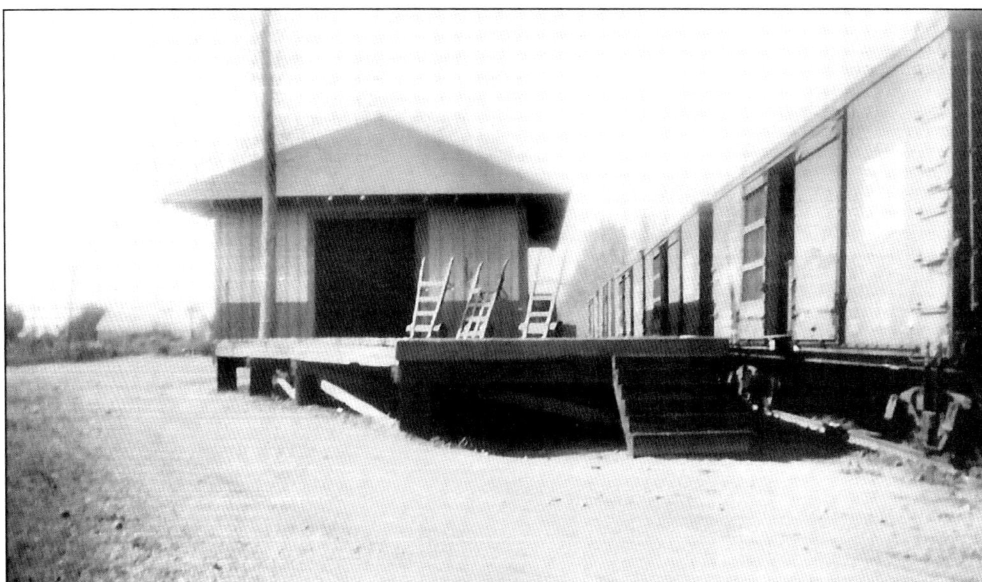

CENTRAL OF GEORGIA, C. 1935. This is a rare photograph of the old Central of Georgia Depot. Notice the platform and train. The Central of Georgia was located on Southern Street across from the Finn Hotel. (Courtesy of Myrtle Leach McDowell in memory of her husband, Bruce W. McDowell Jr.)

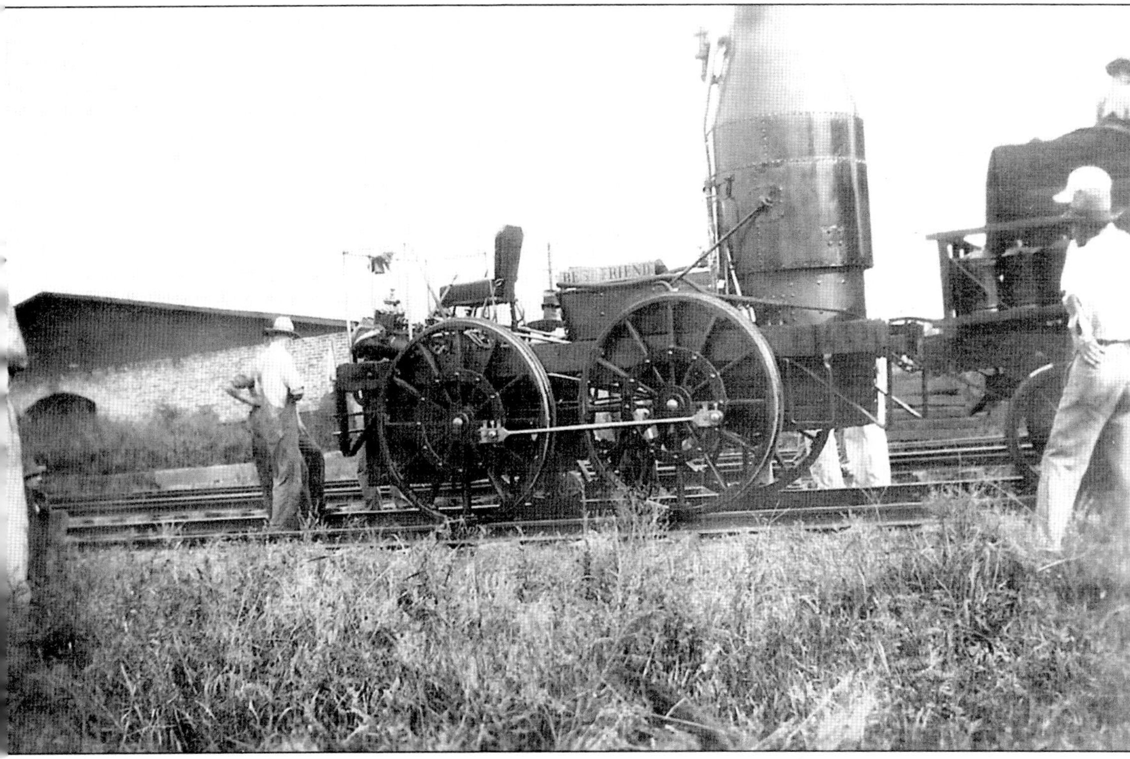

THE *BEST FRIEND* TRAIN, 1930. This photograph was taken at Southern Depot. Notice the sign on the car that says "Best Friend." This train was built in 1928 as an exact replica of its namesake, which was built in 1830 at the West Point Foundry in New York. Six months later in 1831, it was also the first train to explode from its boiler. The replica was used by Southern Railway for parades, conventions, and even later at Jimmy Carter's inaugural parade. It was retired in Charleston, South Carolina, in 1993 and is now housed there. It was donated to the City of Charleston by Norfolk Southern the year it was retired. The original train made its debut on Christmas Day 1830. It was the first steam locomotive in the United States to establish regularly scheduled passenger service, the first to haul freight, and the first to carry the U.S. mail. (Courtesy of the Earle A. Rainwater Memorial Library.)

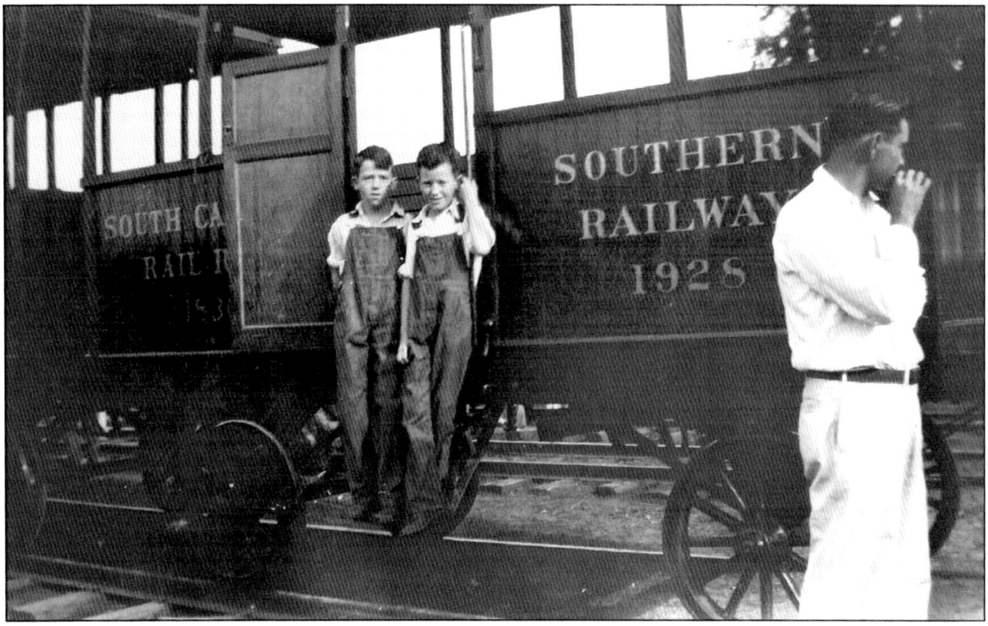

LITTLE RIDDLES ON THE TRAIN, C. 1938. The Riddle brothers, Franklin (left) and Herbert, pose on a train of the Southern Railroad in Childersburg, Alabama. The man at right is unidentified. (Courtesy of Howard "Bucky" Riddle.)

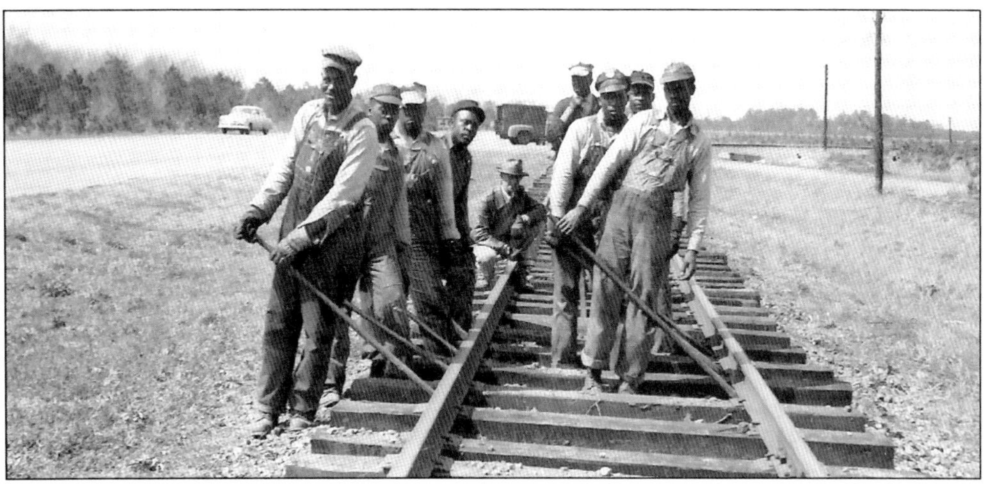

RAILROAD WORK CREW, C. 1952. The men in the photograph are unidentified at this time. Mickey Finn remembers them and said that he loved to hear them sing their cadence while they worked. (Courtesy of Myrtle Leach McDowell in memory of her husband, Bruce W. McDowell Jr.)

Seven

CITIZENS

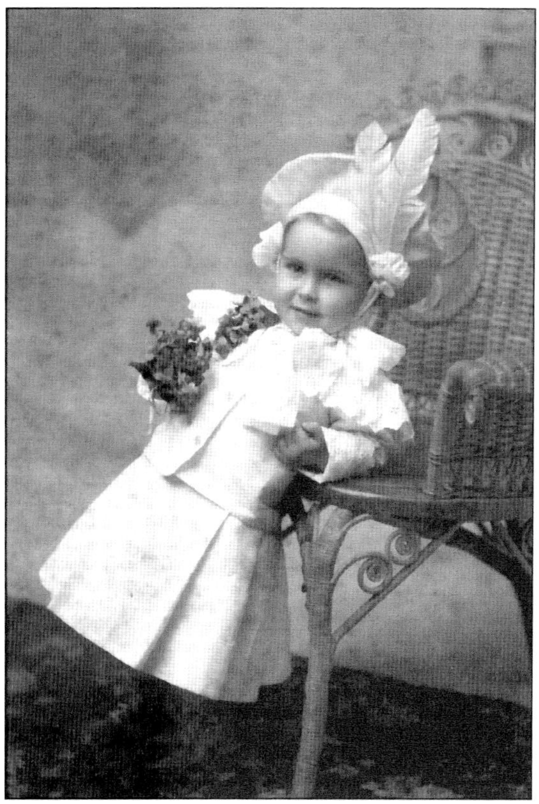

PERCY KEITH, 1871. Percy was born in 1869 to Joseph and Emma Keith in Childersburg. He was educated at Talladega Academy and took his pharmacy courses in Birmingham. He then moved to Marshall, Texas, where he met and married Miss Mac Johnston. He finally settled in Sherman, Texas, where he owned the Keith Pharmacy for 25 years, until his death around 1930. The Keith family was one of the earliest known families of Childersburgh Town. (Courtesy of Monty Powell.)

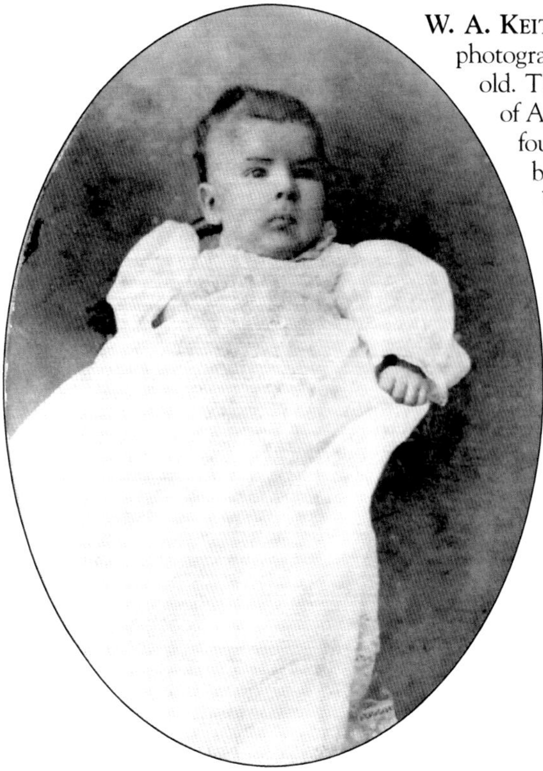

W. A. Keith. Unfortunately it is unknown when this photograph was taken, though it is obviously very old. This photograph was found in the collection of Agnes Cliett. The Keith family was one of the founding families of Childersburgh Town. The back of the photograph identifies the baby as W. A. Keith. (Courtesy of Monty Powell.)

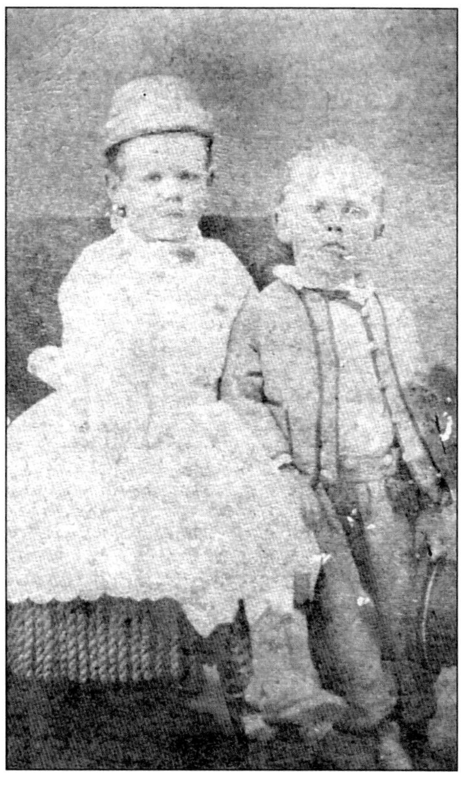

Cliett Children, 1874. Siblings Minnie Cliett and Miner James Cliett pose for this portrait. (Courtesy of Monty Powell.)

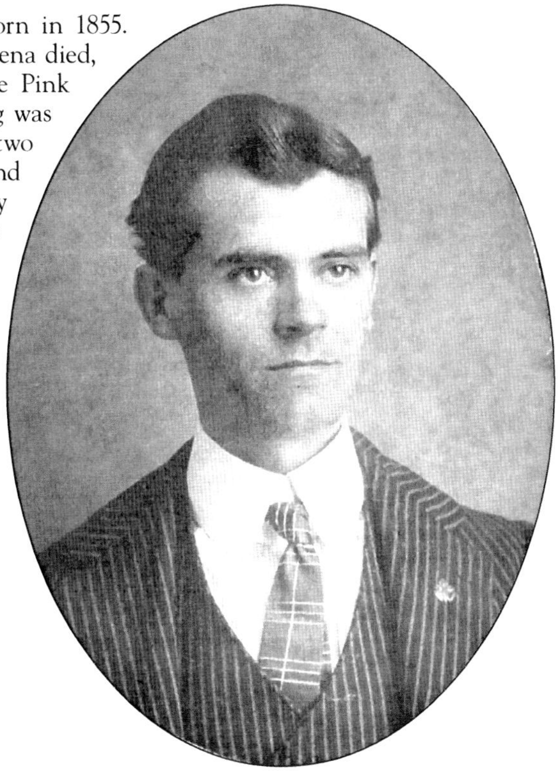

DAVID BRYANT, C. 1875. David was born in 1855. His first wife's name was Rena. When Rena died, he married a woman named Clara. The Pink House on Ninth Avenue in Childersburg was built for him and his wife Rena. He had two daughters by Rena: Bertha (born 1886) and Minnie (born 1888). Bertha married Jerry A. Strickland and had a son, Clarence "Chick" Strickland. David Bryant's son-in-law, J. A. Strickland, was involved in civic affairs and was mayor pro tempore for Childersburg. (Courtesy of Patricia Teague Wesley Godfrey.)

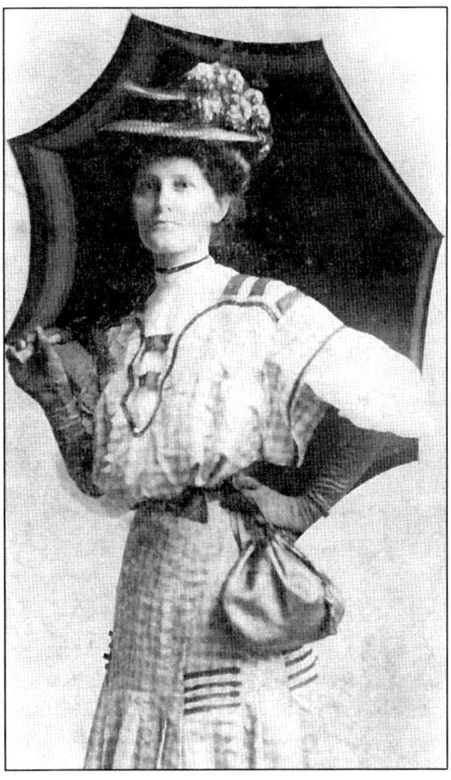

CLARA BRYANT, C. 1880. Clara was the second wife of David Bryant and stepmother of Bertha Bryant Strickland and Minnie Bryant. She and David lived in the Pink House across the street from the library. (Courtesy of Patricia Teague Wesley Godfrey.)

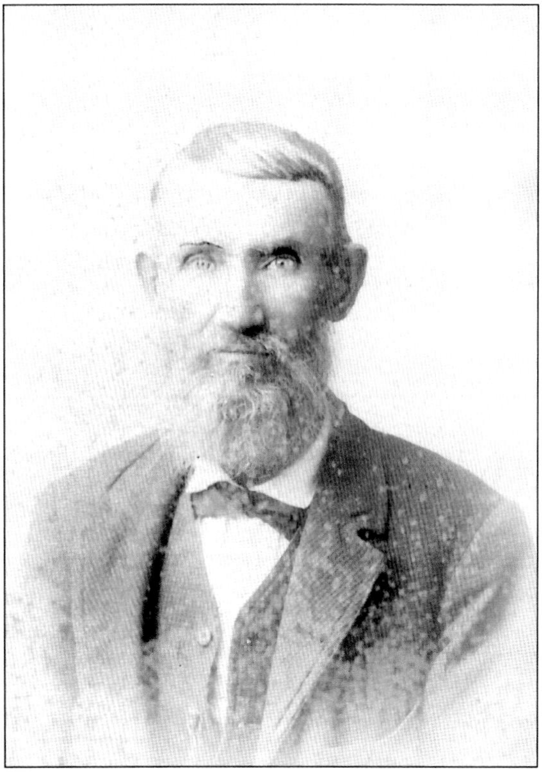

JOSHUA BUSSEY ODEN, C. 1879. Joshua was born in Plantersville, Alabama, (near Selma) in May 1829 and died at his home in Childersburg on September 28, 1892. He married Laura Graham on November 9, 1859. (Courtesy of Patricia Teague Wesley Godfrey.)

ODEN LADIES ON THEIR PORCH, C. 1880. Notice the beautiful wisteria running up the house and across the eves. The eldest woman, in the rocking chair, is Laura Oden. The middle girl, sitting on the steps at right, is Lenore "Sweetie" Oden. The youngest girl, standing on the steps at left, is Bussie Oden. Mrs. Ryder talks about Sweetie in her book *Memoirs of Childersburg*. When Mrs. Ryder was a little girl, Sweetie took her and some other children to Flagpole Mountain to watch the sun rise and cook an outdoor breakfast of eggs and bacon. (Courtesy of Patricia Teague Wesley Godfrey.)

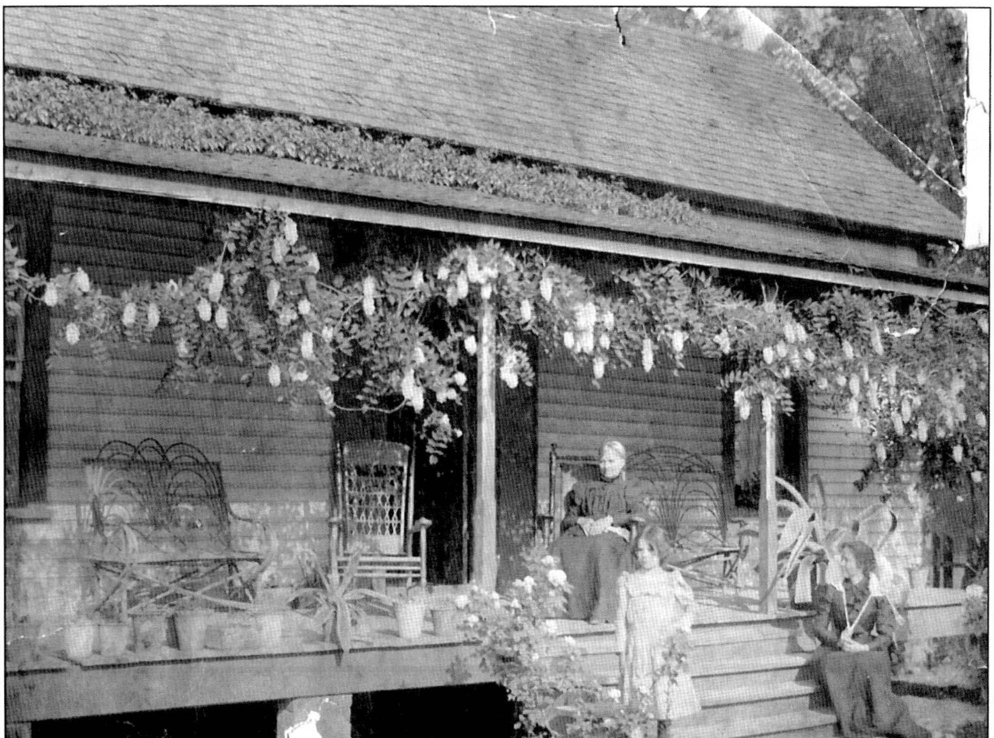

NICHOLS FAMILY PORTRAIT, C. 1888. Judge J. A. Nichols, his first wife, Allie A. Simmons Nichols, and children B. Frank Nichols and Alva Nichols Garlington are pictured here. This photograph was taken when Frank was only two or three years of age. It was presented to Agnes Hamilton by J. A. Nichols on Christmas 1940. (Courtesy of Sandra Donahoo.)

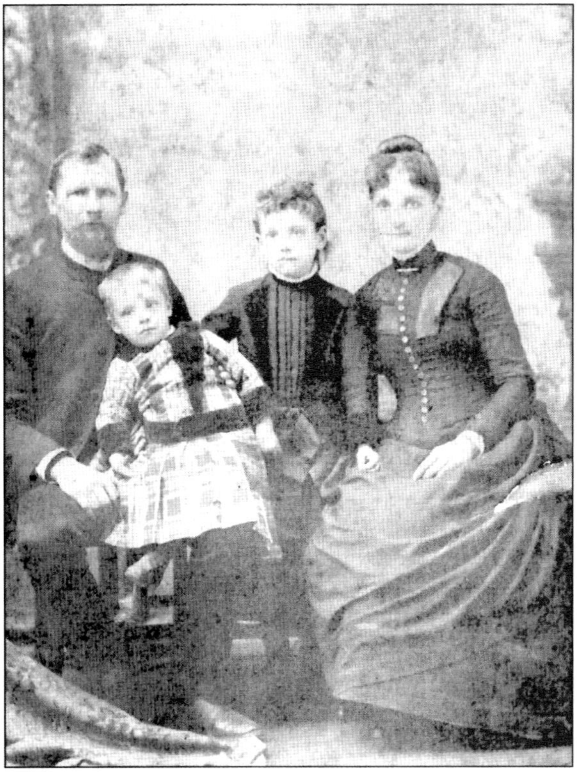

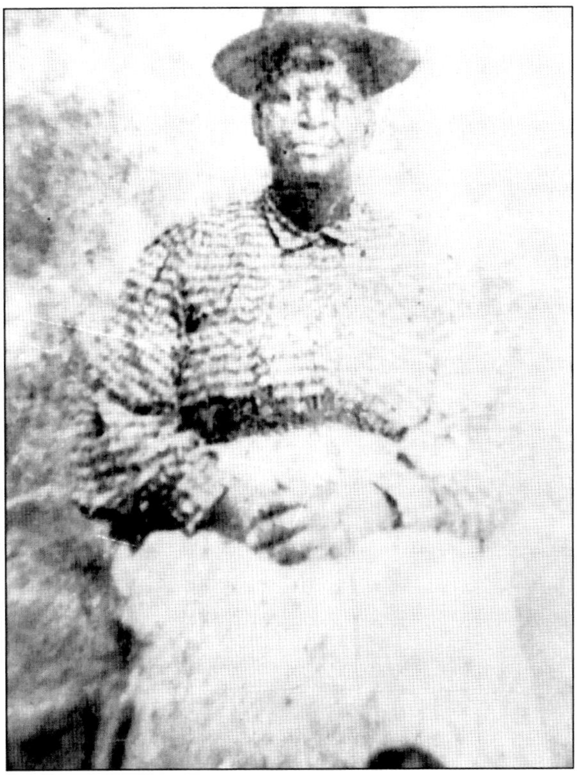

MARTHA MCKINNEY, C. 1890. Martha was the great-grandmother of Gloria McGowan. Due to her age and appearance in the photograph, it is believed that Martha was probably born into slavery. She died in 1905. (Courtesy of Gloria McKinney McGowan.)

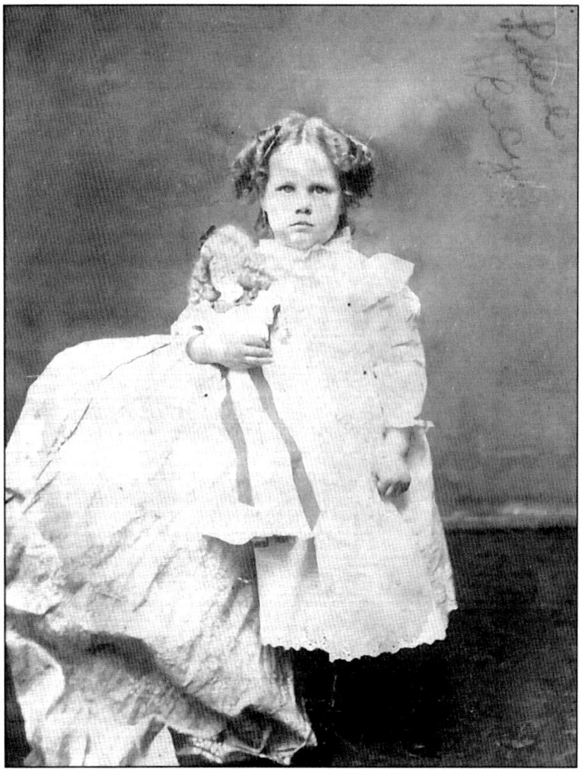

LUCY FINN ROBERTS, 1901. This is a classic Victorian-era baby photograph. Lucy was the daughter of Daniel E. Finn and S. Elizabeth Wood Finn. (Courtesy of Joyce Smith Caldwell Norris.)

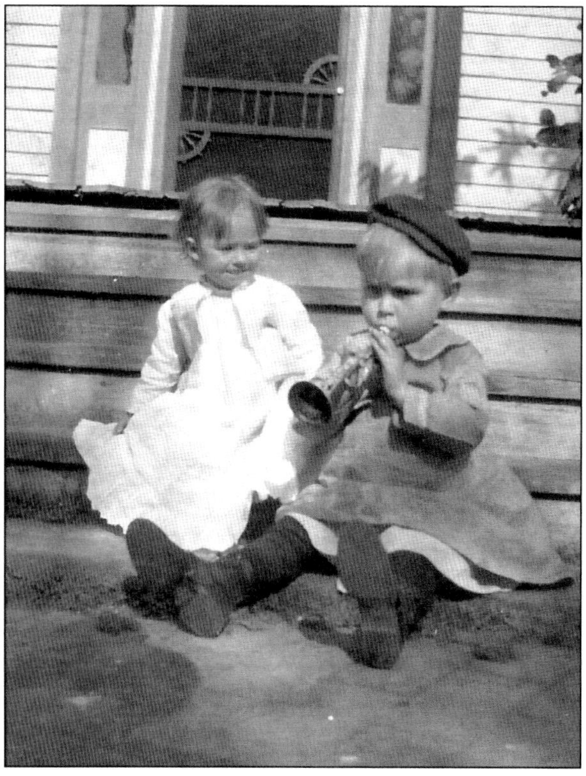

CLIETT CHILDREN ON PORCH, C. 1901. Agnes and her brother William Henry Cliett are playing on their porch steps. Henry appears to be playing Agnes a tune on his horn. Notice the manner in which they are dressed. Henry was to become a successful business owner and mayor of Childersburg. (Courtesy of Monty Powell.)

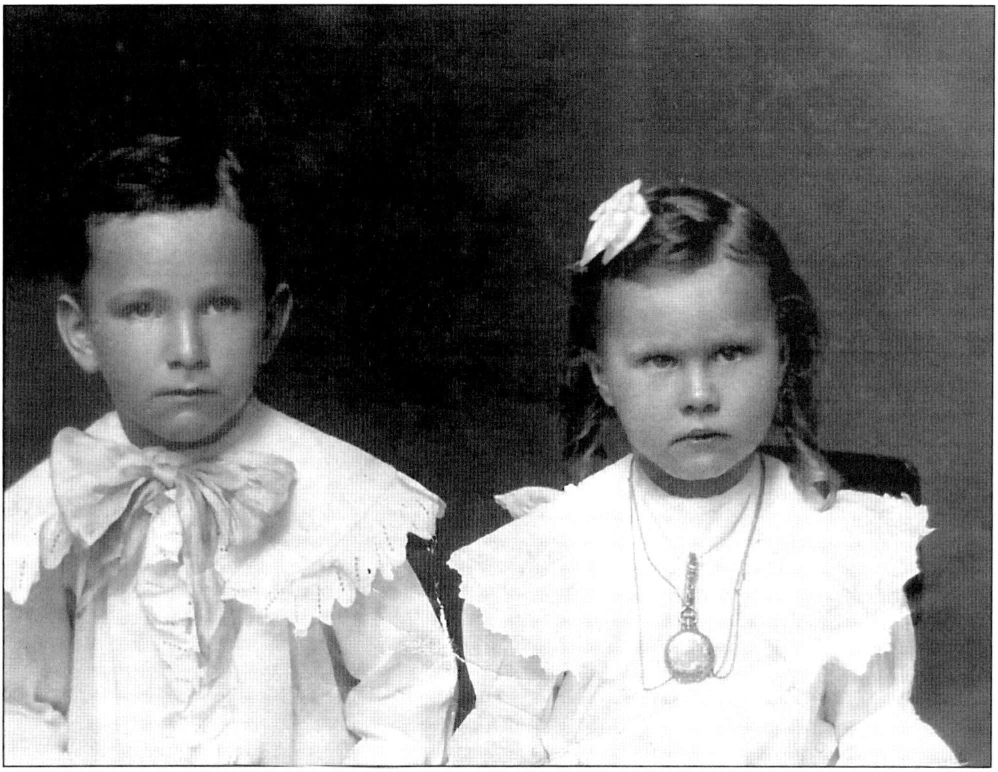

LEON SMITH AND IRENE SMITH PAYNE, C. 1907. The Smith siblings pose for this portrait. Notice her locket and his tie. (Courtesy of Joyce Smith Caldwell Norris.)

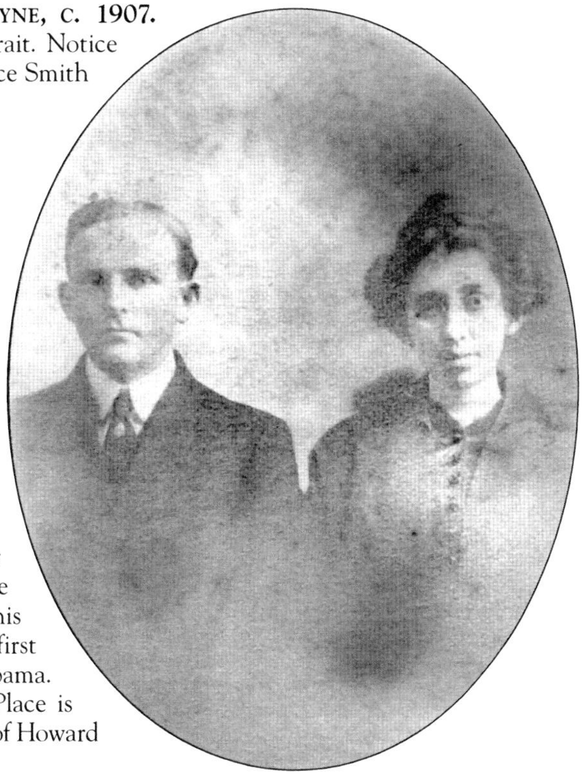

ELON VALENTINE OGLETREE AND CLARA MOSS OGLETREE, C. 1910. This photograph was taken on their wedding day. Clara's father was Flem Moss. When E. V. and Clara asked for his blessing to marry, he told them that they could have his blessing only if they would live with him in his home and if Clara would continue to do his cooking. E. V. Ogletree owned the first electric-powered cotton gin in Alabama. It stood on the property where Pat's Place is now located on First Street. (Courtesy of Howard "Bucky" Riddle.)

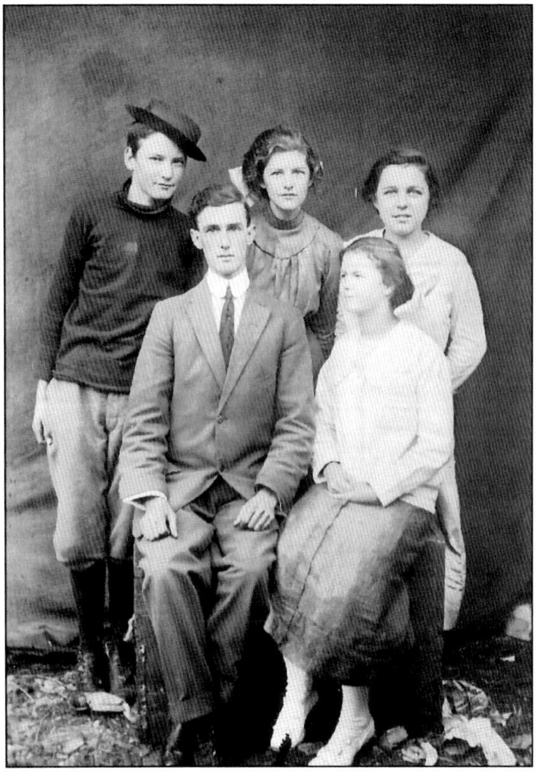

BEST FRIENDS, C. 1910. Pictured here from left to right are (first row) Chancellor Finn and Laura Smith; (second row) Harry Lessor, Thelma Butts, and Esther Adams. (Courtesy of Joyce Smith Caldwell Norris.)

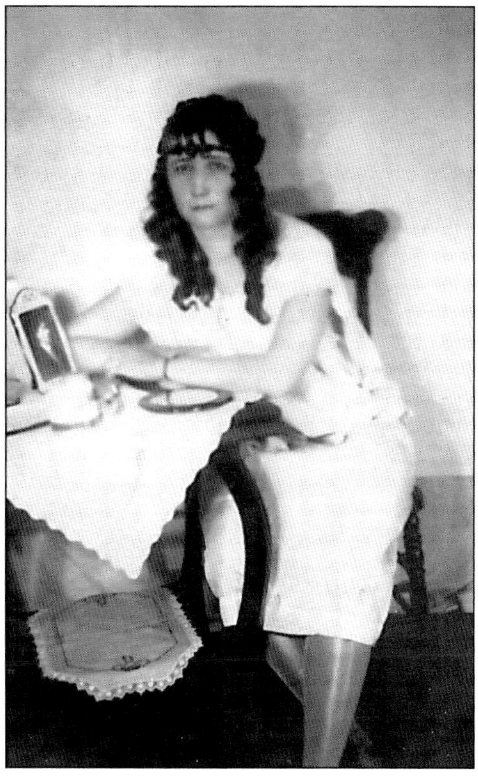

YOUNG LAURA ELLEN FINN AROUND 1910. Laura was born on September 6, 1896. She was the daughter of James Alonza Finn I and Virginia Hughes Finn. This photograph was taken when she was about 14 years old. (Courtesy of Clarence Edwin "Mickey" Finn.)

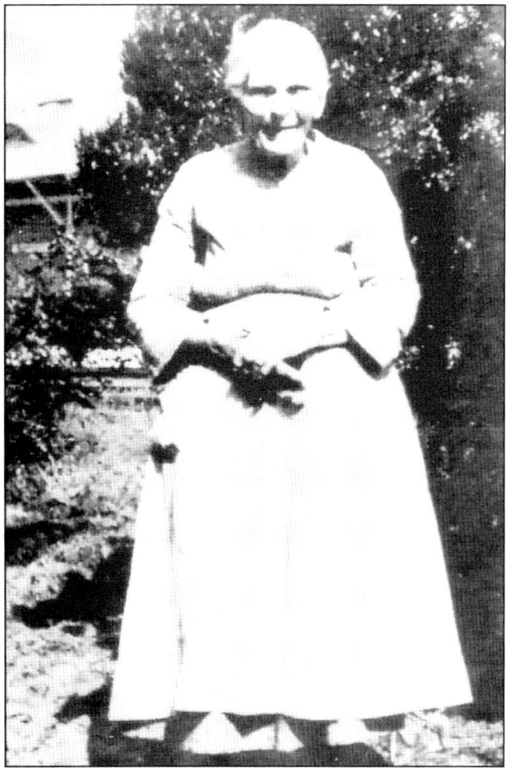

SARA BLACK LEE, C. 1910. Mrs. Sarah Black Lee was born in 1840. This is an outdoor photograph of her at age 70. (Courtesy of Robert E. Lee.)

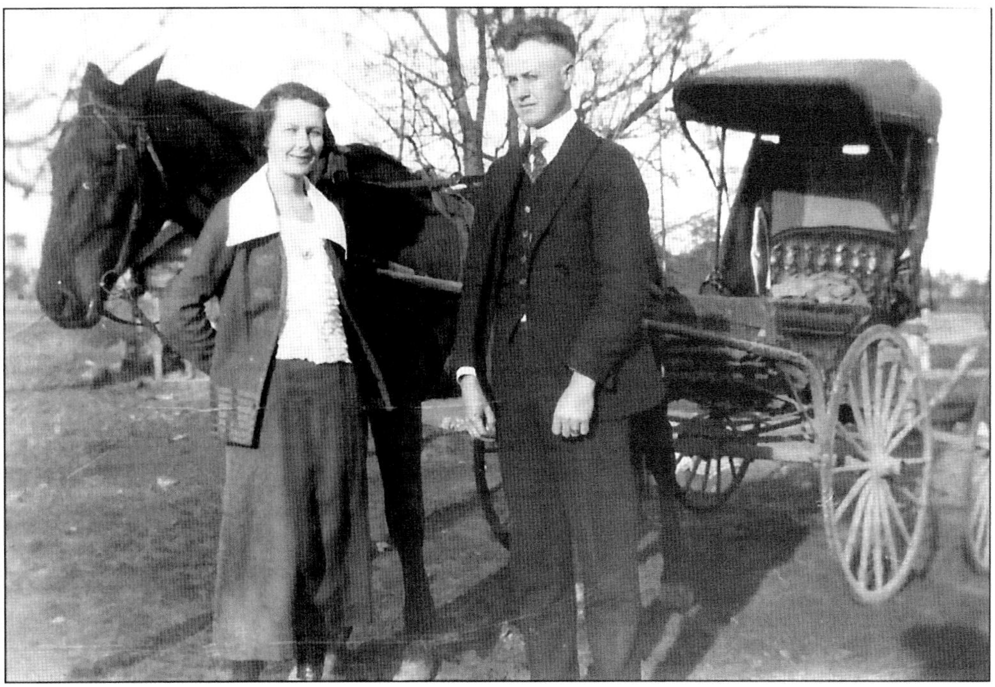

LENA CHANCELLOR AND UNIDENTIFIED FRIEND, C. 1910. Lena and her friend are very charming in this early photograph with horse and buggy. (Courtesy of Mary Farr Stone Hamby and Mike Hamby.)

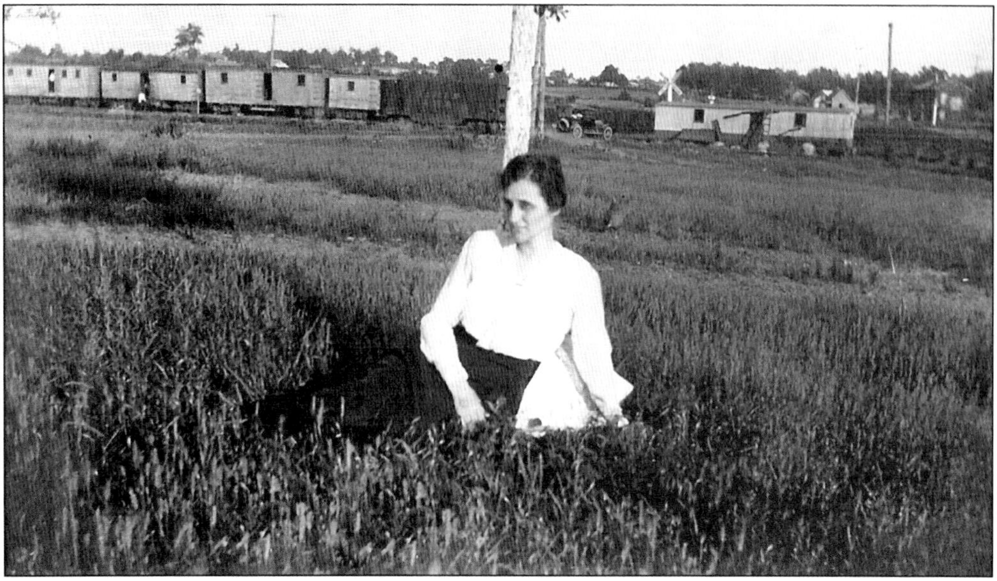

WILLIE PAULINE MONTGOMERY CLIETT, C. 1910. Notice the train in the background. Willie Pauline (born 1876) was the daughter of William Henry Montgomery and Sarah Cleveland Cliett. She was the wife of Miner James Cliett, who was the mayor of Childersburg. Willie was responsible for starting the Church of Christ in Childersburg. Her daughters, Agnes and Mildred, remembered their mother with pride and respect. She was very exacting in everything she did, whether it was raising her children, sewing, worship, or artwork. Her maternal grandfather was a close relative of Pres. Grover Cleveland. (Courtesy of Joyce Smith Caldwell Norris.)

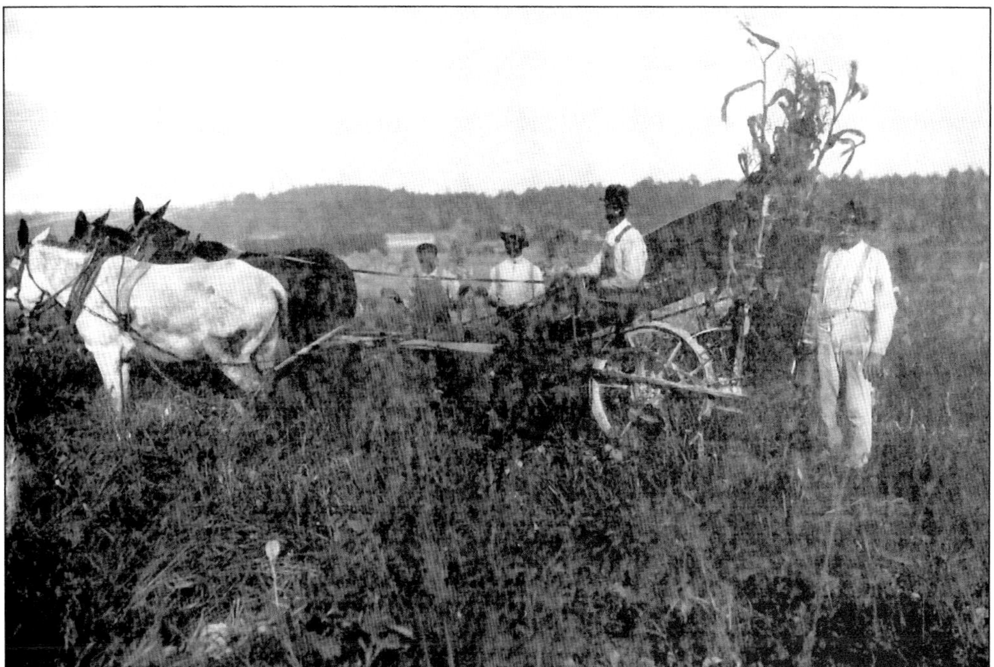

CORN HARVEST TIME, 1911. Turner Benjamin Ogletree, standing, harvests his corn. The other workers are unidentified. (Courtesy of Howard "Bucky" Riddle.)

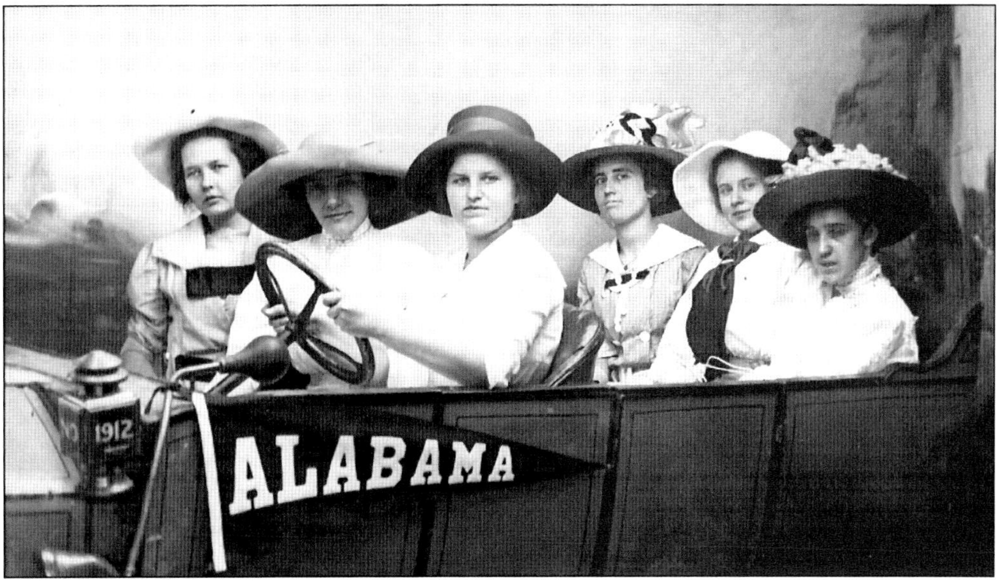

'BAMA FANS IN 1912. Unfortunately the only individual identified in this charming photograph is Lena Chancellor, riding shotgun. (Courtesy of Mary Farr Stone Hamby and Mike Hamby.)

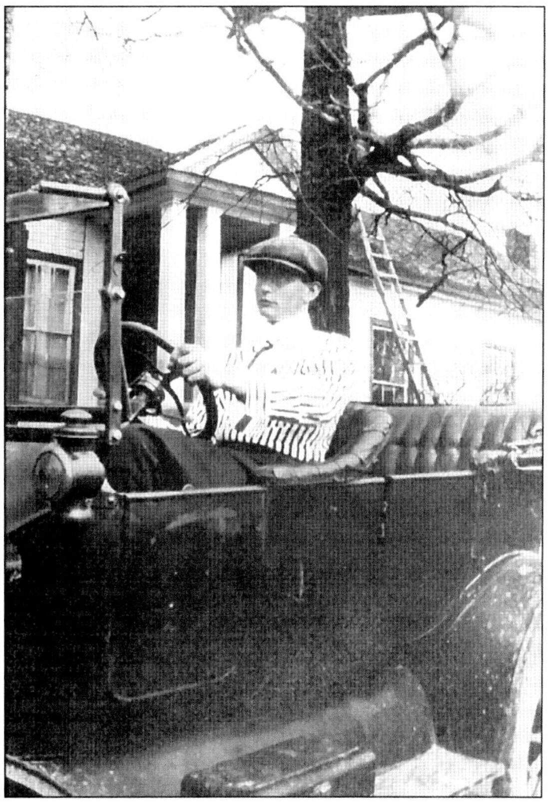

WALTER H. CHANCELLOR, C. 1915. In this photograph, Walter is sitting in his car. Walter was part owner of Chancellor's Ferry. He lived right on the Shelby County side of the river. He could hear the cars and buggies on the Childersburg side and would always wake in the middle of the night to go and get them with his ferry. (Courtesy of Mary Farr Stone Hamby and Mike Hamby.)

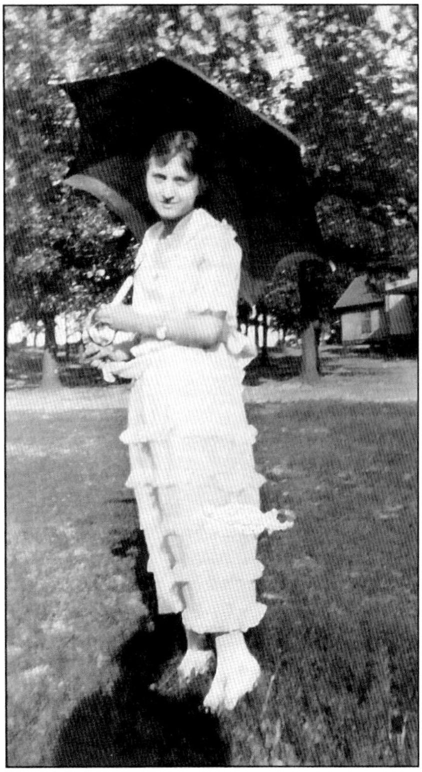

Agnes Cliett, c. 1918. Agnes is sporting her swimming attire and her shade umbrella. Agnes was the daughter of Miner J. and Willie Pauline Montgomery Cliett. (Courtesy of Joyce Smith Caldwell Norris.)

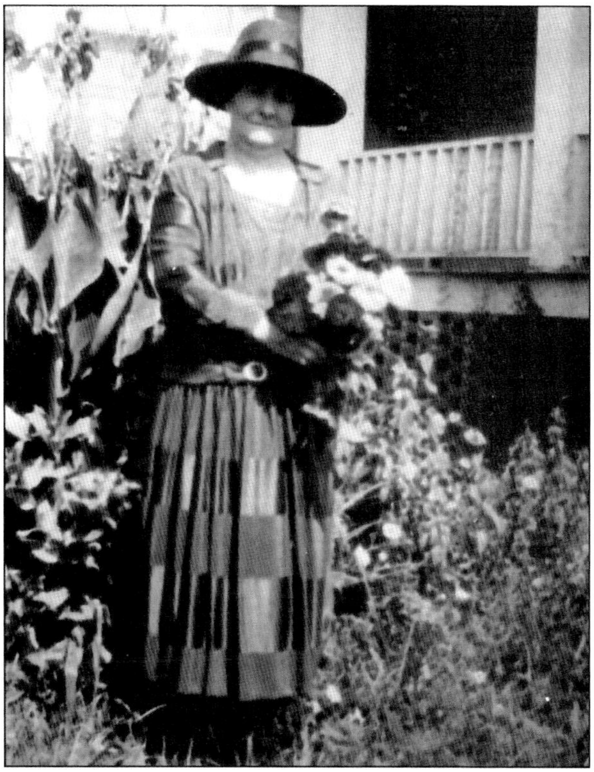

Virginia Hulley Hughes Finn, c. 1918. Virginia was the daughter of Ira Hughes and Laura Jones and the wife of James Alonza Finn I. They owned the Finn Saloon and the Finn Hotel before passing the hotel on to their son Daniel E. Finn. (Courtesy of Clarence Edwin "Mickey" Finn.)

SHEALEY LIMBAUGH, BEFORE 1920. The Shealey Limbaugh known by all for his selfless civic work in Childersburg was named after this man, his uncle, who died in 1920. (Courtesy of Jane Limbaugh Allen.)

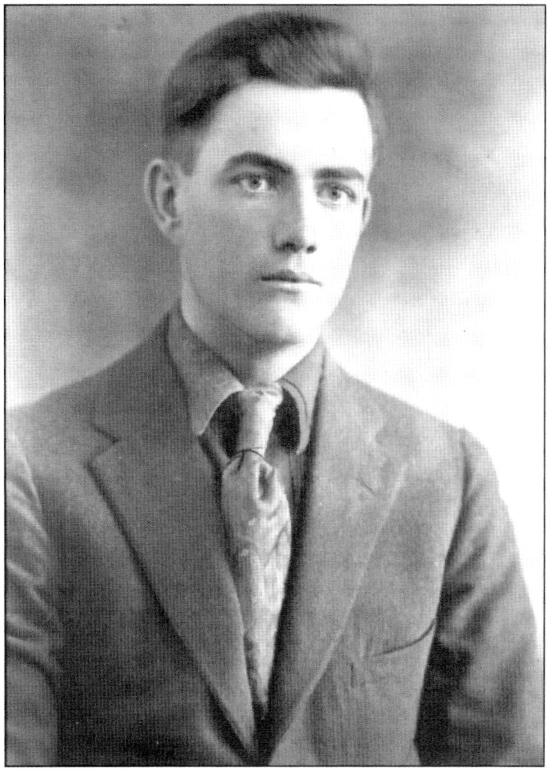

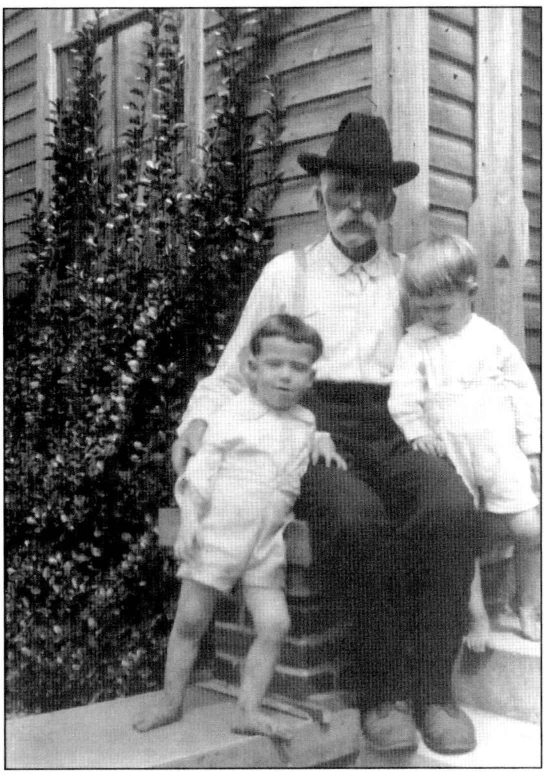

TURNER BENJAMIN OGLETREE, 1920. This is a photograph of Ogletree with his grandsons Franklin "Red" (left) and Herbert Riddle in 1920. (Courtesy of Howard "Bucky" Riddle.)

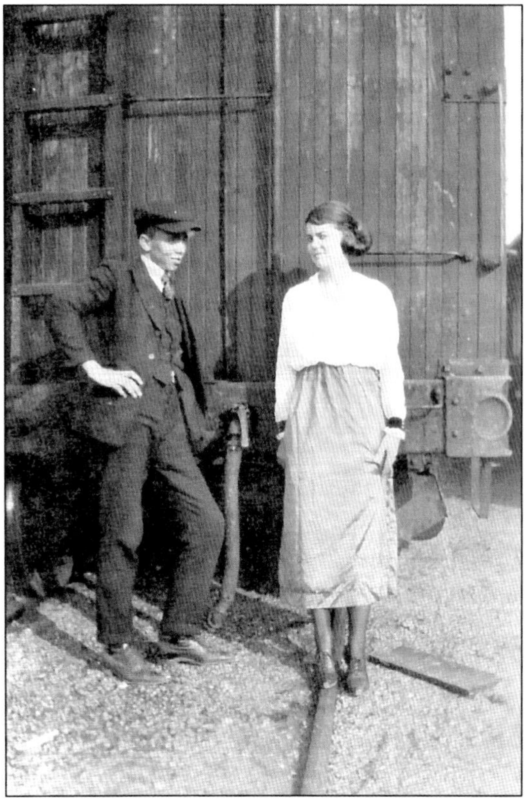

William E. Tate and Ruby Riley, c. 1922. William and Ruby appear to be standing in a barn. Notice the way they are dressed. (Courtesy of Joyce Smith Caldwell Norris.)

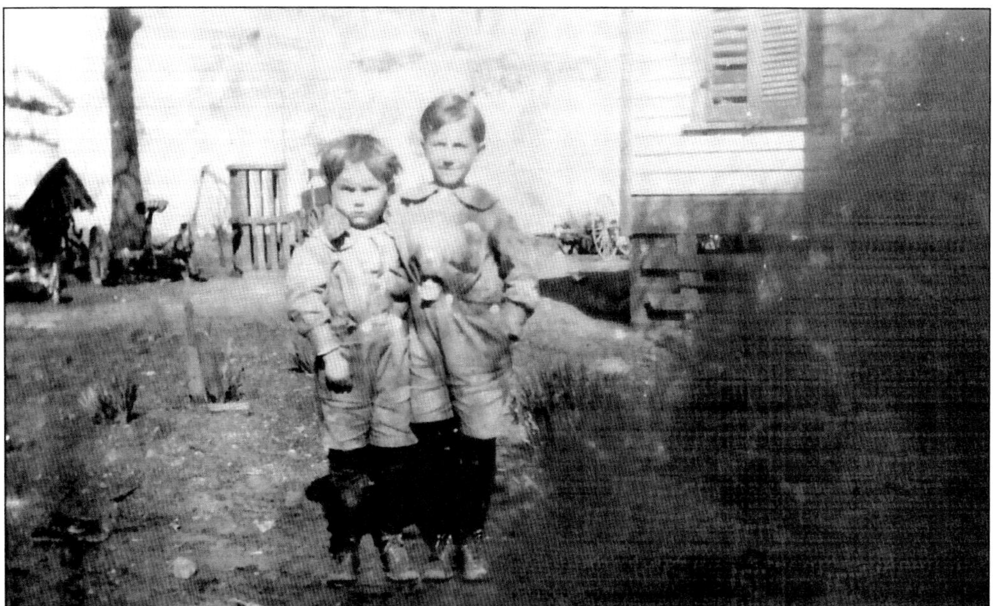

Siblings Lamar (Left) and Earl Smith, c. 1920. It appears that these brothers may have been playing in their yard and just stopped for a photo opportunity. (Courtesy of Joyce Smith Caldwell Norris.)

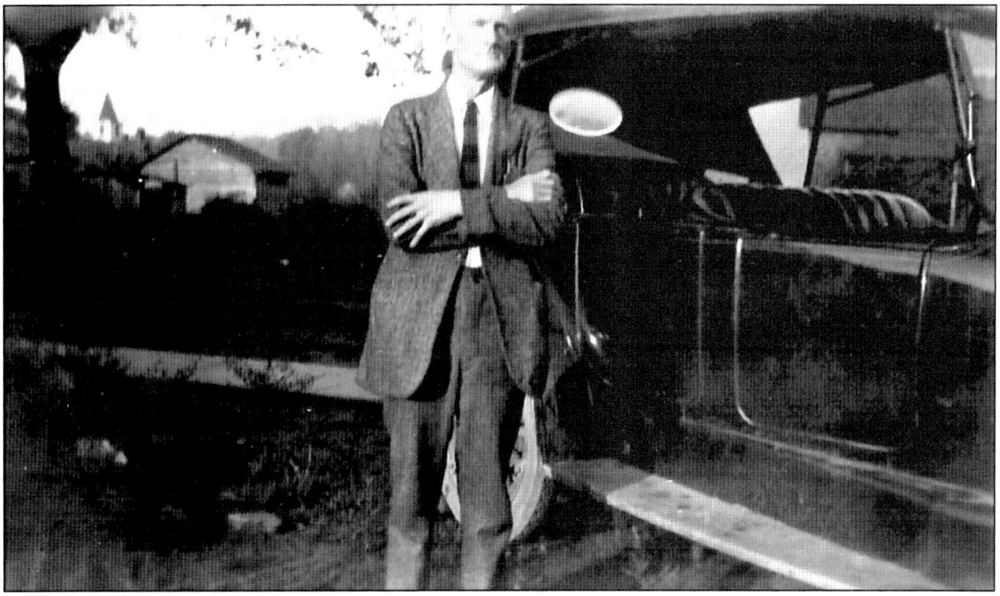

DANIEL EDWIN FINN, C. 1920. Mr. Finn was the proprietor of the New South Finn Hotel. In this photograph, he is standing near his car. (Courtesy of Joyce Smith Caldwell Norris.)

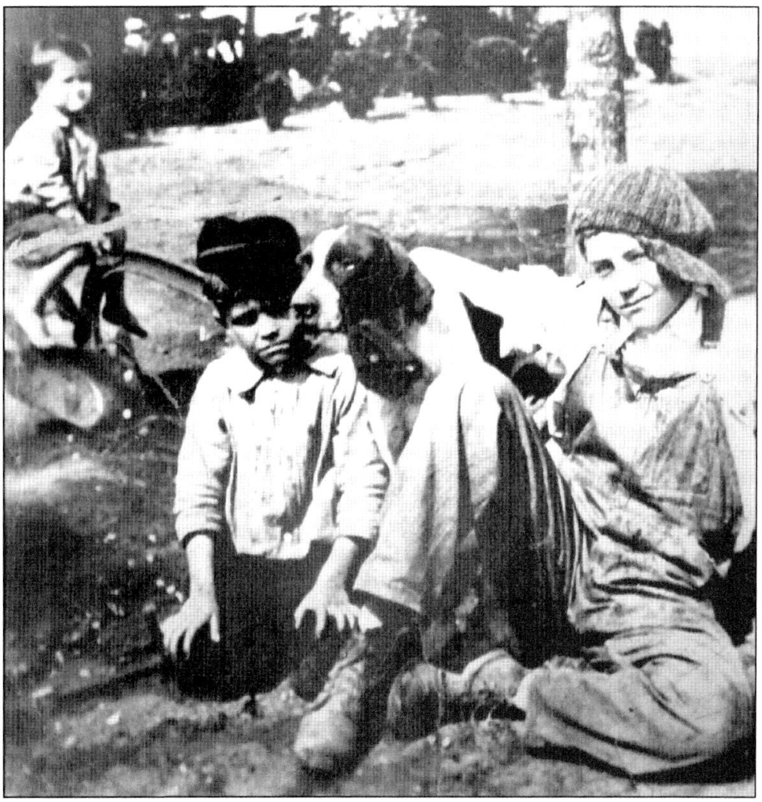

YOUNG LIMBAUGH BROTHERS, C. 1923. Robert (left), Roston (center), and Joe Limbaugh are pictured here. The dog's name was Dixie. (Courtesy of Jane Limbaugh Allen.)

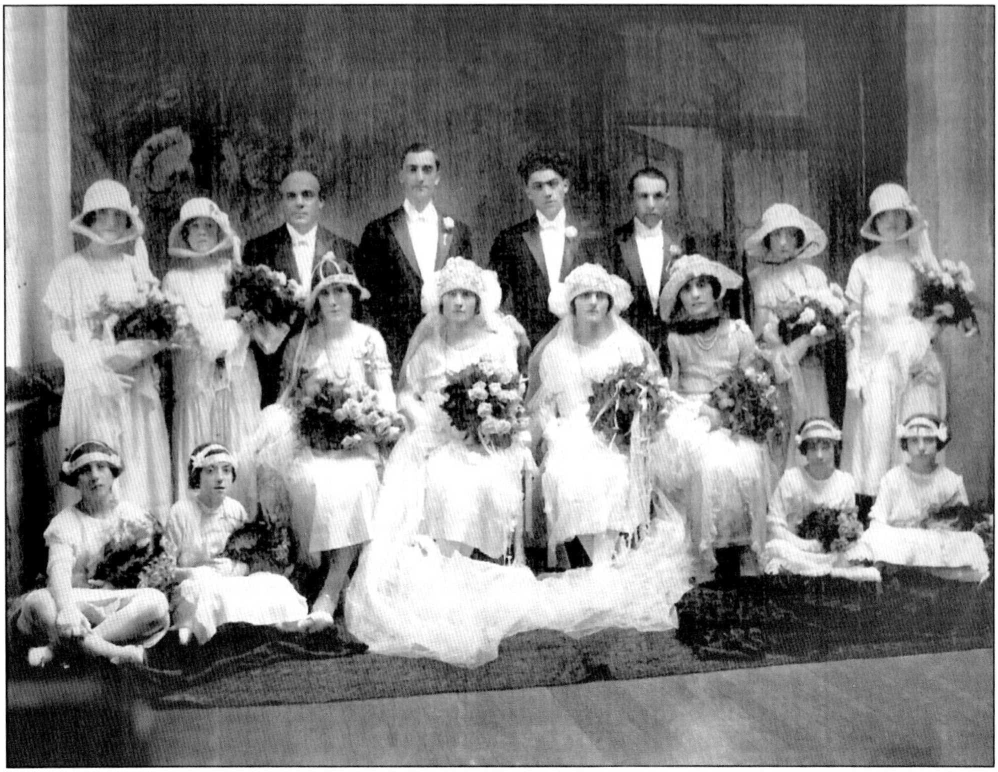

Double Wedding, 1924. Emma Finn is the bride on the left center and Tony Herrera is the groom on the right center. At this time, the others are unidentified. Tony Herrera was an immigrant from Spain. Emma was from Childersburg and was raised at the old Finn homeplace on Lucy Finn Road. Tony answered Emma's ad in the *Chicago Tribune*'s Lonely Hearts Club, and they were married shortly thereafter. (Courtesy of Clarence Edwin "Mickey" Finn.)

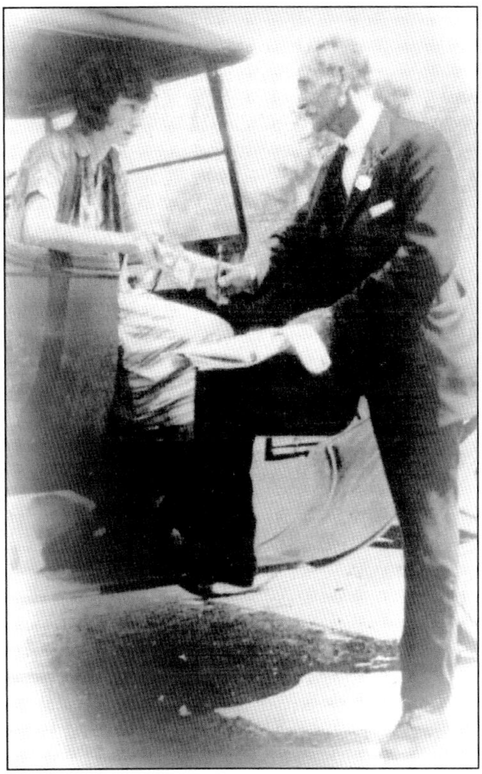

W. Jesse Limbaugh (1858–1936). William Jesse Limbaugh was the husband of T. Elizabeth Shealey Limbaugh. Their son, George Malley Limbaugh, was the father of the Limbaugh brothers who have done so much for Childersburg. Jesse sold insurance policies. This photograph was an advertisement for the company that employed him. Notice the exchange going on between Jesse and the lady in this photograph. (Courtesy of Jane Limbaugh Allen.)

SHELLEY AND LURA FINN, C. 1925. Edgar Shelly Finn (1893–1975) and his wife, Lura R. Finn (1897–1978), are posing with a huge log. This photograph was either taken on a visit to Yakima, Washington, or in Childersburg at one of the old sawmills. (Courtesy of Ralph and Dolly Finn.)

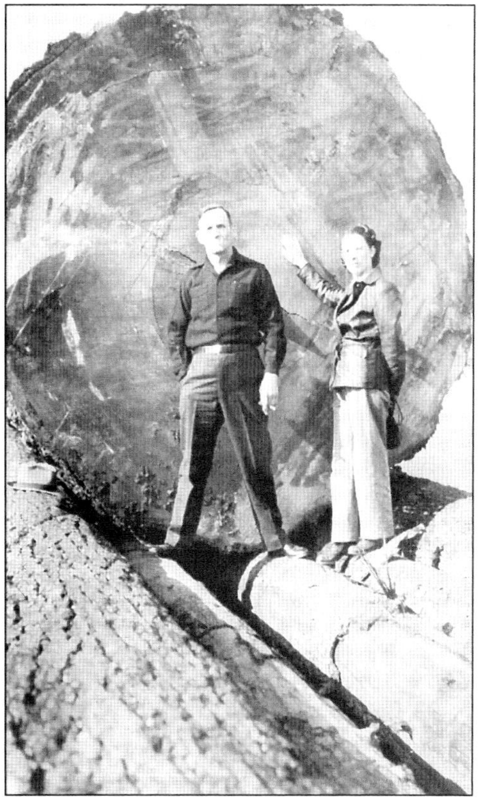

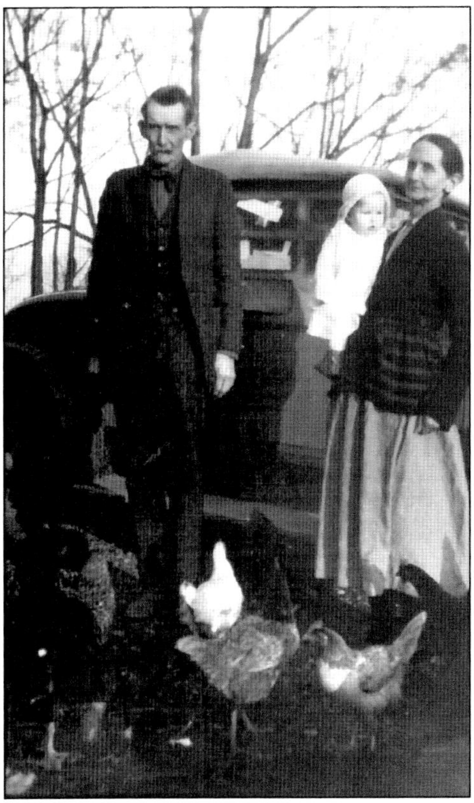

TIME FOR GRANDBABY, 1928. Isaac Suttle Chancellor and his wife, Mary Elizabeth Hughston Chancellor, hold their granddaughter, Mary Farr Stone (Hamby), in 1928. (Courtesy of Mary Farr Stone Hamby and Mike Hamby.)

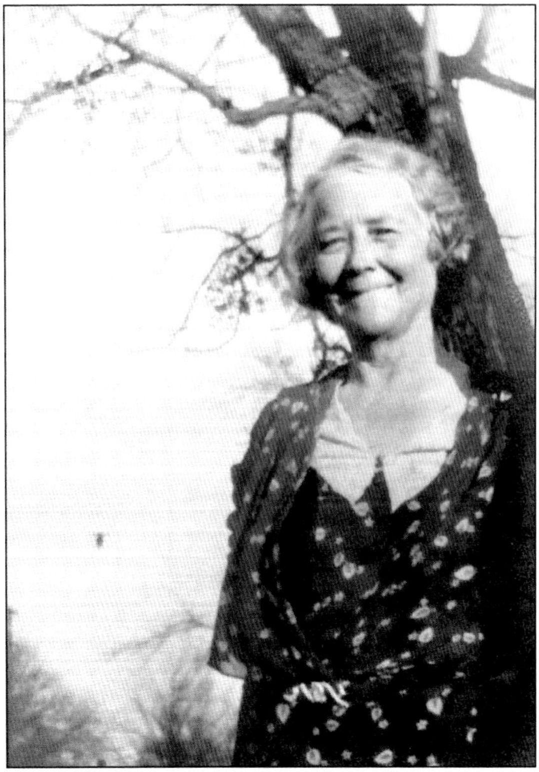

LENORE "SWEETIE" ODEN NICHOLS, C. 1930. Sweetie was born in September 1868 to Joshua Bussey Oden and Laura Graham Oden. She married John A. Nichols. She never had children of her own, but she had two stepchildren, B. Frank and Alva Nichols. They lived in what is now known as the Donahoo House on Ninth Avenue in Childersburg. The Donahoo family is descended from John A. Nichols's first marriage to Allie Simmons. B. Frank's daughter Dorothy married Ed Donahoo. (Courtesy of Patricia Teague Wesley Godfrey.)

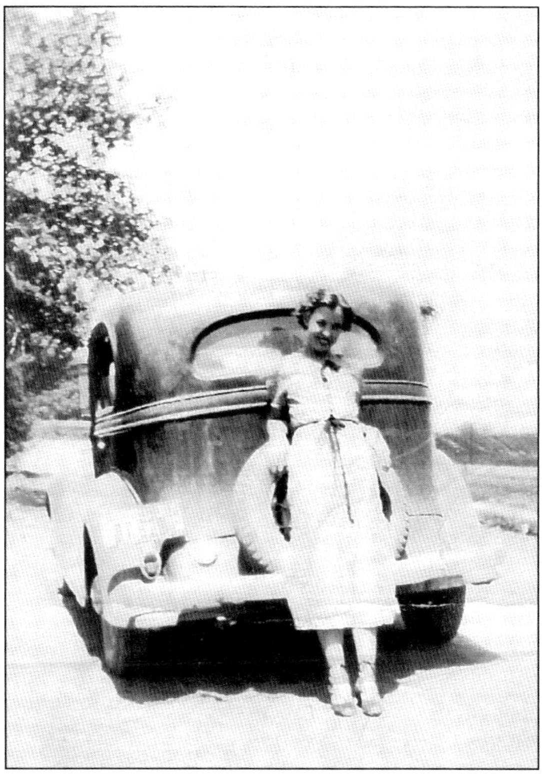

GRACE ELIZABETH EDWARDS MCSWEEN, C. 1930. Grace was born October 24, 1914. Her parents were W. O. and Ira Edwards. She had one sibling, Dorothy Edwards McGathey. Grace graduated from Childersburg High School in 1932. She got her bachelor of science degree from the University of Montevallo in 1937. That same year, she was employed by the Talladega County Board of Education, where she taught her entire career of 35 years. She married John Finley McSween in 1938. John was killed in Italy in 1944, during World War II. They had one son, William "Bill" McSween. At this time, Grace lived with her parents on Eighth Avenue in Childersburg. The house was located between Frontier Bank and the Antique Car Garage. Grace died on July 2, 1998, and was buried at the Old Childersburg Cemetery. (Courtesy of Clarence Edwin "Mickey" Finn.)

ANNIE HAMMETT GIDDENS, C. 1930. Annie Hammett Giddens (1866–1951) was the daughter of William Bethel Hammett and Miriam Hawkins Brasher and the wife of Madison Whitfield "Babe" Giddens. She is best remembered as being a gentle woman and fervent Baptist. (Courtesy of Ralph and Dolly Finn.)

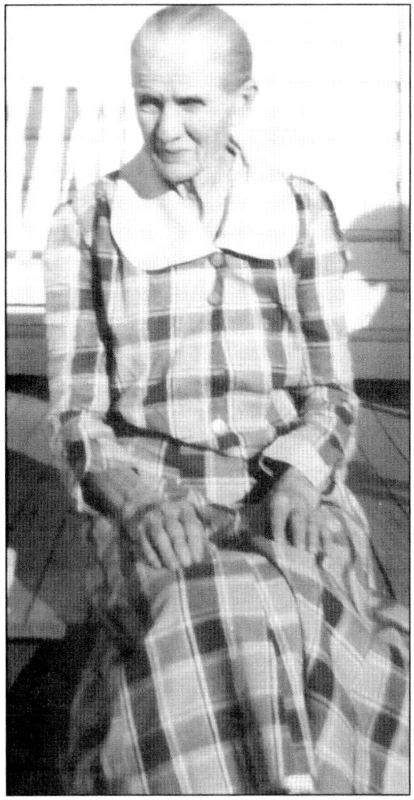

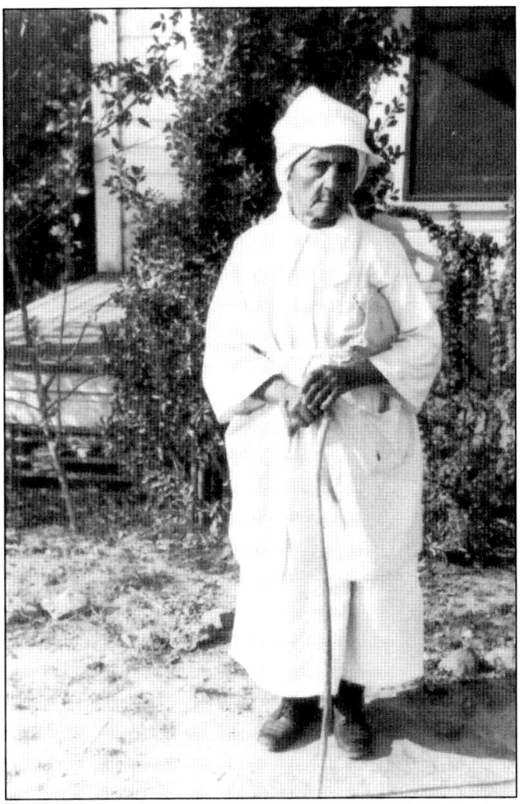

AUNT MARIAH, C. 1932. Aunt Mariah was probably born into slavery. She was someone whom the people of Childersburg saw every day. Not much is known about her except that she always went barefoot and wore spotless white in thick layers. Every day, she would go door to door asking for a cup of sugar or flour and people always gave her what they could. Everyone in town just called her Aunt Mariah. One day, Aunt Mariah told everyone she saw that she was going to heaven on a white horse. The next day, she was hit by a truck and killed. (Photograph by and courtesy of Katherine Frangopoulos Commander Blackerby.)

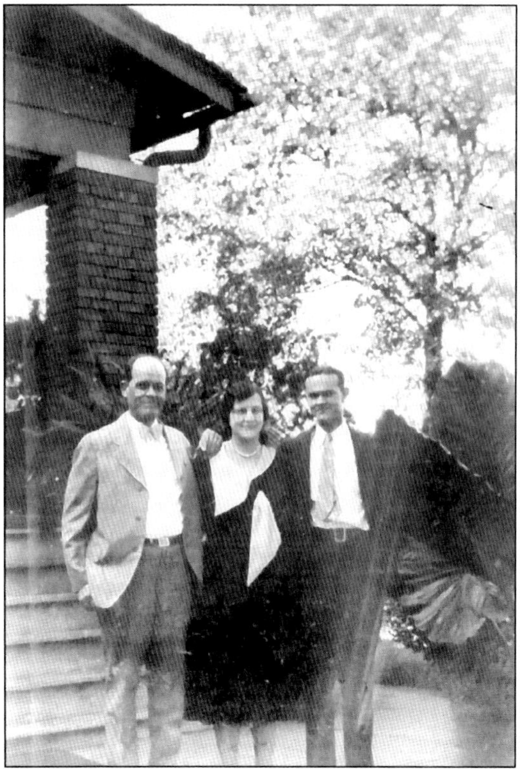

STRICKLAND FAMILY, C. 1935. From left to right are Jerry Strickland, Bertha Bryant Strickland, and Clarence "Chick" Strickland. (Courtesy of Patricia Teague Wesley Godfrey.)

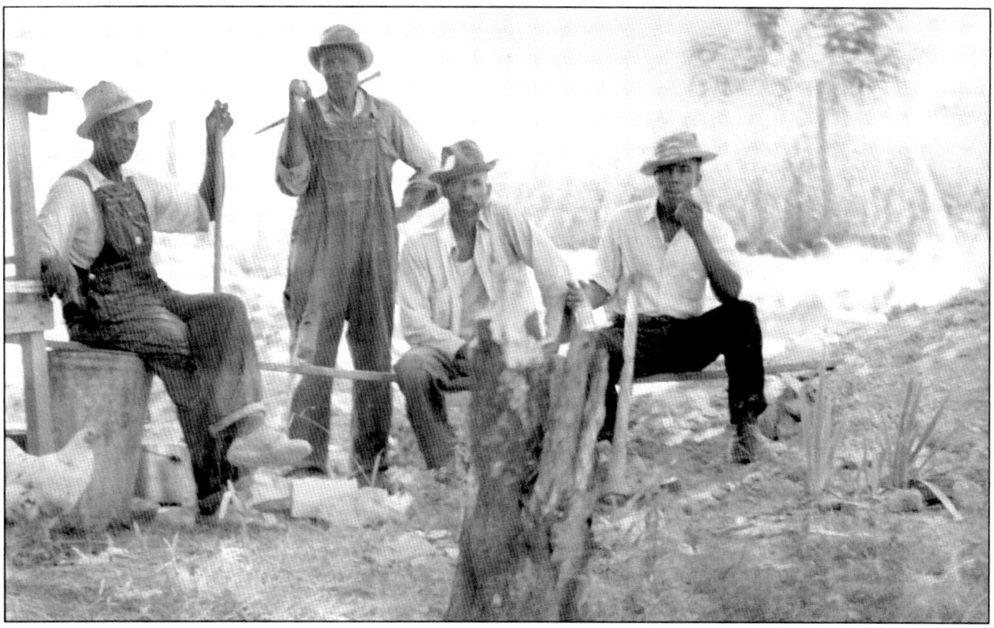

TAKING A BREAK, C. 1935. These hard-working men take a break for this photograph. They are, from left to right, John Rhoden, John Templeton, Willie Lee, and unidentified. Notice the ingenuity of the bench on which they are sitting. It is a wooden plank propped between the dirt pile and the garbage can. Also notice the pickax John Templeton is holding. (Courtesy of Clarence Edwin "Mickey" Finn.)

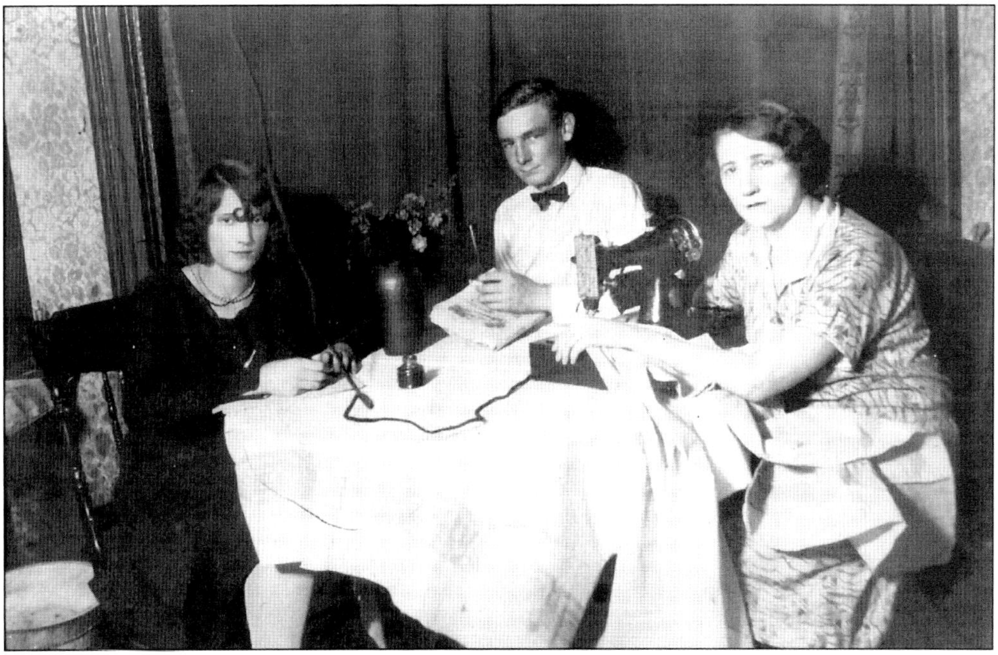

FINN SIBLINGS, C. 1935. Shown here are, from left to right, Emma Herrera, Dennis Finn, and Laura D'Aston. Notice the style of the sewing machine. (Courtesy of Clarence Edwin "Mickey" Finn.)

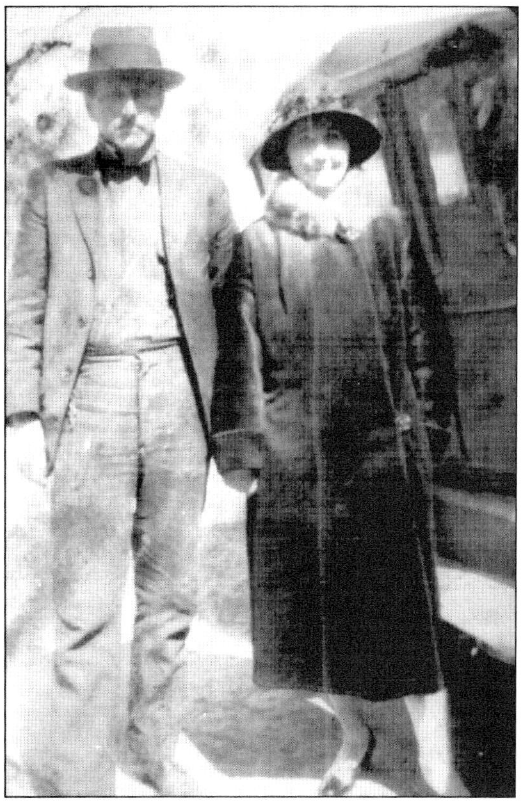

WILLIAM OSCAR SMITH AND WIFE, WILLIE LIPSEY SMITH, C. 1935. Oscar and Willie still have descendants in Childersburg. Their six children were Lemuel, Irene, Maenetta, Lynwood, Earl, and Lamar Smith. (Courtesy of Joyce Smith Caldwell Norris.)

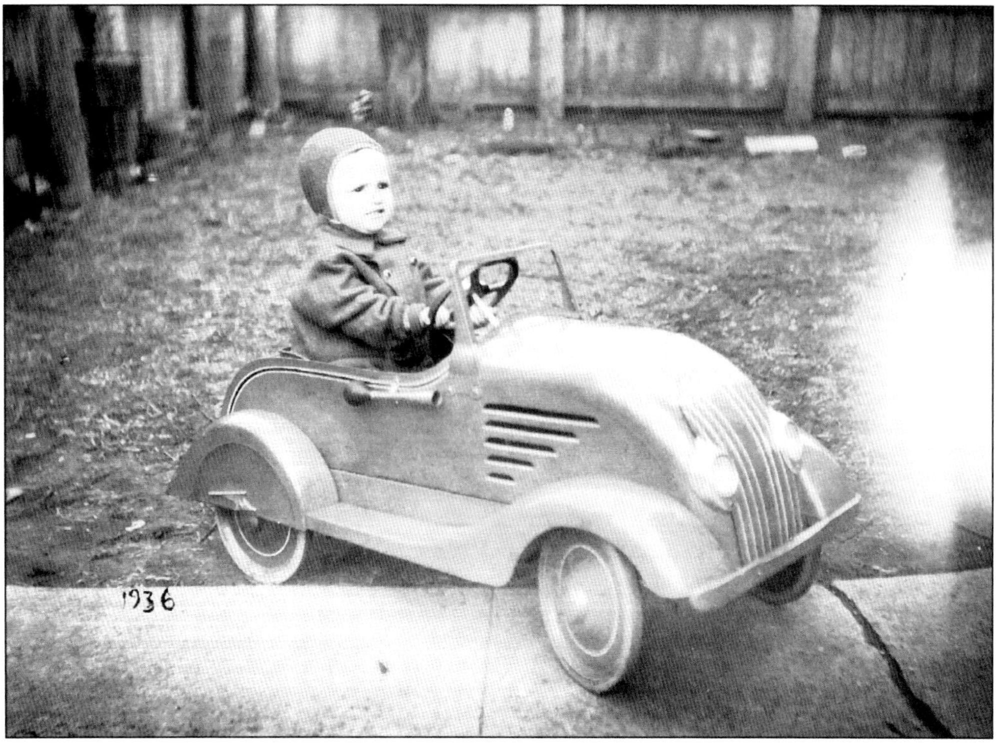

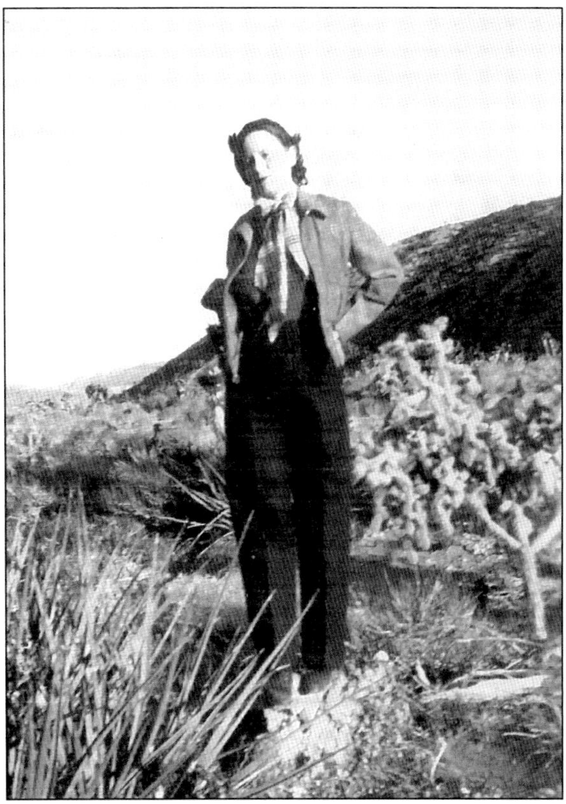

MILLARD HERRERA, 1936. Millard is riding in his toy car. (Courtesy of Clarence Edwin "Mickey" Finn.)

LUCY ESTHER FINN WEARING PANTS, 1936. This is the progressive woman from which Lucy Finn Road gets its name. There were actually three Lucy Finns: Lucy M. Finn (born 1853), Lucy Finn (Roberts) (born 1899), and the one in this photograph, Lucy Esther Finn (Howard) (born 1903). They are all from the same family. Notice the cacti in the background. They probably belonged to her sister's husband, botanist and cactus expert Joshua D'Aston. (Courtesy of Clarence Edwin "Mickey" Finn.)

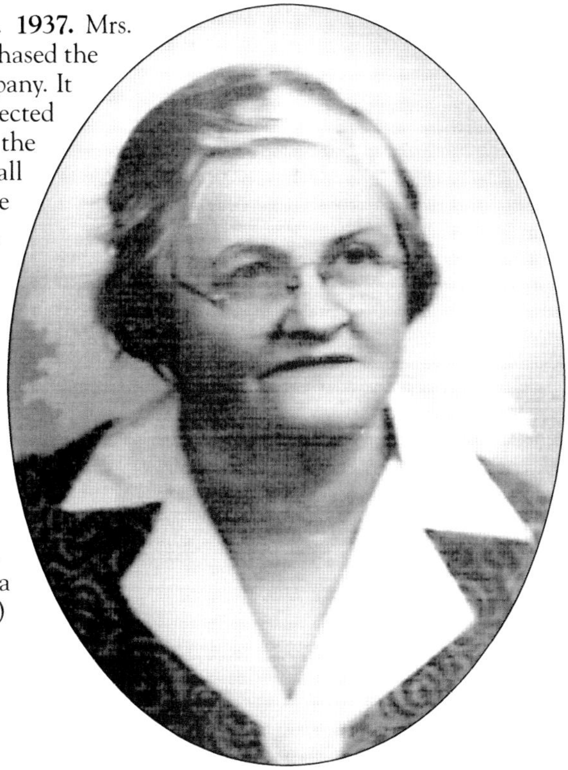

Ernestine Lessor Bryant Bates, c. 1937. Mrs. Bates and her husband, W. L. Bates, purchased the holdings of the Childersburg Land Company. It is an oral tradition that they were not expected to be able to meet the requirements of the loan and the land company expected all property to revert back to them at some point. Soon after the initial transaction, World War II broke out and the U.S. government bought a large piece of property from the Bateses to build part of the Alabama Ordnance Works. The AOW was massive, and they bought property from many residents. The sale of this property secured the loan. Some of their property is known today as Bates Addition and Lakeside Drive. The property for the former Childersburg High School was donated by W. L. and Ernestine Bates for the purpose of a school. (Courtesy of Kim Veazey Knight.)

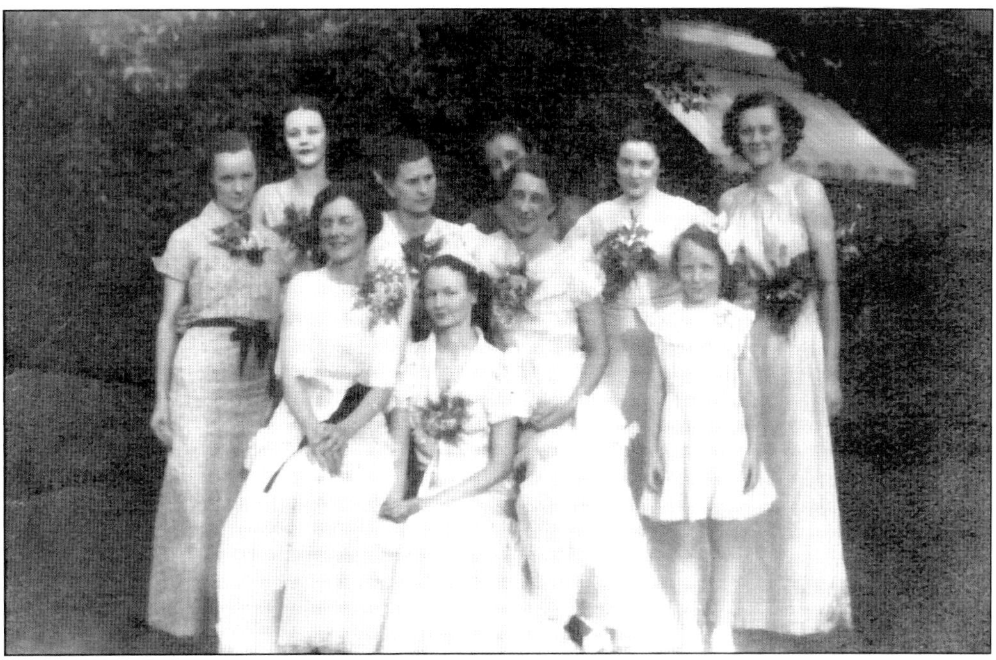

Formal Ladies, 1937. Shown here from left to right are (first row) Agnes Taylor Riddle; (second row) Miss Nellie Glazner, Helen Chancellor Biles, and Grace Riddle; (third row) Rebecca Hines, Mildred Oden Strickland, Evelyn Richardson, Grace Edwards, Elizabeth Stewart, and Dot Edwards. (Courtesy of Howard "Bucky" Riddle.)

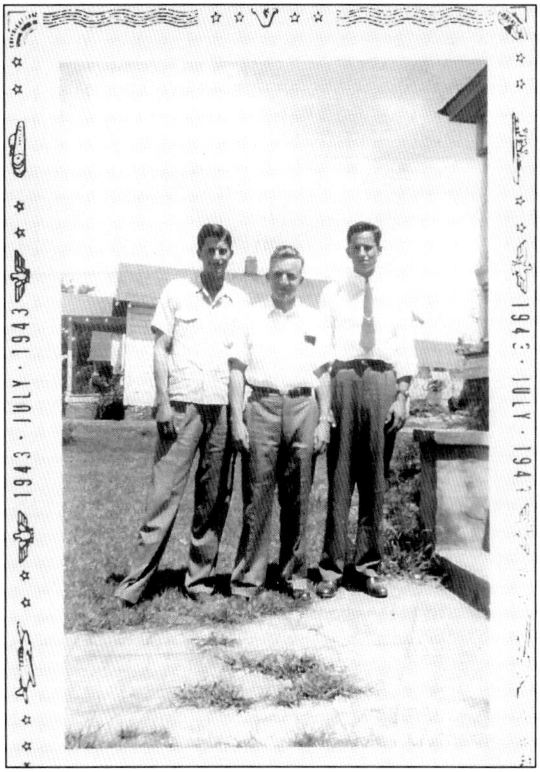

Frank Limbaugh (left), Mickey Finn (center), and Shealey Limbaugh, c. 1943. These three handsome young men stop to smile for the camera. (Courtesy of Clarence Edwin "Mickey" Finn.)

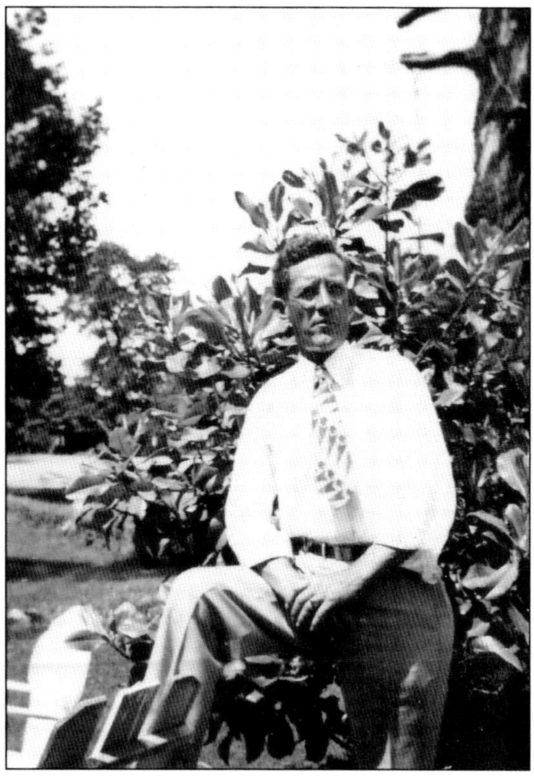

Wallace H. Veazey, c. 1940. Mr. Veazey owned Veazey Grocery Store in downtown Childersburg as well as the Shell service station. He was an entrepreneur and a businessman. He moved to Childersburg from Chilton County. He died during his third term on the city council of Childersburg. Veazey was a deacon at the First Baptist Church, a postman, and a gentleman farmer. (Courtesy of Kim Veazey Knight.)

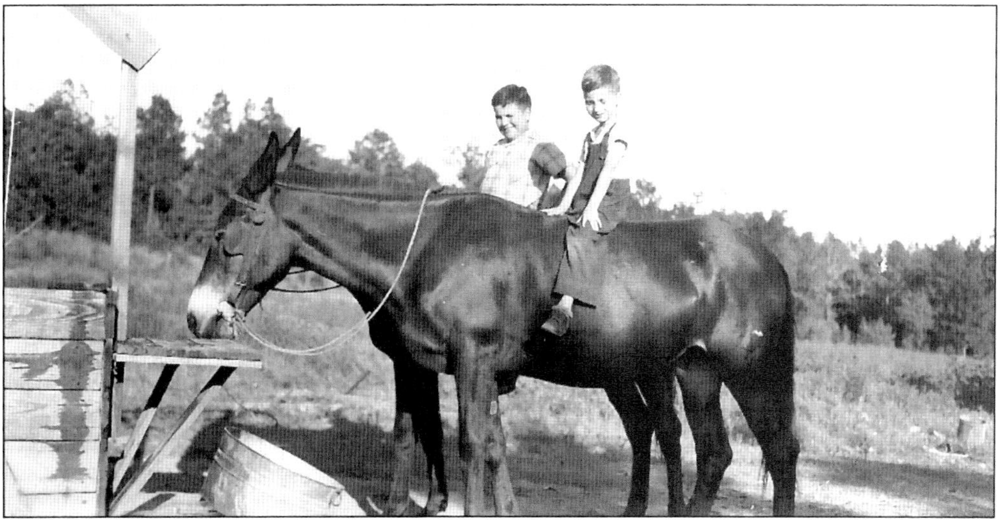

MILLARD (LEFT) AND DENNIS HERRERA, C. 1941. These boys are having fun riding donkeys. (Courtesy of Clarence Edwin "Mickey" Finn.)

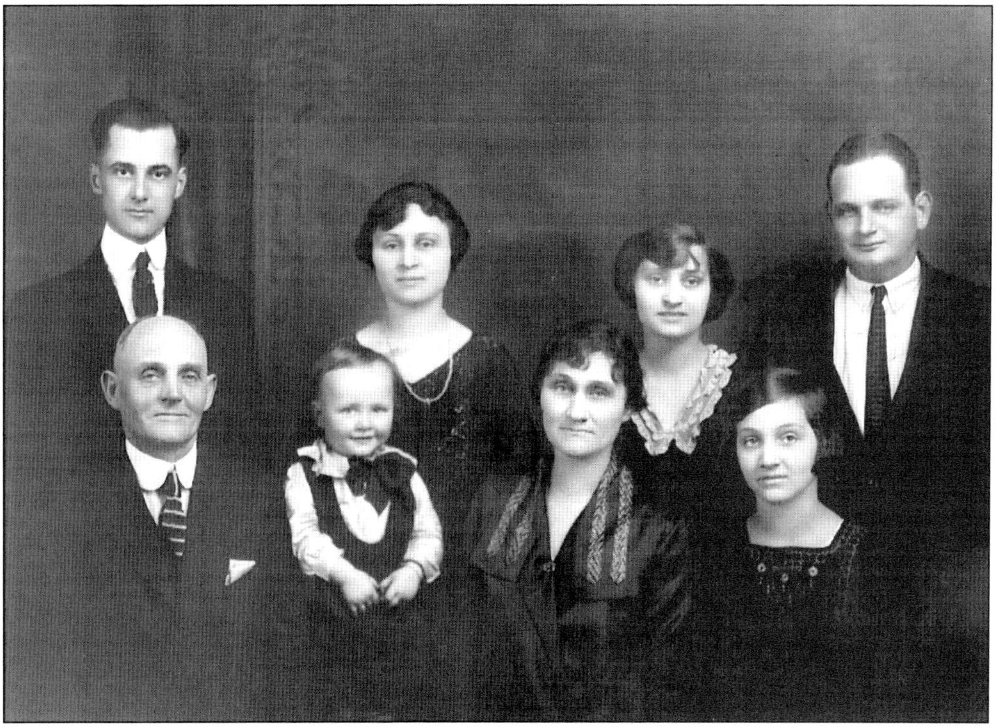

CLIETT FAMILY. The Cliett family was one of the first families in Childersburg. Pictured in this family portrait are, from left to right, (first row) Miner James Cliett, Cordell, Pauline, and Mildred; (second row) B. C. Goodpasture, Cleveland, Agnes, and Henry Cliett. (Courtesy of Monty Powell.)

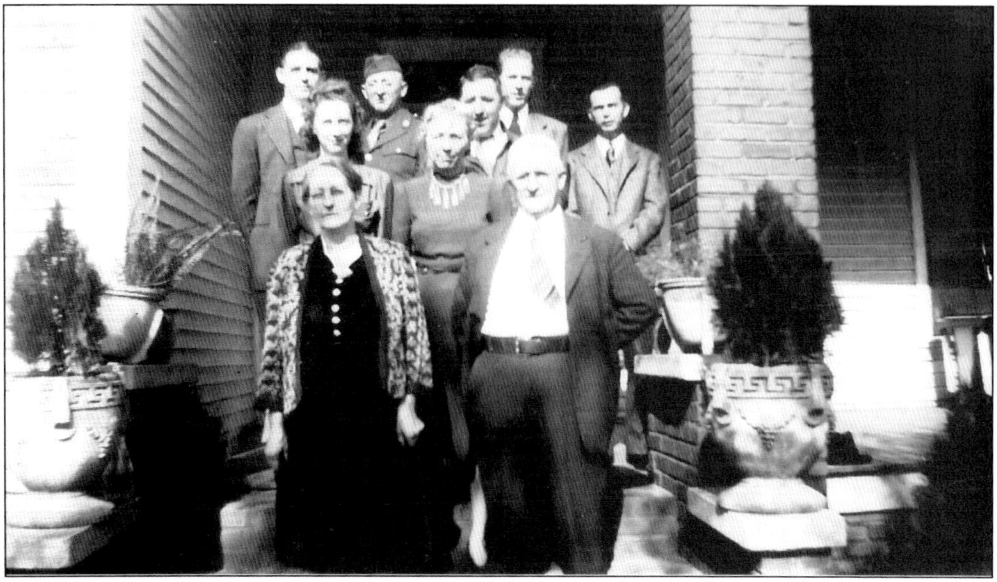

MOODY FAMILY, 1942. From left to right are (first row) mom Frances and dad George; (second row) Helen and Lillian; (third row) Henry, Jack, Walter, Dee, and Casey. Chuggy Moody took the photograph. (Courtesy of Dr. Marcus "Dee" Moody.)

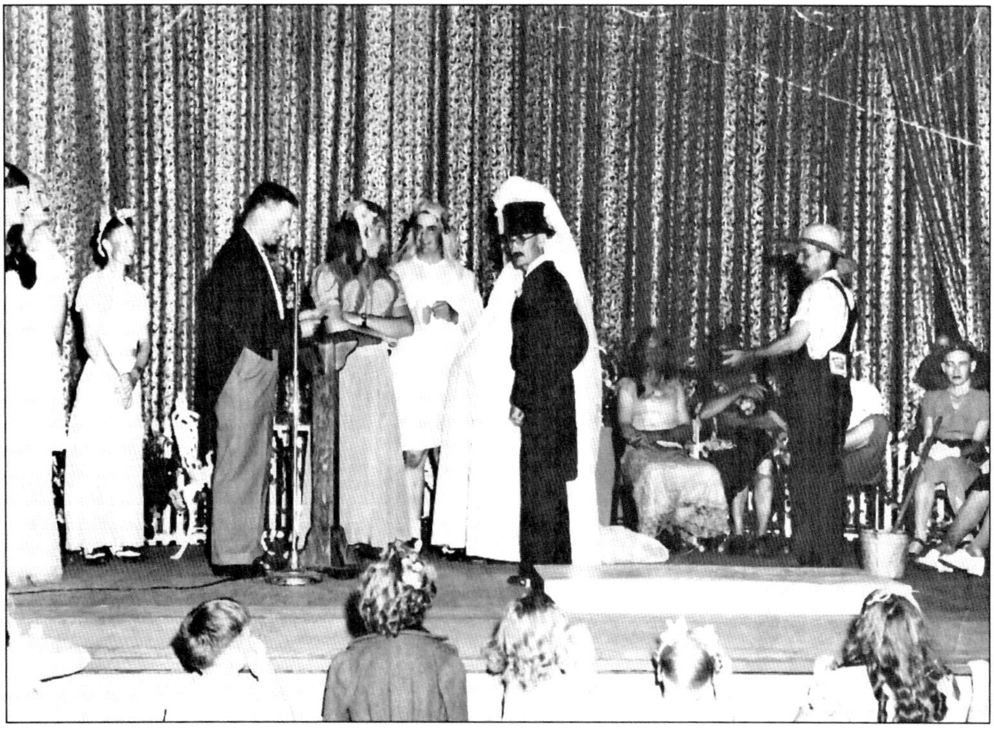

WOMANLESS PLAY, 1942. Though it would be such a treasure to have this on film, we can be thankful that at least we have the photograph. The minister is Joe Harris, the bride is Police Chief Tim Finn, the groom is Mr. Aderholt, the father of bride is Lamar Smith, and the maids are, from left to right, Ed Bolton, George Limbaugh, and Fred Conville; seated from left to right are Wallace Veazey, Shealey Limbaugh, and Clarence Cooke. (Courtesy of Jane Limbaugh Allen.)

HAPPY COUPLE. This is a portrait of Kempis W. McKinney and wife Callie O'Neal McKinney. This photograph was taken after World War I. They lived their whole lives in Childersburg. (Courtesy of Gloria McKinney McGowan.)

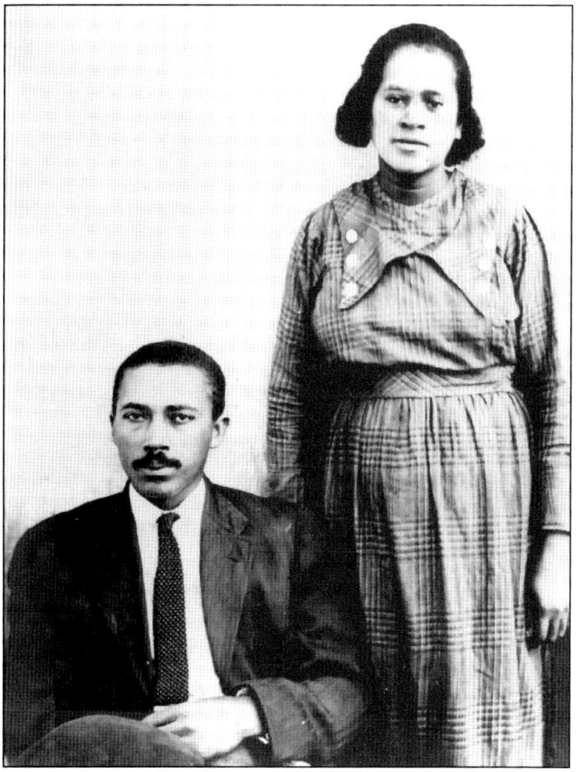

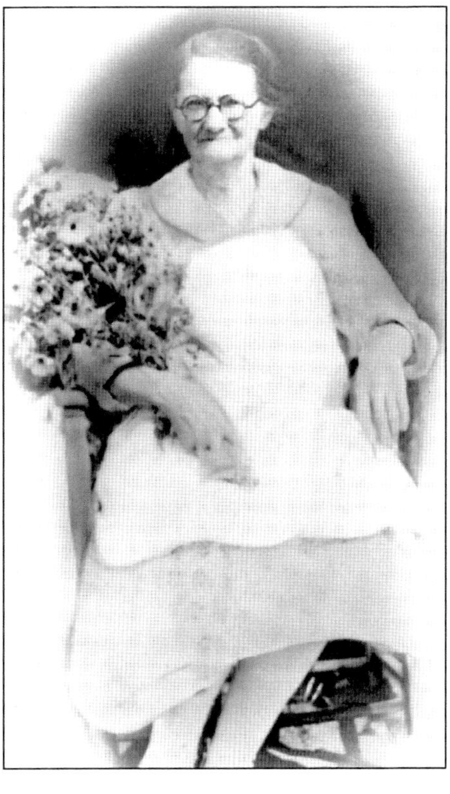

T. ELIZABETH SHEALEY LIMBAUGH. Mrs. Limbaugh was the wife of Jesse Limbaugh and the mother of Malley Limbaugh. Malley was the father of the Limbaugh brothers who have all given so much to this city. Mrs. Limbaugh left a great legacy to our city in the fine family she raised to serve Childersburg so well. In this photograph, she is holding a bouquet of flowers. (Courtesy of Jane Limbaugh Allen.)

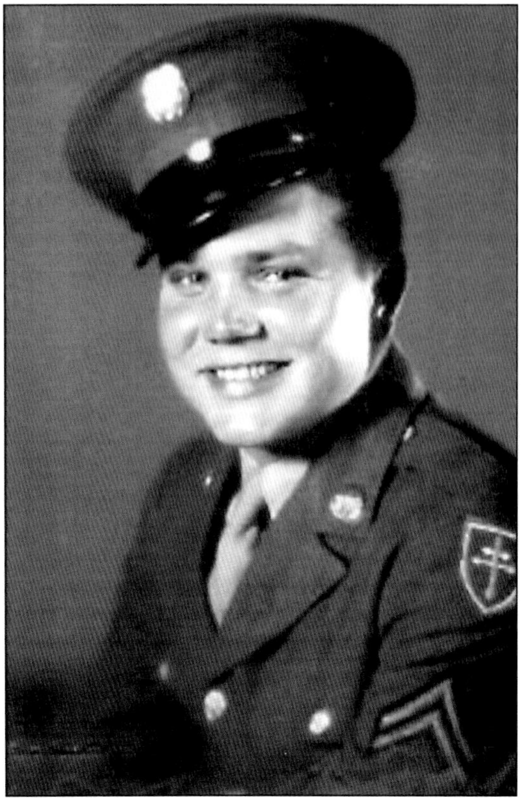

SGT. JOHN WILBUR COX, C. 1944. Sergeant Cox fought in the European theater in World War II. While there, he earned the Bronze Star. A graduate of the University of Alabama, Coach John W. Cox's biography can be found in the 1991 Alabama High School Athletic Association Hall of Fame. He coached football at Childersburg High School for 33 years, earning a 204-109-15 record. He also coached basketball for 13 years with only one losing season. Coach Cox also had six winning seasons of baseball. (Courtesy of the Childersburg National Veterans Association and Museum.)

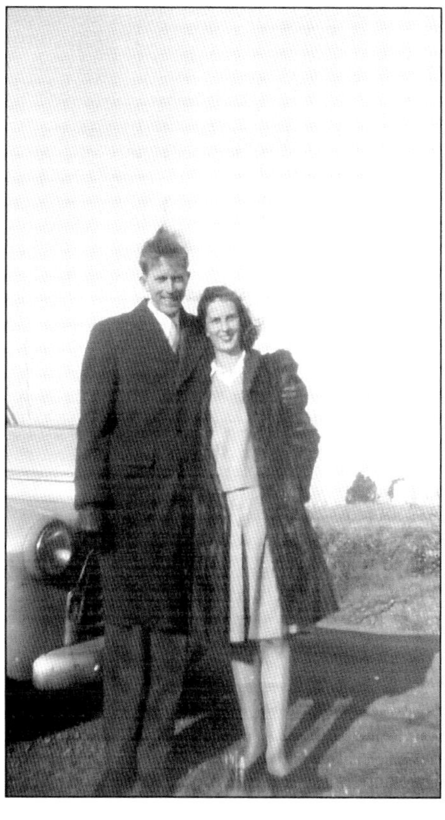

HENNY AND DR. DEE MOODY, 1945. Henny and Dee are at the funeral of Dee's father, George W. Moody. (Courtesy of Marcus Dee Moody.)

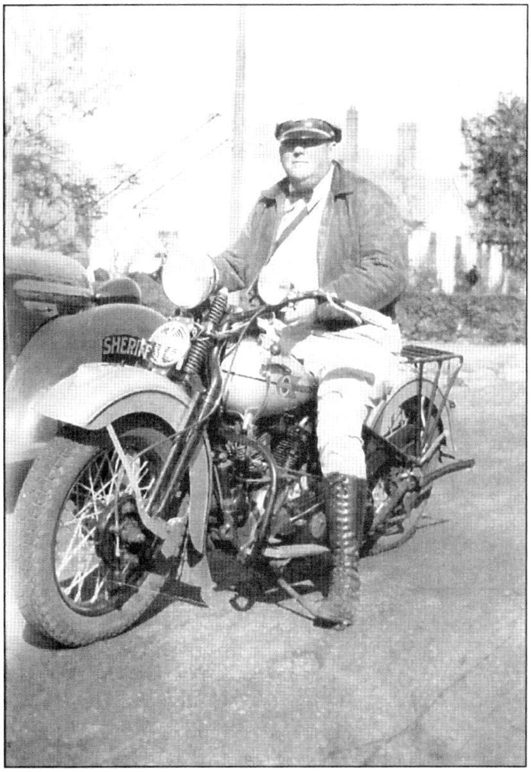

TIM FINN, SHERIFF, C. 1949. Tim also served as fire chief, constable, and police chief of Childersburg (though not all at the same time) while owning a service station. He is riding his sheriff's motorcycle. Notice his boots and bow tie. Tim Finn was known in Talladega County as a detective of amazing talent. He woke at 4:00 every morning and could solve a tough case before dark the same day. Tim was not only a brilliant officer of the law but a very generous man, giving away more than he kept. (Courtesy of Clarence Edwin "Mickey" Finn.)

FINN SIBLINGS, C. 1949. From left to right are (first row) Emma Finn Herrera, Laura Finn D'Aston, and Lucy Finn Howard; (second row) Edgar Shelley Finn, William Michael "Bill" Finn, Ira Forney Finn, Joseph Magnus Finn, and Dennis Millard Finn. (Courtesy of Ralph and Dolly Finn.)

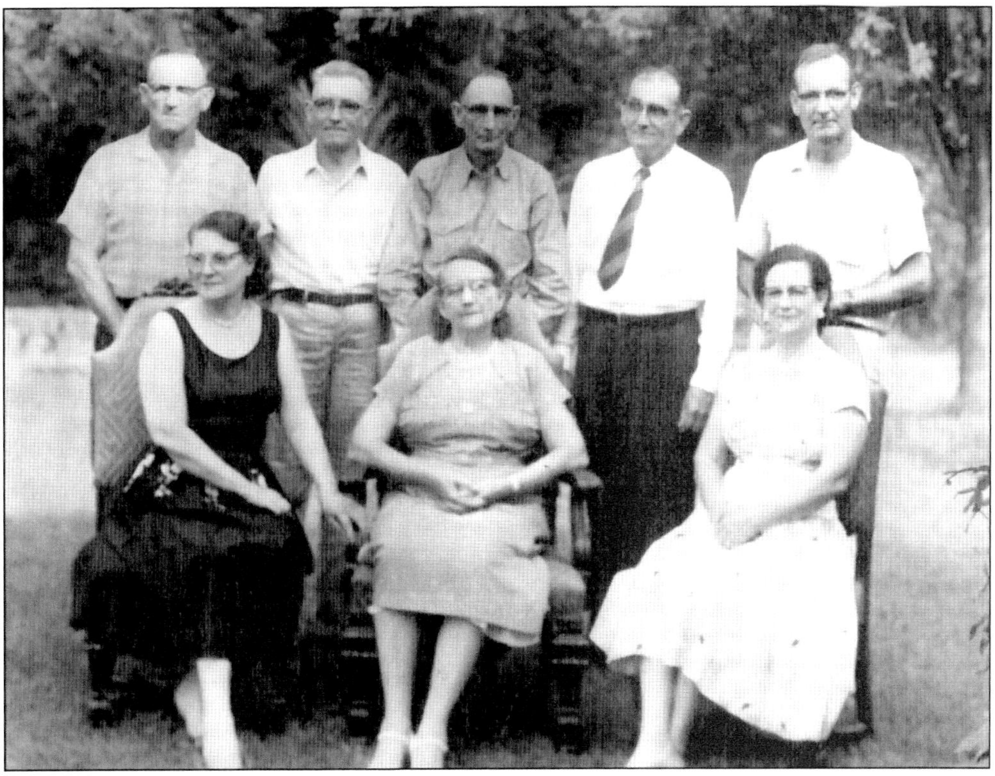

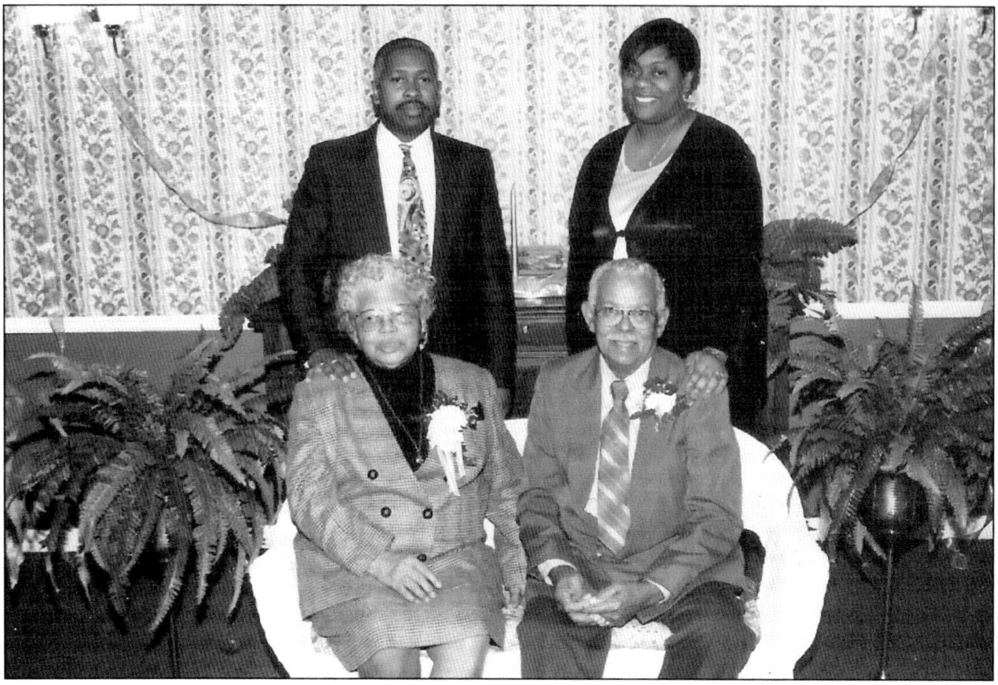

THE 50TH WEDDING ANNIVERSARY. This photograph of Beasley and Coreen Martin was taken on their 50th wedding anniversary. Behind them are their son, Beasley Martin Jr., and his wife, Marian Vincent Martin. (Courtesy of Beasley Martin Sr.)

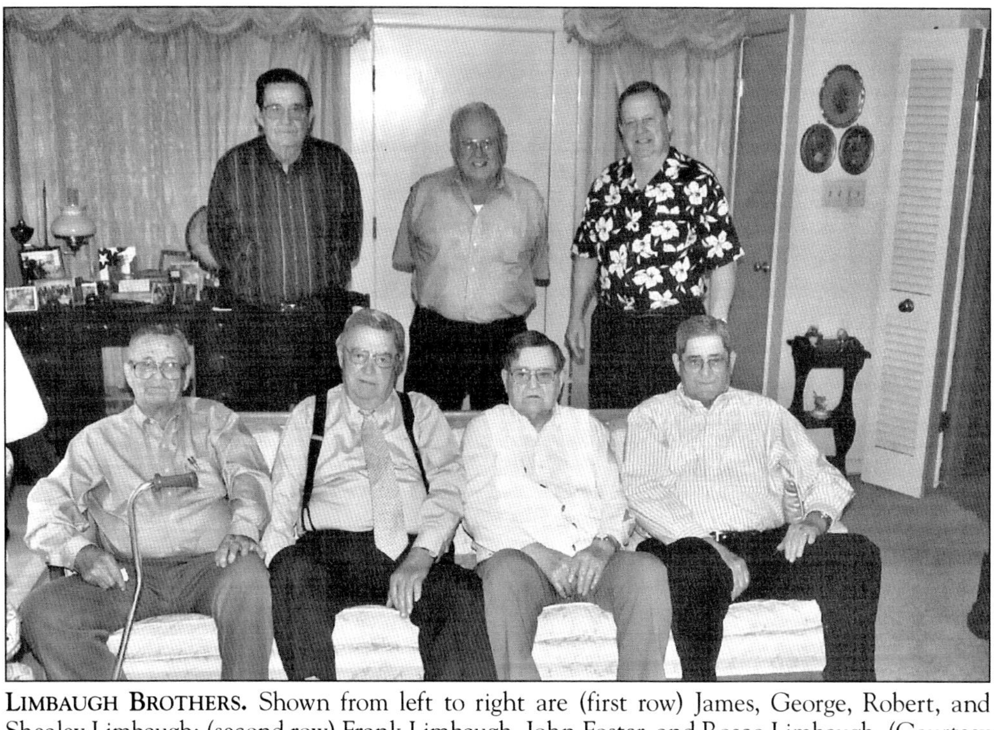

LIMBAUGH BROTHERS. Shown from left to right are (first row) James, George, Robert, and Shealey Limbaugh; (second row) Frank Limbaugh, John Foster, and Rosco Limbaugh. (Courtesy of Joy Thompson Limbaugh and Shealey Limbaugh.)

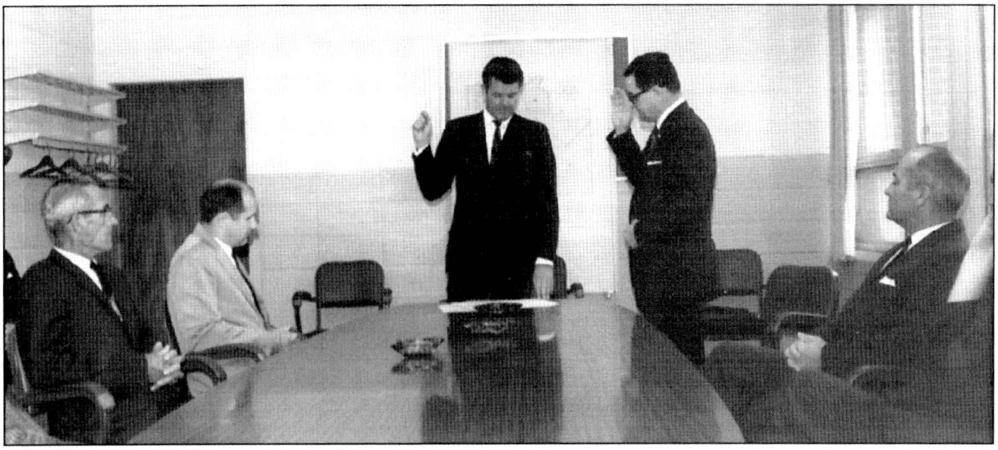

ROBERT LIMBAUGH SWORN IN AS MAYOR OF CHILDERSBURG. Robert Sheror Limbaugh (December 27, 1914–February 14, 2005) served the city of Childersburg for 24 years. He was on the city council for eight years before he was elected mayor, an office he held for 16 years. Rescuing a city deep in debt, he accomplished a great deal in those years. He established a savings account for the city that was worth over $250,000 when he retired as mayor. He had all 32 roads in Childersburg paved in just a year's time. He brought the police department into the 21st century, created the first zoning board and board of adjustments and appeals, and organized the East Alabama Planning Commission. Mayor Limbaugh created the first full-time fire department and established the first senior citizens center in Alabama. He created several parks in the community and even a community boat launch. He opened Limbaugh Hardware on First Street in 1949 and operated it for 39 years. Robert Limbaugh lived by the Golden Rule. His life and example defined the term "service to community."

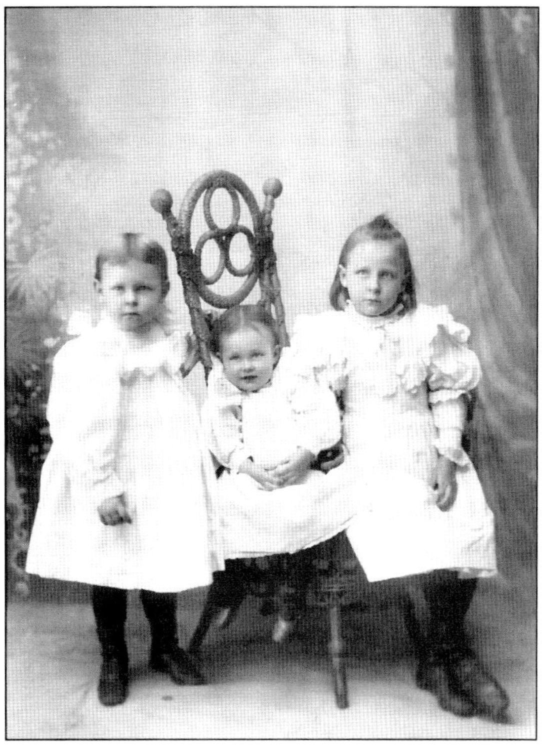

CHILDREN OF J. MAC BARNES. Mac Barnes, a graduate of Bethany College, started Highland Home School to educate people in the way of the Church of Christ. W. Pauline Montgomery Cliett attended this school and started the Church of Christ in Childersburg. These are the children of her mentor. (Courtesy of Monty Powell.)

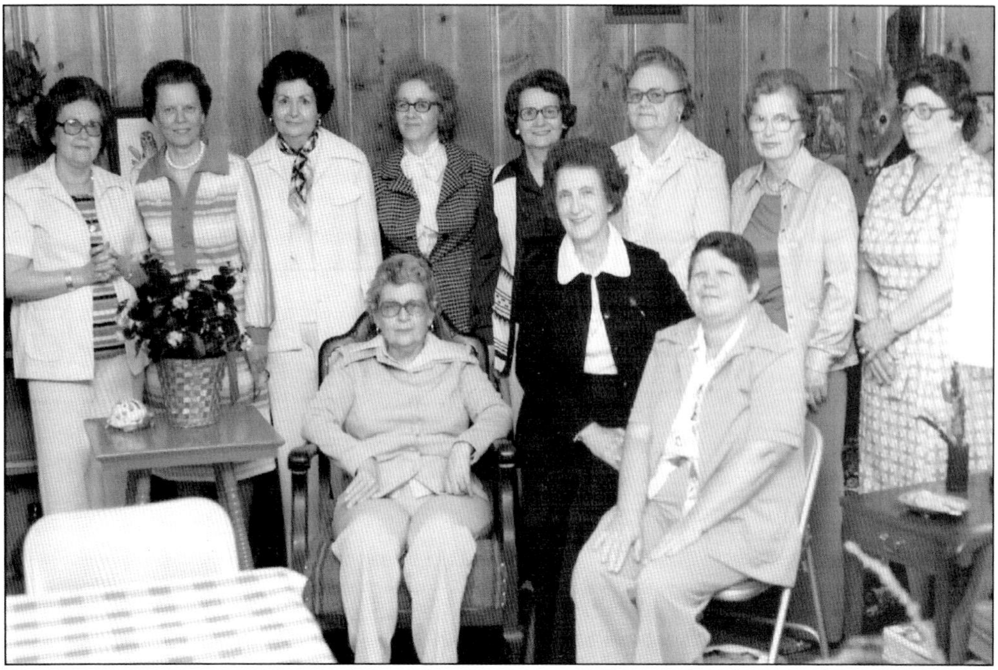

CHILDERSBURG LADIES. Pictured From left to right are (first row) Velma Bush Brooks, Leona Jones McCallum, and Betty Veazey; (second row) Ellen Rainwater, Laurie Maxwell, Betty Shem Helison, Ethel McSheridan, Irene Richardson Holt-Wood, Suzie M. Veazey, Helen McCaffrey, and Alma Bush McMillan. (Courtesy of Jane Limbaugh Allen.)

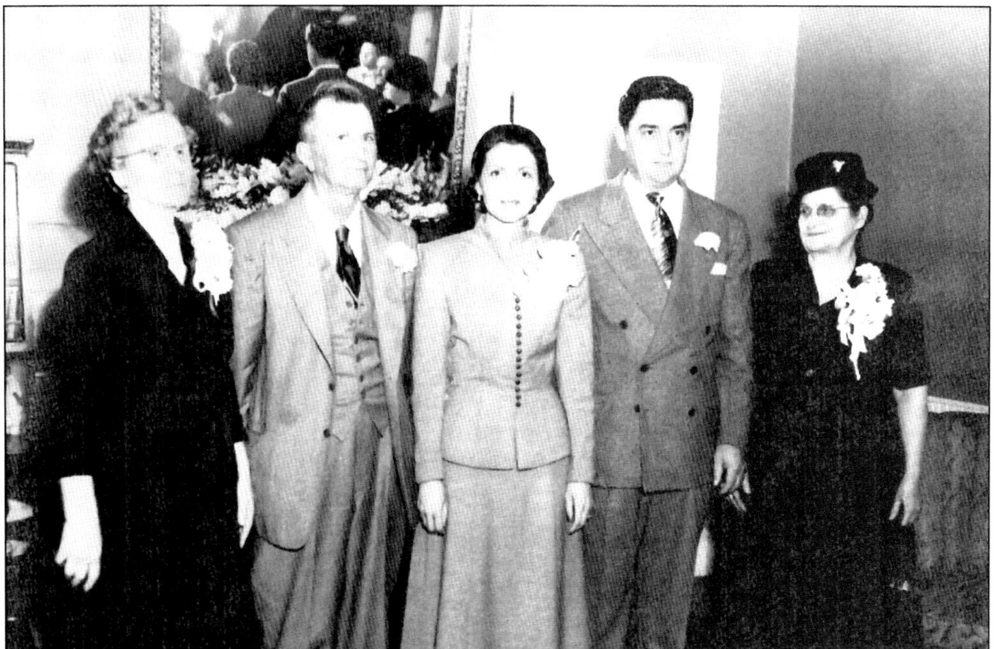

GEORGE AND OLLIE LIMBAUGH FAMILY, C. 1952. Pictured here from left to right are Alva Garrett Thompson; her husband, John Thompson; their daughter, Ollie Thompson Limbaugh; their son-in-law, George Limbaugh; and George's mother, Hattie Limbaugh.

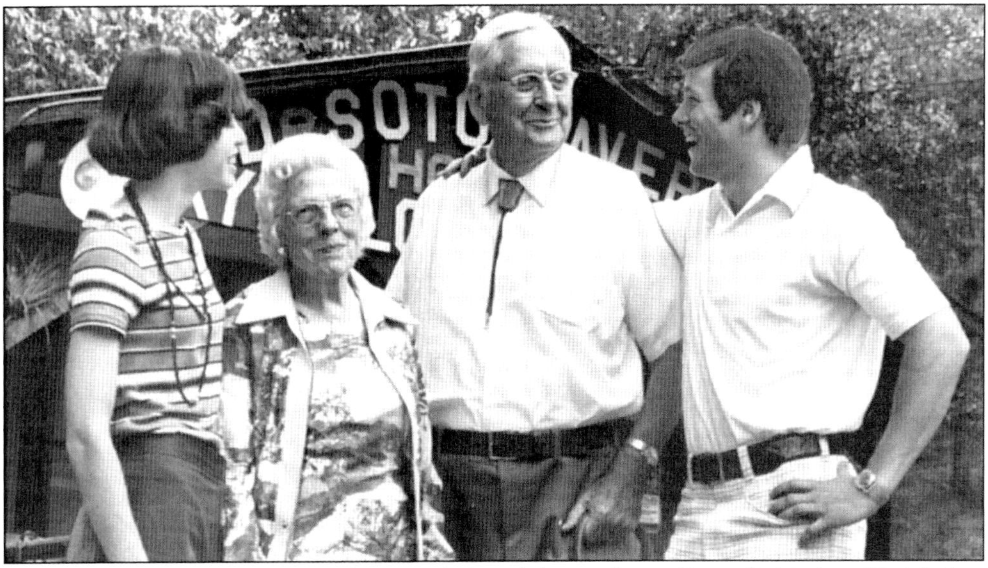

MATHIS FAMILY. Shown in this photograph from left to right are Danielle Mathis, Ola Mathis, Allen W. Mathis Sr., and Allen W. Mathis III. In 1975, when Fred Layton left the caverns, Allen W. Mathis Sr. turned over the cave to his grandson, Allen W. Mathis III, who changed the name to DeSoto Caverns Park in honor of Hernando de Soto's visit to Childersburg in 1540. It only seemed fitting since this very cave was described in de Soto's chroniclers' letter to Spain. (Courtesy of Allen W. Mathis III.)

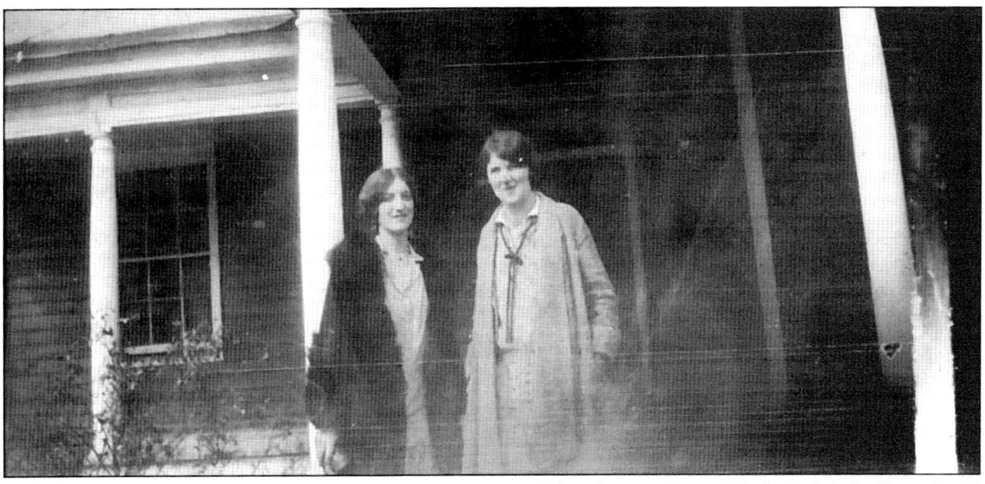

LEONA JONES AND LAVERNE MEADOWS, C. 1930S. Mrs. Leona Jones Nichols McCallum (left) was one of Childersburg's most dedicated civic and community service leaders. She graduated from Jacksonville State Normal College and taught elementary school for 12 years. In 1941, she began work at the Childersburg post office, where she worked for 31 years. In 1977, she was the first woman elected to the city council. She was a founding member and secretary on the board of the Earle A. Rainwater Memorial Library, the Cheaha District Library Council, and the Talladega County representative at the Governors Council on Library Information Service. She was also on the Talladega County Historical Society. The Alabama Historical Commission honored her with an award of merit for her service. She was a longtime member of the Coosa Garden Club and was instrumental in the club's creation of Sally West Park. (Courtesy of the Earle A. Rainwater Memorial Library.)

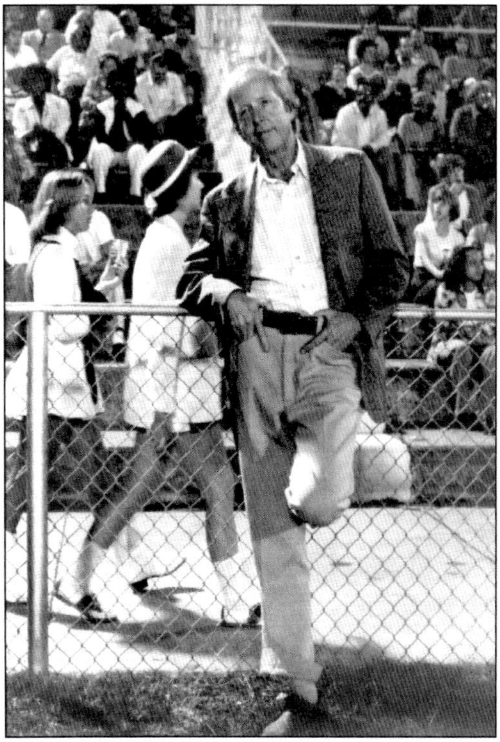

Dr. Marcus "Dee" Moody, c. 1968. Dr. Moody was the team doctor for the Childersburg High School football team for 25 years. He graduated from Childersburg High School in 1936. Dr. Moody studied pre-medicine at Birmingham Southern College, went to the University of Alabama in Tuscaloosa for two years, and finished at the Medical College of South Carolina in Charleston, where he met and married his wife, Henrietta "Henny" White Moody, in 1945. After serving in the U.S. Army for about two years, he began practicing medicine in 1947 with Dr. Stock at the old Childersburg Hospital on Seventh Street, SW. He moved his practice to the second story of the old Powell Building on Eighth Avenue in 1949 and, in 1952, moved to an office on Seventh Avenue, SW, now occupied by his son's business, Mort Moody Accounting. Dr. Moody retired in 1985. In 2004, he became the 20th person inducted into the Childersburg Chamber of Commerce Hall of Fame. (Courtesy of Dr. Dee Moody.)

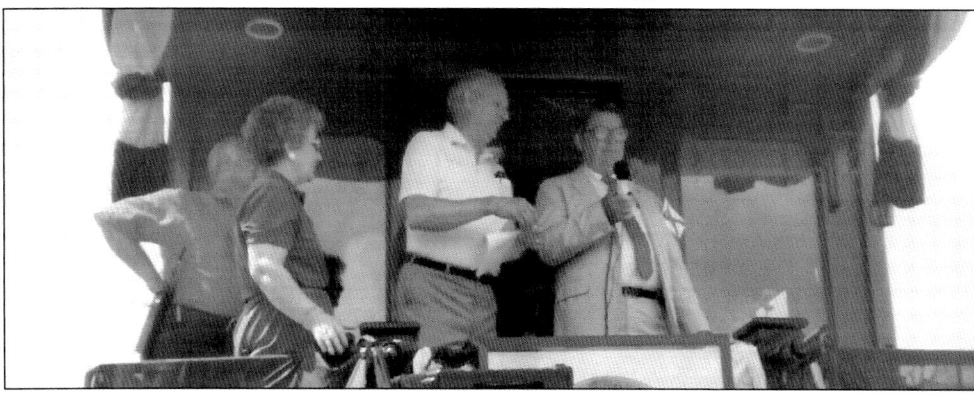

George Limbaugh and Gov. Guy Hunt, 1990. This photograph was taken at the Alabama Reunion in Childersburg aboard the *Alabama Reunion Special*, a train on a mission to fulfill a 900-mile journey. George was born in 1917 to George Malley and Hattie Johnson Limbaugh. He was an army captain during World War II in the European theater. He served on the Childersburg waterworks, industrial development, and parks are recreations boards and on the board of the Alabama Institute for the Deaf and Blind, and he is the chamber of commerce executive director. He is president of the Kiwanis Club and Heritage Society, chairman of Coosafest Committee, and captain of the Childersburg Quarterback Club. Limbaugh was responsible for the sale of bonds to finance the Childersburg High School football stadium and the purchase of the Kymulga Grist Mill. He also helped to secure funds to buy the land to donate to what is now Central Alabama Community College. George was also instrumental in developing the first system of gas lines in Childersburg. He was co-owner of Limbaugh Hardware as well as Talladega Materials Company. George is referred to lovingly as "Mr. Childersburg" for all his service to his beloved city. (Courtesy of Billy Atkinson Sr.)

Eight

HOMES

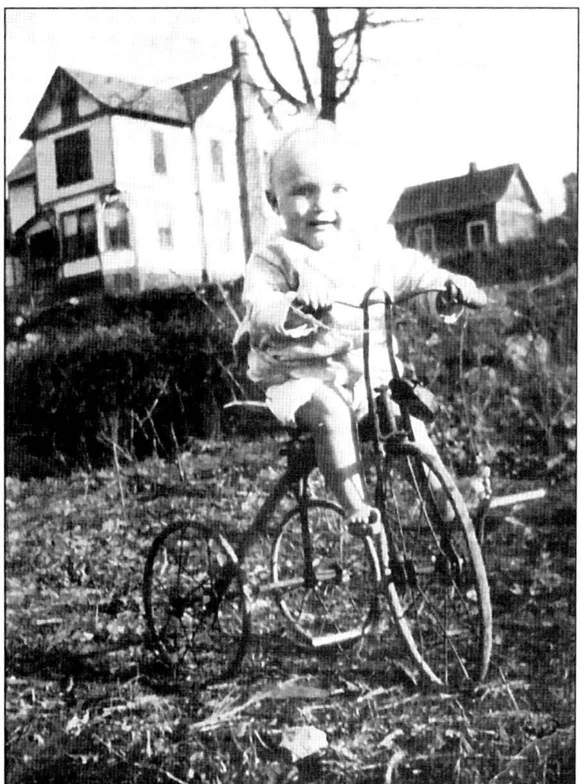

MICKEY FINN RIDING HIS TRICYCLE, C. 1925. The old Hunt house is the large house in the background. It sat on the hill near the Rainwater House (Museum). (Courtesy of Clarence Edwin "Mickey" Finn.)

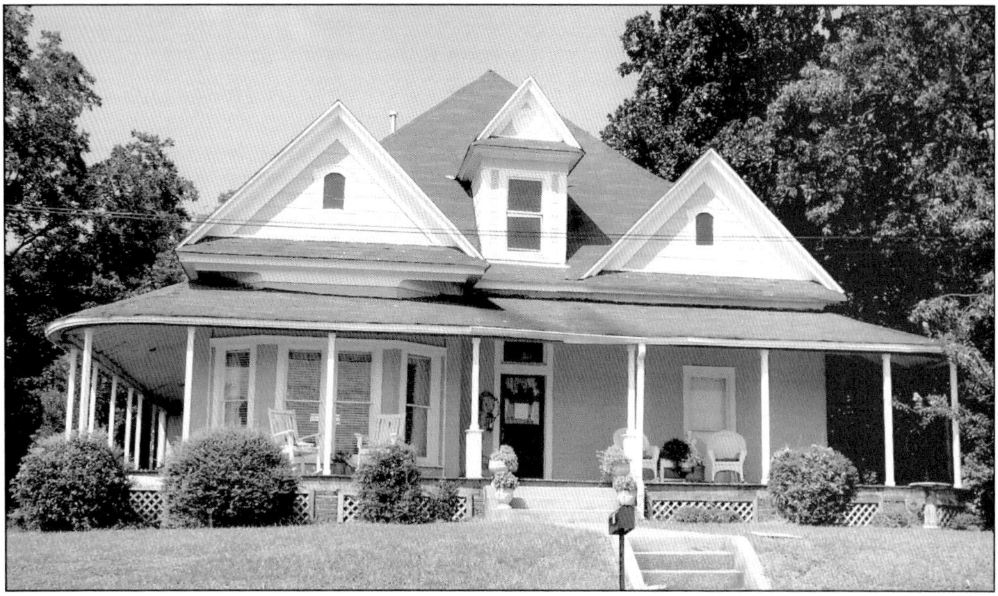

THE PINK HOUSE. The Cochran home, also known as the Pink House, was built in 1902 for Rena and David Bryant. It was purchased later by Jesse and Betsy Ryder, who lived there for many years. This folk Victorian-period home has 3,000 square feet of living space. It contains the original five fireplaces, a nine-foot-wide grand central hallway, and original wood floors. Much later, owners Ray and Dawn Reeves added two full baths and a new kitchen. It was purchased in 2004 by Jamie and Hope Cochran, the current owners.

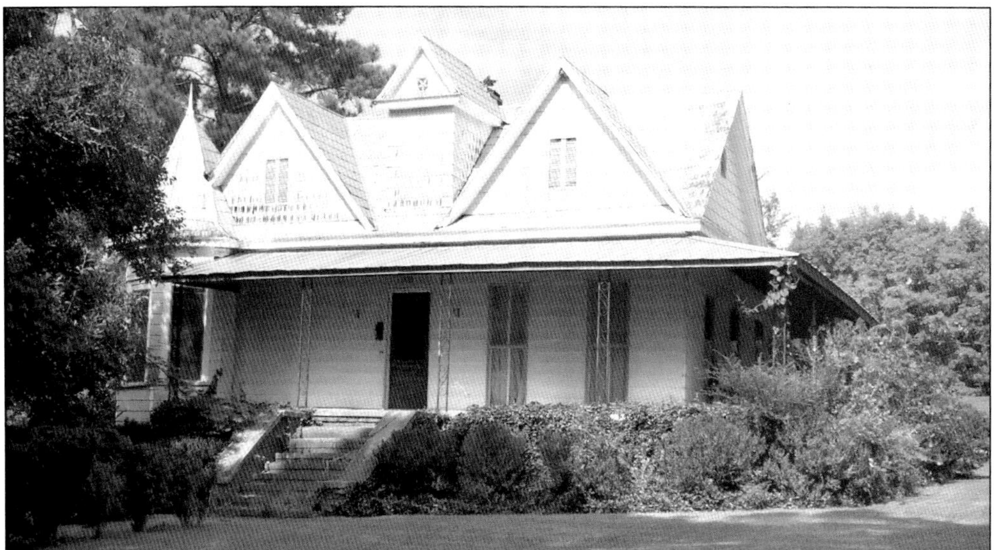

THE DONAHOO HOUSE. This Victorian home was built in 1881 by Judge John A. Nichols for his wife, Allie Simmons, a music teacher from Cove Springs. He was the son of Dr. Benjamin F. Nichols, a Civil War doctor. J. A. Nichols was one of the five-member board of deacons responsible for rolling the Methodist church from the area close to the Old Childersburg Cemetery to its present location. The house once had a gingerbread design and banisters around the porches. John and Allie's two children, Frank and Alva, and three grandchildren, Agnes, John, and Dorothy Nichols Donahoo, were all born in this house.

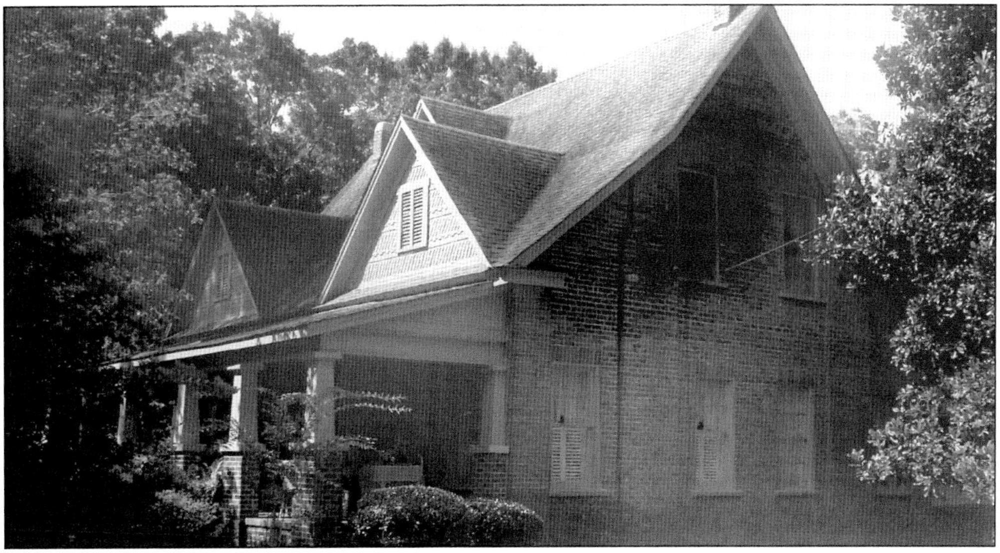

THE VINCENT HOME. The Childersburg Bicentennial Commission named this house the oldest house in Childersburg. There is a brick on the front of the house with the date August 11, 1873. This house was built by Demps Oden Sr., one of the founders of the Oden Elliot Lumber Company in Birmingham, Alabama. It has been an oral tradition that the house was built with bricks that were made by slaves. There is evidence that the house was put together by handmade bricks and pegs. There is a remnant of an old well in the back yard. The kitchen was originally in a smaller building connected to the house by a breezeway. (Courtesy of Mrs. Eugenia Vincent.)

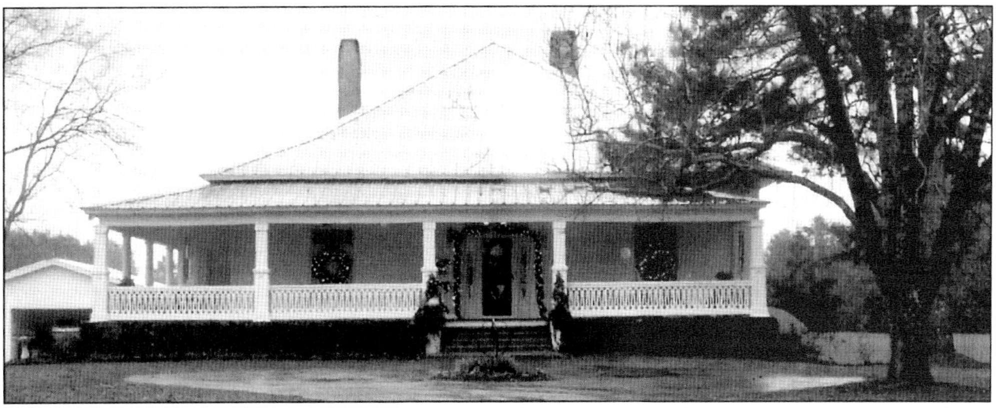

THE ALFORD VEAZEY KNIGHT HOME. This 1910 Queen Anne Victorian was originally built by Bennett Alford, a cotton broker, for his wife, Claudia. Though they did have two children, Claudia died shortly after the home was completed in 1911. Claudia's mother, Sally West, donated land to the City of Childersburg for use as a park in the early 20th century. This home has a Bermudian roof line, grand central hall, and five original fireplaces. It was renovated in 1992 by Roland and Kim Veazey Knight. Kim's father, Bob Veazey, constructed the 232 individual handrails in Dothan, Alabama. The home features pocket doors, pocket windows, 13-foot ceilings, cut glass, transoms, and original fireplace mantels. It was awarded the Camellia Award and Award of Merit in 1996 for restoration of a historic residence. These awards were presented by actress Polly Holliday, who was born and raised in Childersburg. You probably remember her as Flo from *Mel's Diner*, the grandmother on *Tool Time*, and the next-door neighbor in *Mrs. Doubtfire*. (Courtesy of Kim Veazey Knight.)

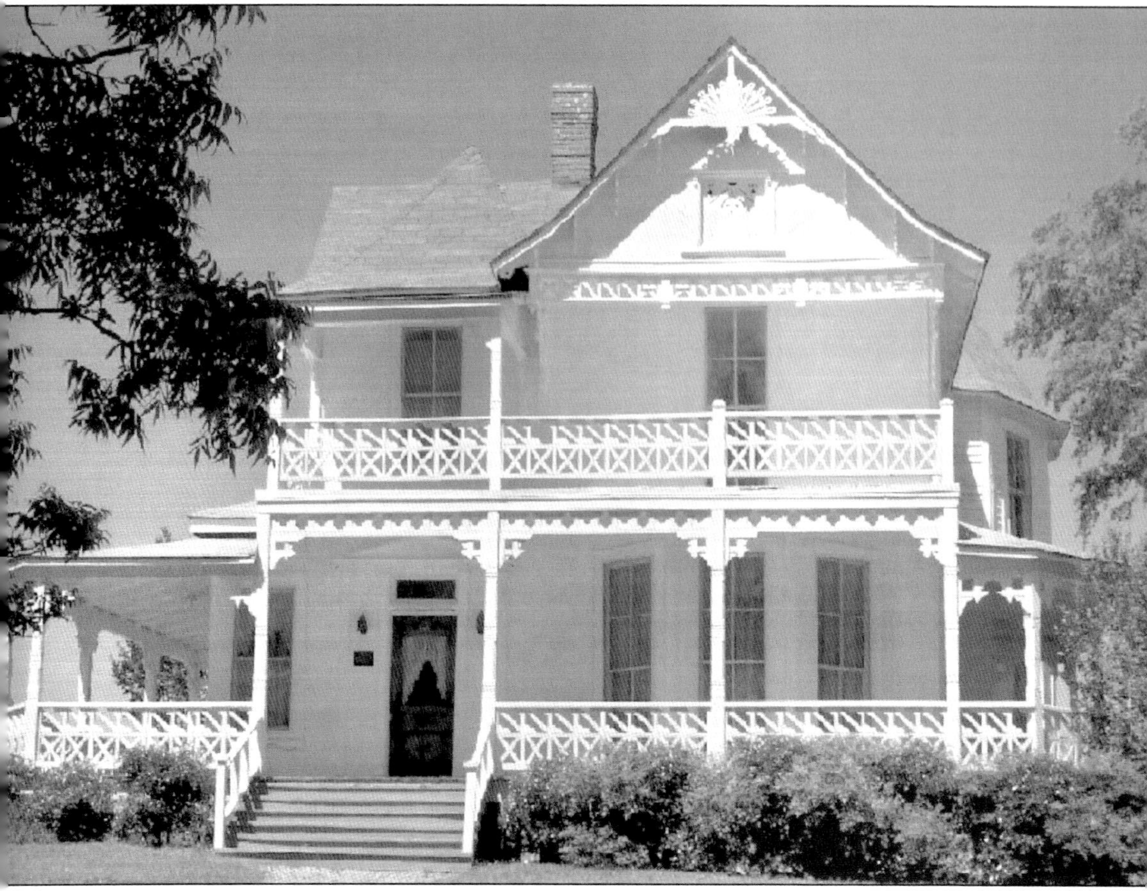

THE BUTLER-HARRIS-RAINWATER MUSEUM. This beautiful Eastlake-style Victorian was built in 1894 by George Butler as a wedding gift for his son, Charles Butler. Charles deeded the house to his wife, Eliza "Lide" Nichols Butler. The home was purchased by Sophie Harris in 1922. She and her twins, Virginia and Joe, moved into the house. Sophie's husband was Dr. Joseph Harris, who came to Childersburg to practice medicine in 1905. Mrs. Harris was postmistress for Childersburg from 1914 to 1924. One of their twins, Virginia Harris, was married in the house in 1923 to Earle A. Rainwater. Mr. Rainwater was elected mayor in 1948. In 1994, the house was purchased by the city, and the Childersburg Historic Preservation Commission was appointed to its renovation and care. The first floor has been renovated and furnished. It has gingerbread gables and trim, a wraparound porch, etched-glass front door, banister stairway, 12 rooms, and 9 fireplaces. It stands proudly on a hill overlooking downtown Childersburg.

Nine

COUNTRY

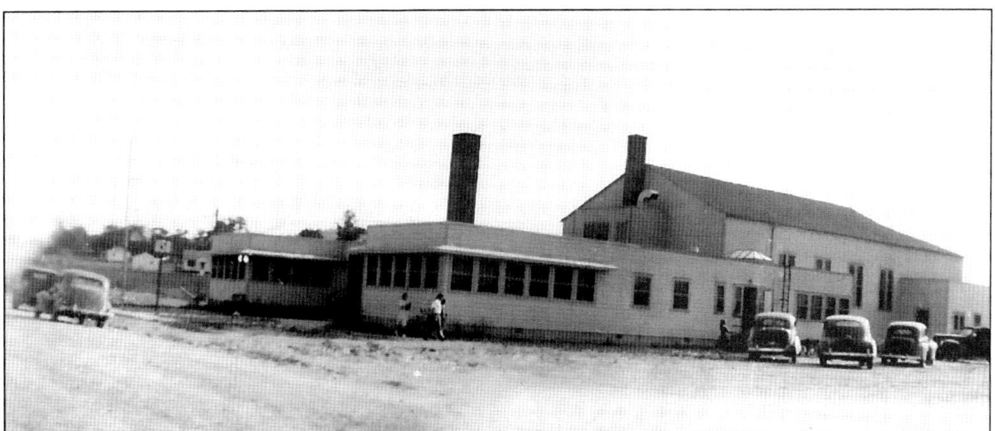

USO BUILDING, C. 1943. The USO was located on Seventh Street and Sixth Avenue. It was the hub of entertainment and social occasions in Childersburg during World War II. Col. Eston Lovingood was the commanding officer. The building was torn down in the 1970s. (Courtesy of the Earle A. Rainwater Memorial Library.)

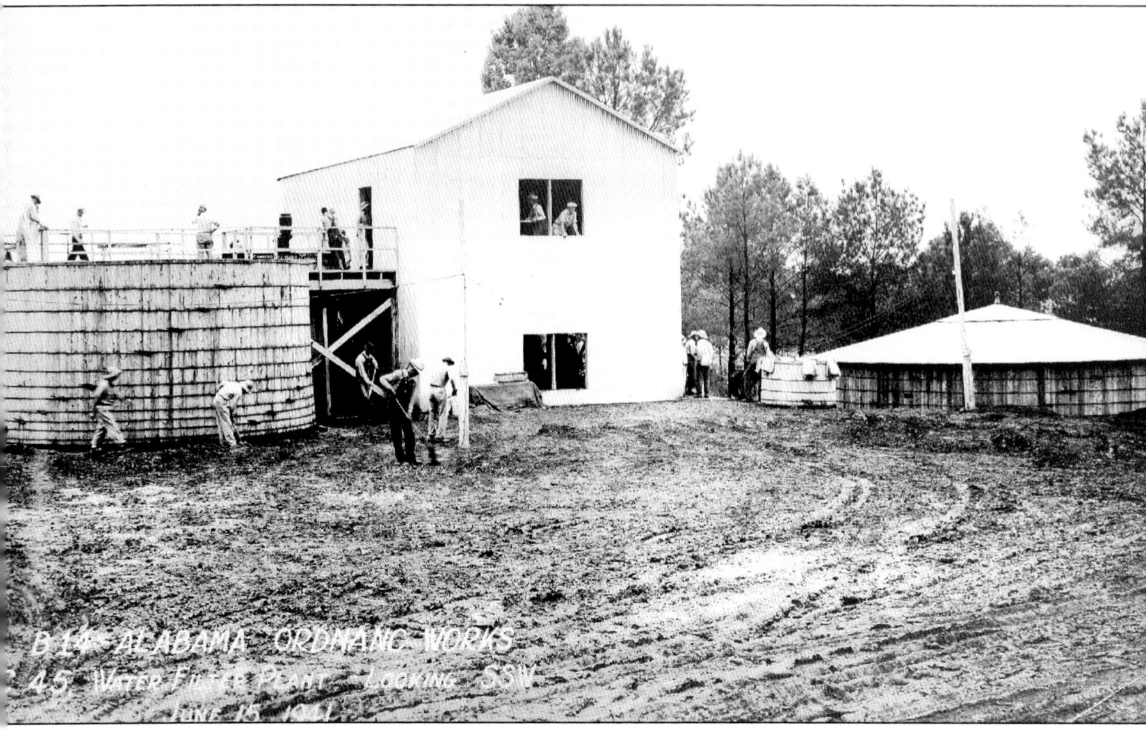

Alabama Ordnance Works. On January 1, 1941, the War Department announced that they would be building a massive, $100-billion complex of munitions plants in Childersburg, Alabama. People came from everywhere in the country to work here. The war had not begun, but Hitler had taken over most of Europe already. The government purchased 13,500 acres of land from local farmers. The construction itself provided employment for about 25 companies. One plant would go into operation as another one was being built. The government built the plants and provided workers, but the expertise was provided by DuPont, the contractor that ran the plants. The population of Childersburg went from 498 to 15,000 in just a few months. The population boom happened overnight. The streets weren't even paved. The plant itself ultimately employed 25,000 workers. (Courtesy of the Earle A. Rainwater Memorial Library.)

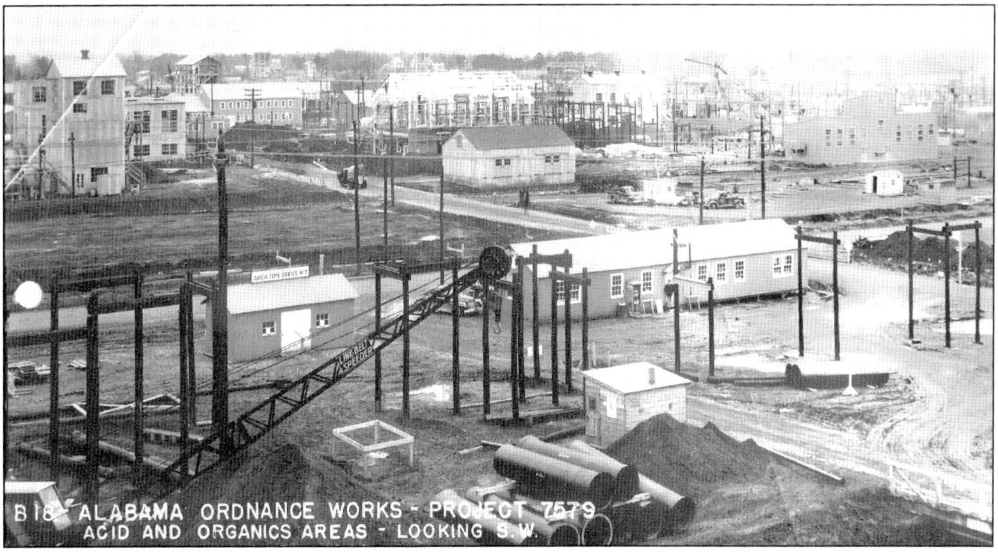

DuPont AOW. This is an official government photograph of the Alabama Ordnance Works in Childersburg. (Courtesy of the Earle A. Rainwater Memorial Library.)

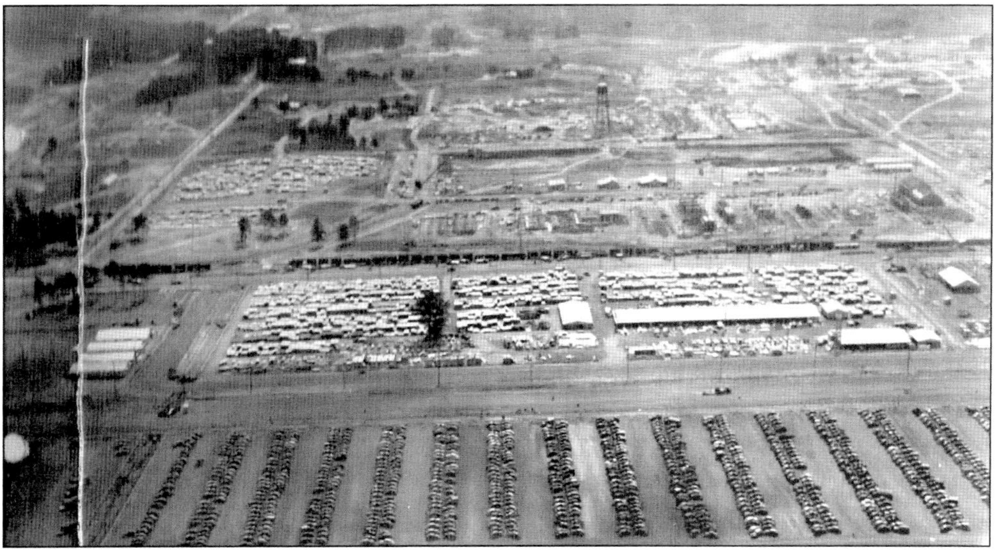

Alabama Ordnance Works. This is an aerial view of the DuPont AOW, which gives some idea of its massive size. There were several plants within the complex. Plant 1 produced rifle powder and artillery powder. Plant 2 produced TNT. Plant 3 was the nitric acid plant. Plant 4 was the sulfuric acid plant. These plants were very dangerous, and much training was provided to the workers on how to safely do their jobs. The fifth plant was top secret. It was part of the P-9 project—the Manhattan Project. DuPont was also the primary contractor for the Manhattan Project. The top-secret plant produced one gallon of heavy water per day. Heavy water was used for the production of plutonium and uranium to go in the atomic bomb. The heavy water was shipped to Oak Ridge, Tennessee. On Sunday, December 7, 1941, the Japanese bombed Pearl Harbor. On Monday morning, the road to the plant and the rooftops had heavily armed soldiers stationed at intervals. As one-third of Alabama's draft-age men went into the army, a labor shortage caused women to take their places at work. (Courtesy of the Earle A. Rainwater Memorial Library.)

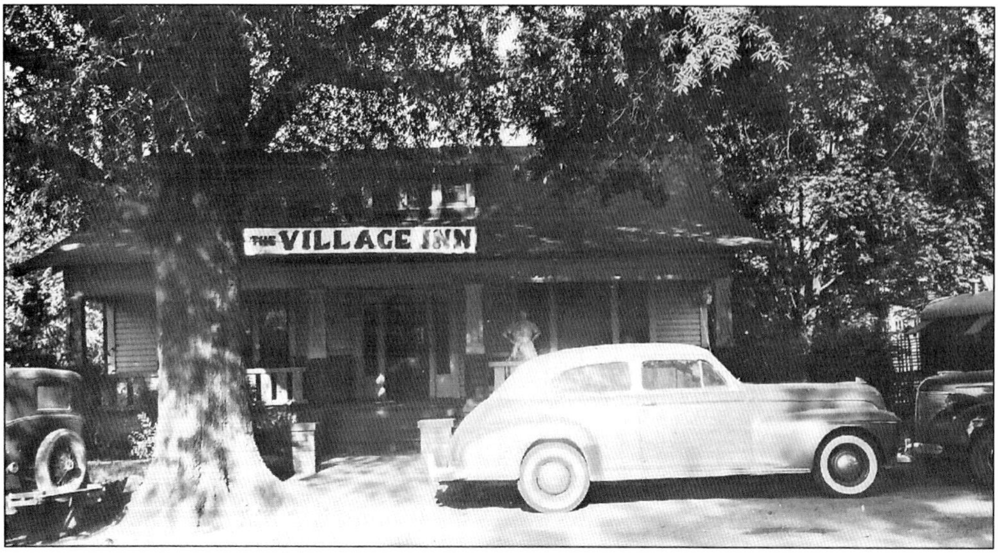

VILLAGE INN. During World War II, every home was an inn or boarding house. This in was the old Oden homeplace, built by Joshua Bussey Oden and Laura Graham Oden. At this time, it was used as the Village Inn. (Courtesy of Patricia Teague Wesley Godfrey.)

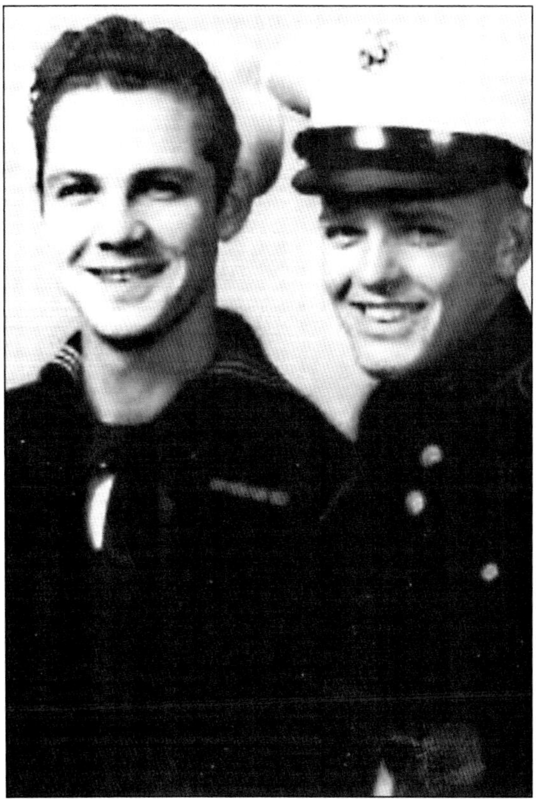

DAVIS BOYS. Brothers Harold (left) and Howard Davis served their country during World War II. Harold was in the U.S. Navy, while Howard served in the U.S. Marine Corps. (Courtesy of George Cosper and the Childersburg Veterans Museum.)

SGT. HOLMAN ROWLAND. Sergeant Rowland fought in the Spanish-American War. (Courtesy of George Cosper and the Childersburg Veterans Museum.)

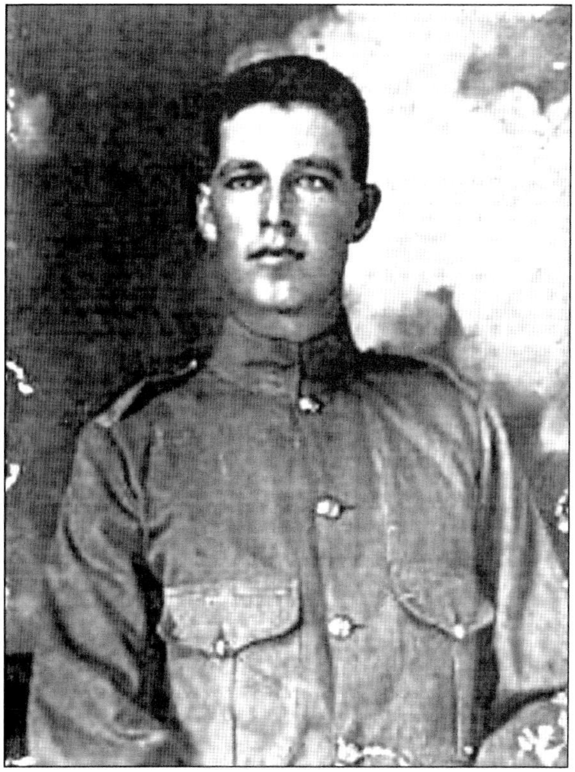

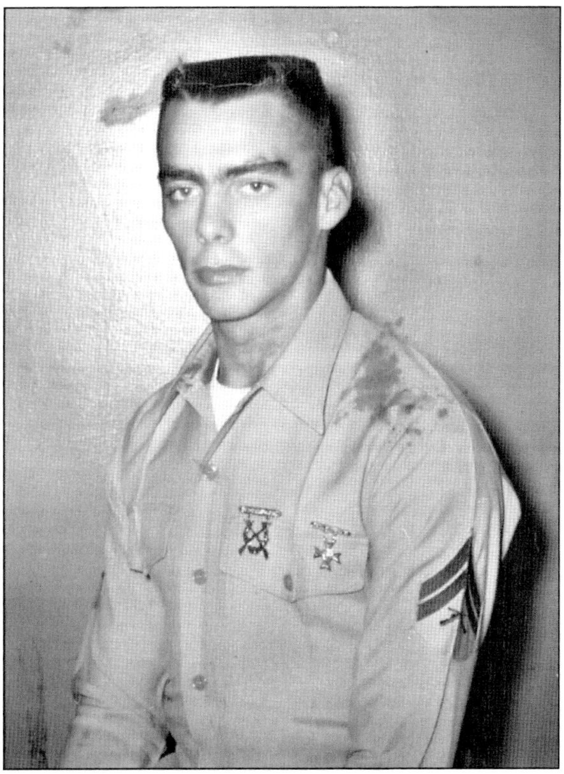

SGT. JERRY FINN. Jerry served his country in the U.S. Marine Corps. Jerry did security detail for the White House during the presidency of John F. Kennedy. He stood guard during presidential state dinners and all White House functions. He also worked security for Blair House, across the street from the White House. Blair House was where all visiting dignitaries stayed. He stood guard for Prime Minister Nehru of India, Prime Minister MacMillan of England, King Saud of Saudi Arabia, and many others. He spent two weeks of every six weeks as security at Camp David. Sergeant Finn also worked security for arrivals and departures of dignitaries and funerals at Arlington Cemetery. His second two years in the Marines, he was in charge of security for presidential helicopters. (Courtesy of Hilda Faye McGrady Finn.)

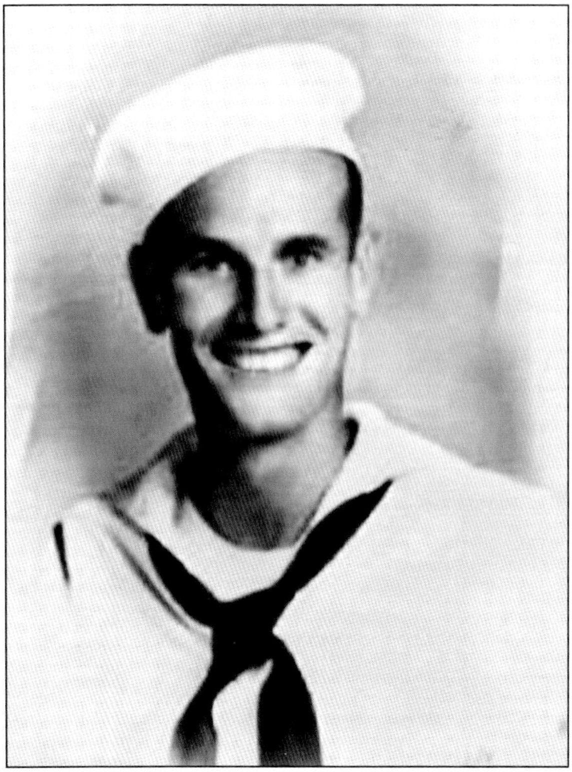

PO2 J. E. Rainwater. Mr. Rainwater served in the U.S. Navy during World War II. He spent his duty in the Pacific aboard the USS *Chimon* (LST-1102).

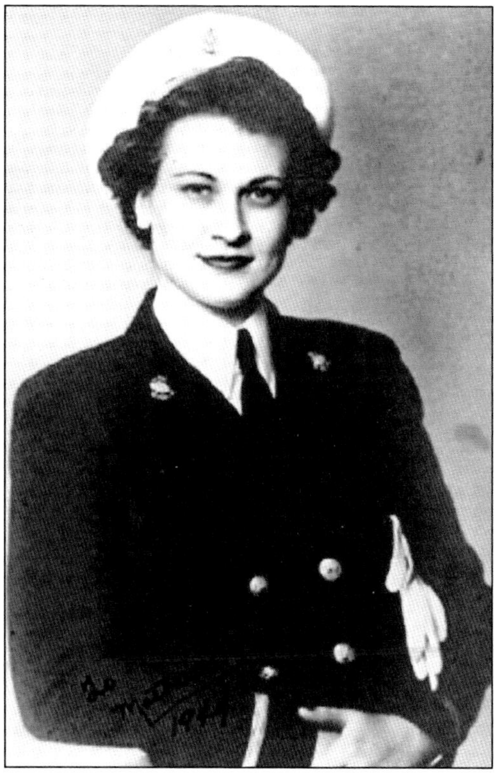

Martha Hallman, 1944. This is a photograph of Ens. Martha Hallman. She was in the nurse corps in World War II. Martha lived in Childersburg all her life. (Courtesy of George Cosper and the Childersburg Veterans Museum.)

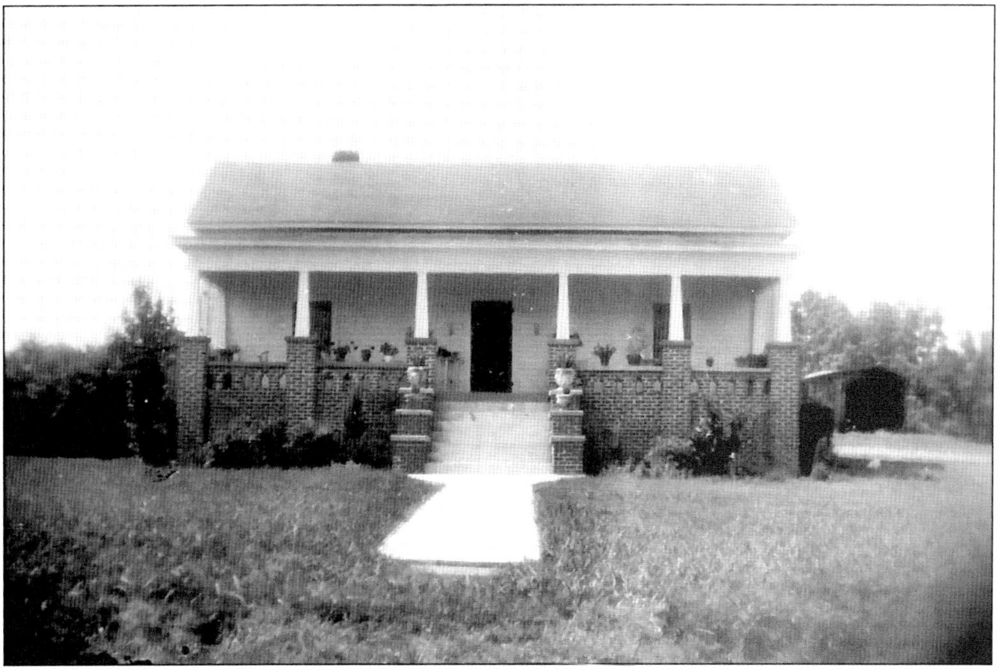

TIM FINN HOME. This house is located on Pecan Road across the street from the old Childersburg High School gymnasium. During the 1980s, it was the home of Reuben and Susan Abernathy, but during World War II, it was the home of Tim and Estelle Finn. They had boarders staying in their barn, in the chicken house, and in tents in what was previously their garden area. (Courtesy of Clarence Edwin "Mickey" Finn.)

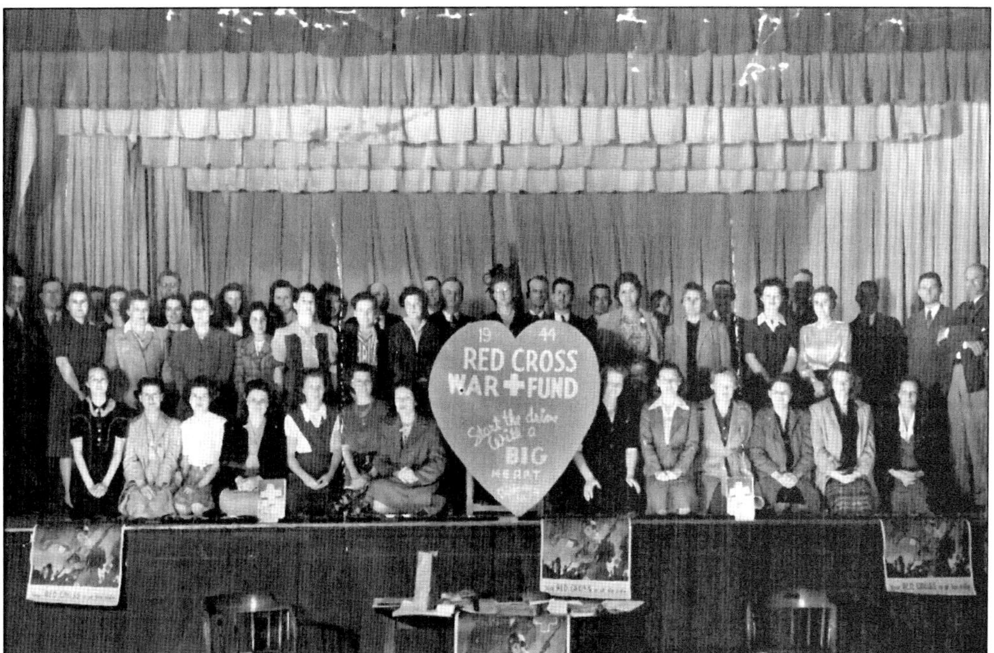

RED CROSS BENEFIT. This benefit was held at the Childersburg USO during World War II. (Courtesy of the Earle A. Rainwater Memorial Library.)

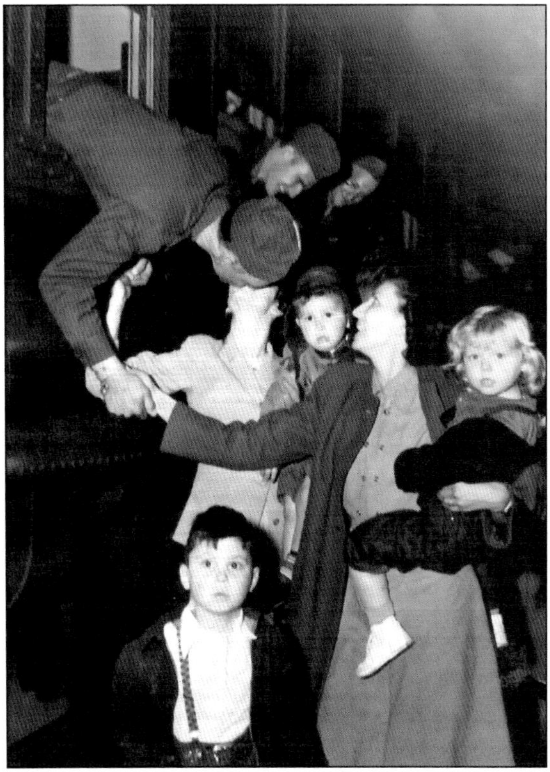

GOING OFF TO WAR. It is unknown at this time who these World War II soldiers on the train and their families are. (Courtesy of the Earle A. Rainwater Memorial Library.)

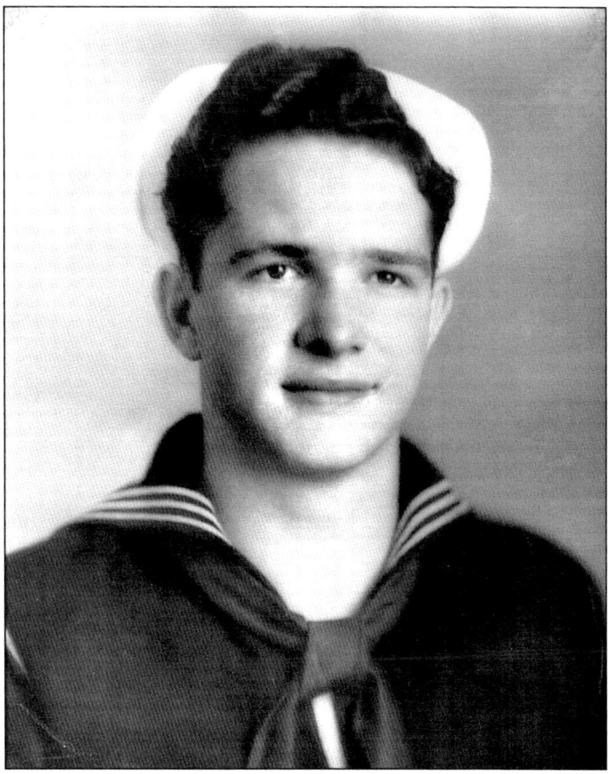

RALPH JOSEPH "DOC" RATLIFF. Born in 1925, Dr. Ratliff was in the U.S. Navy during World War II. He served two campaigns, one in the European theater and the other in the South Pacific. He earned a Purple Heart and an Expert Marksman Badge. He married Antoinette "Toni" Rady in 1951. Dr. Ratliff was a Mason for 51 years of his life. In the 1950s, he opened his chiropractic office in Childersburg, where he worked until his death in 2005. (Courtesy of Antoinette Ratliff.)

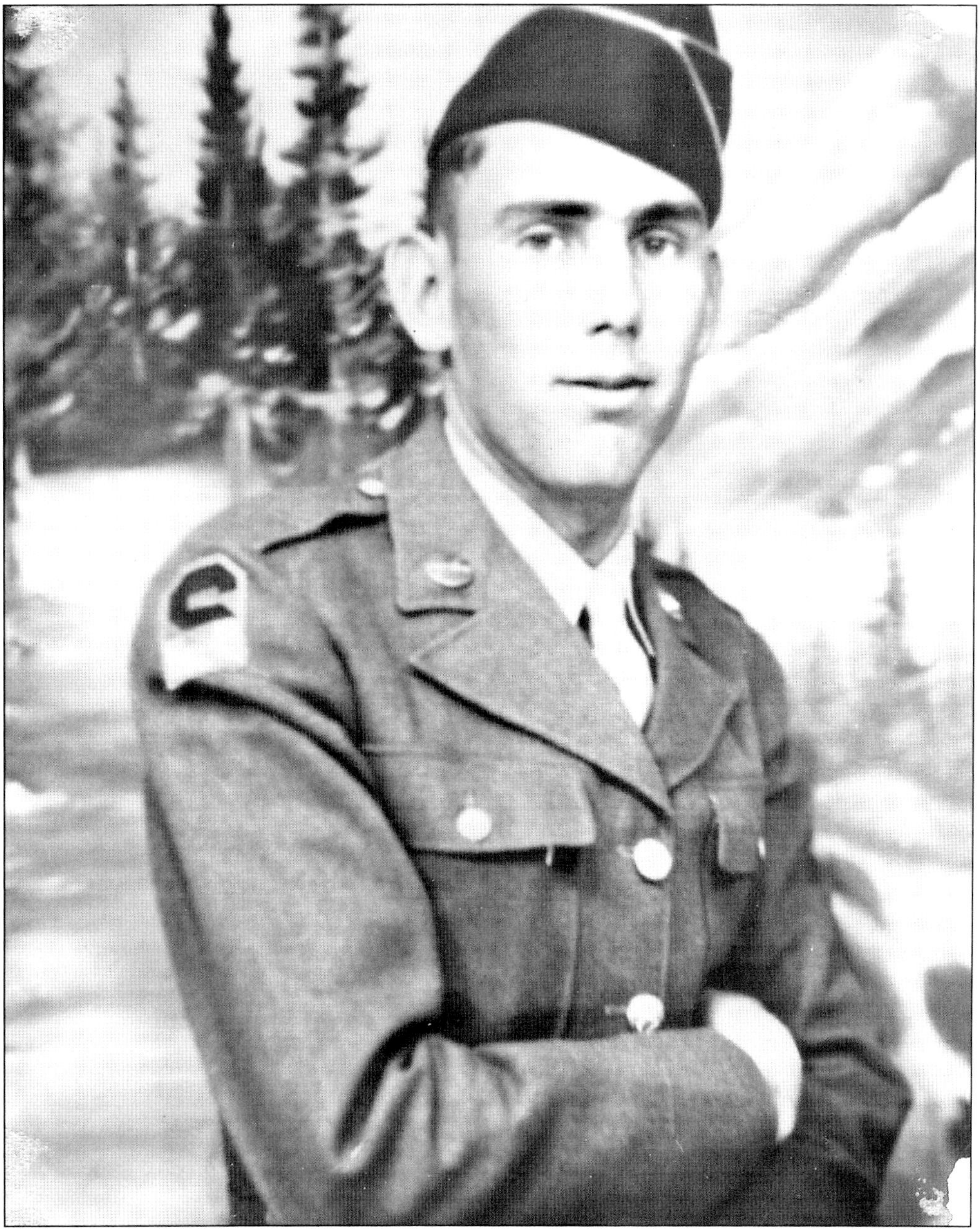

FRED MATHIS JR. Fred Mathis Jr. was in the U.S. Army during World War II. He was in Easy Company of the Americal Division. Fred was trained on skis in Colorado Springs, Colorado, for the European theater. After they trained him for snow fighting, the army sent him straight into the hot jungles of the South Pacific on an island-hopping campaign, though he had no training in jungle fighting. He was the company's BAR man and carried the Browning Automatic Rifle everywhere he went. He lost his leg to a mortar, and his hand was in a permanent claw position from all his bullet wounds. When he came home, he was awarded the Purple Heart. He graduated from Howard University, which is now Samford, with a degree in accounting. He married Annie Lou Brown and was the father of four sons: Erskine, Paul, Clinton, and David. (Courtesy of Erskine and Doris Mathis.)

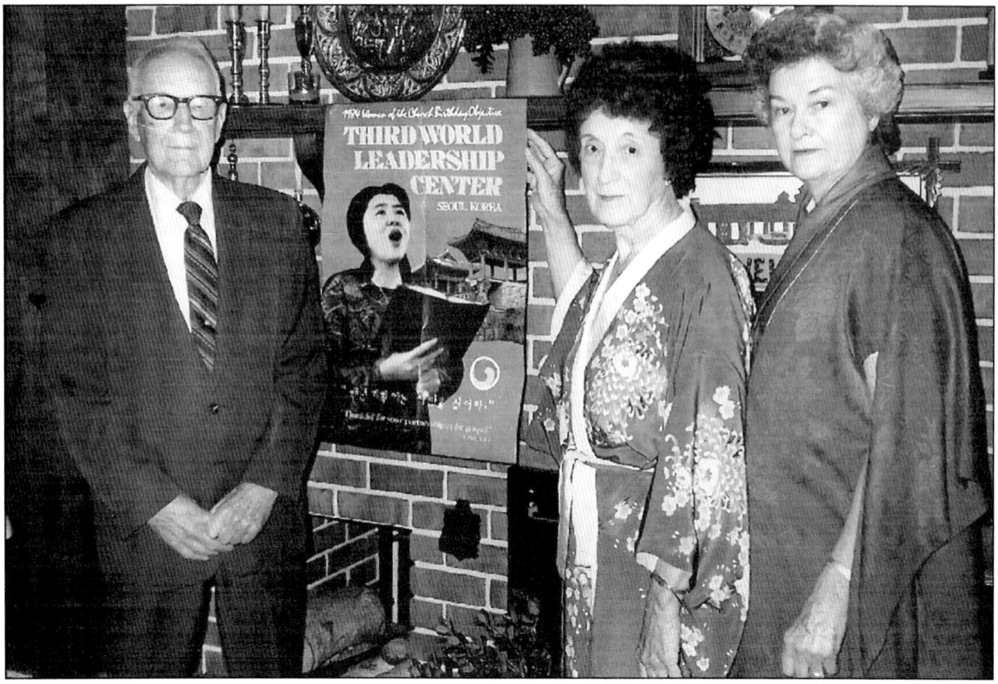

PRESBYTERIAN MISSION, C. 1984. Pictured from left to right are Col. Eston Lovingood, Leona Jones Nichols McCallum, and Inez Comer. (Courtesy of the Earle A. Rainwater Memorial Library, Presbyterian Church collection.)

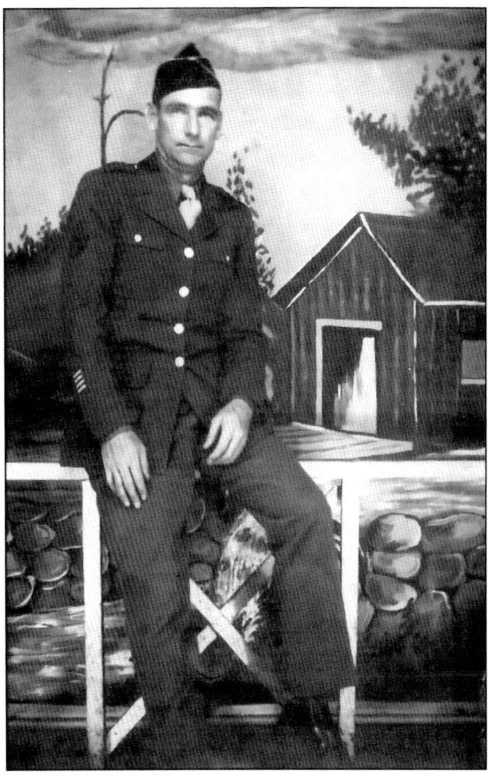

DENNIS FINN. Mr. Finn served in the U.S. Army during World War II. He was born in Childersburg on October 8, 1909, to James Alonza Finn I and Virginia Hughes Finn. (Courtesy of Ralph and Dolly Finn.)

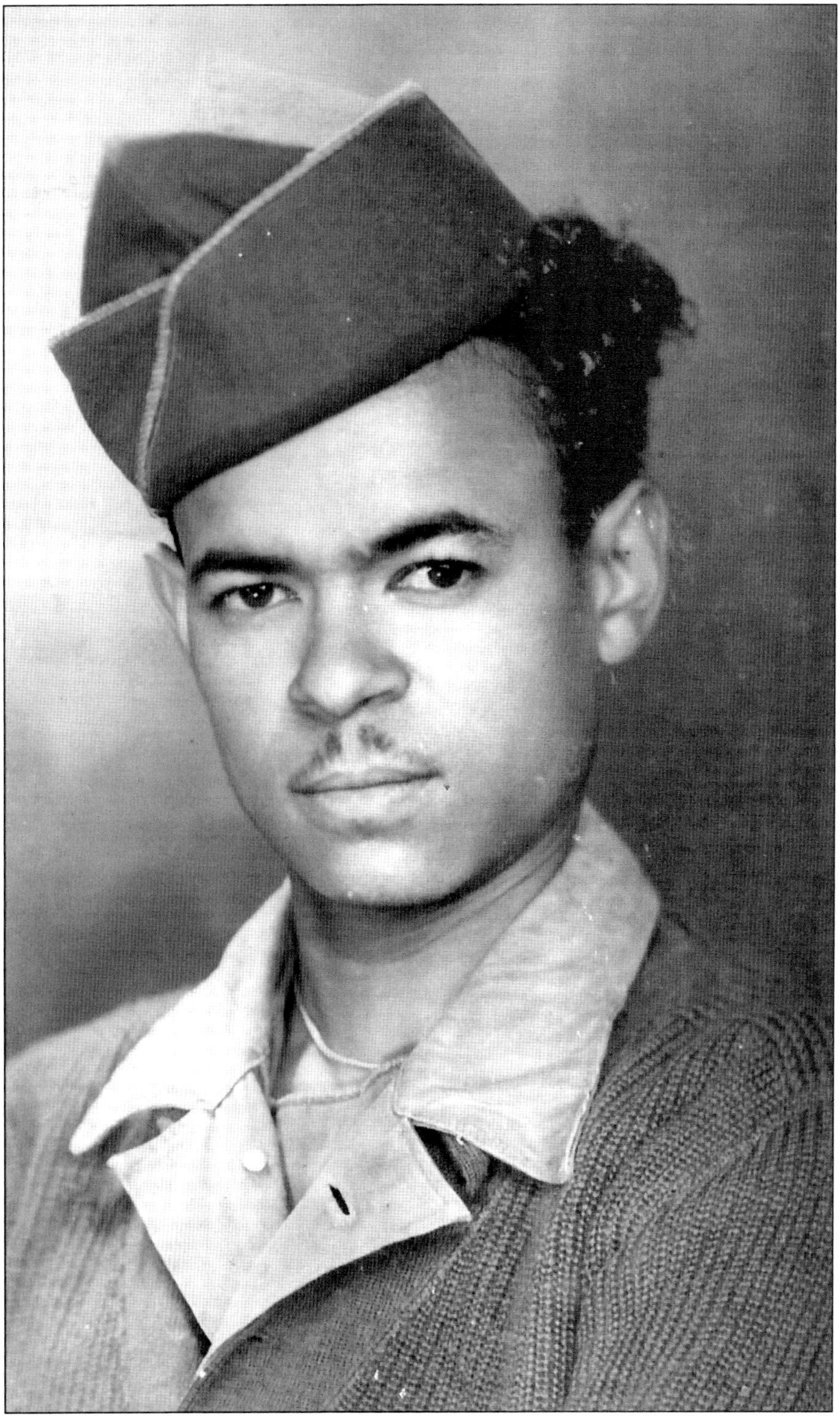

BEASLEY MARTIN, 1943. Mr. Martin served in the U.S. Army during World War II. He was in the European theater. This photograph was taken in France. (Courtesy of Beasley Martin.)

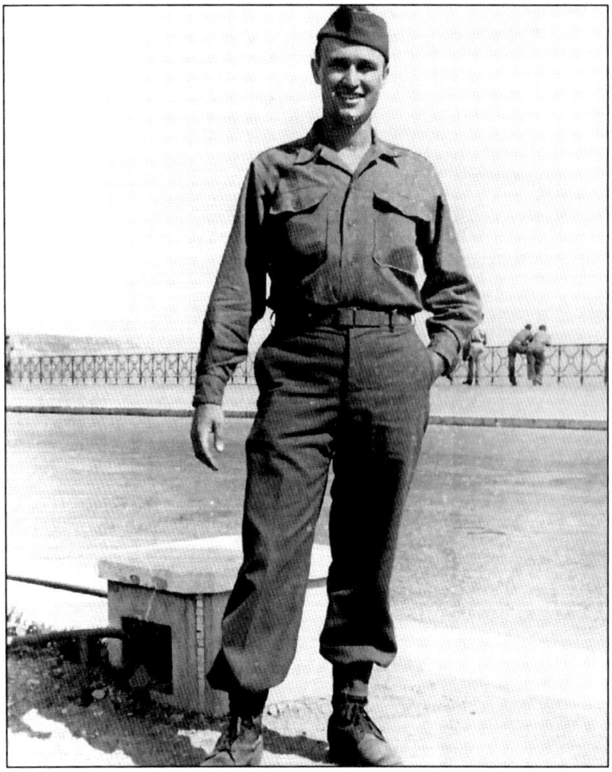

Major Harold Downs. Major served in the U.S. Army during World War II. He was born on November 19, 1919, to Florence Downs. He was husband to Beatrice Marveline Duncan and the father of five children. Major worked at Beaunit Mills until his death in April 1964. (Courtesy of Randy Downs.)

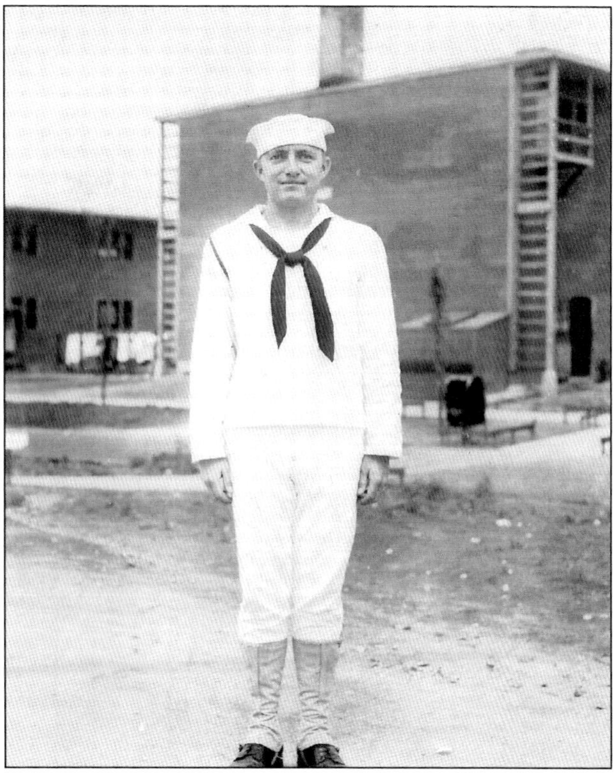

Mickey Finn. Mickey was in the U.S. Navy. He was a motor machinist mate first class. He was trained in Melville, Rhode Island, and served in the South Pacific during World War II. Mickey started in PT (Patrol Boat, Torpedo) Squadron 7. He was on the same boat the entire war, PT-130. They were the first PTs that ever fuelled up at sea. (Courtesy of Clarence Edwin "Mickey" Finn.)

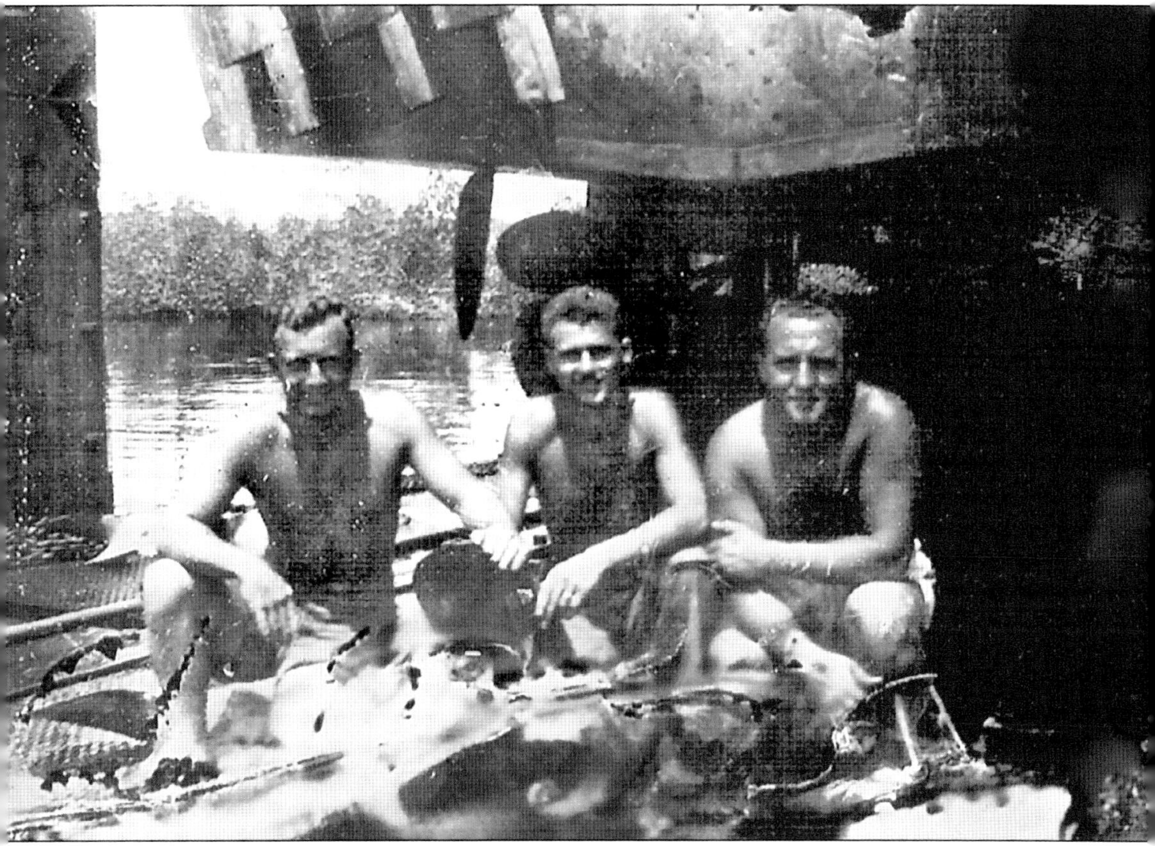

BATTLE OF SURIGAO STRAIT, 1944. On October 14, 1944, Mickey Finn and his squadron were in the Battle of Surigao Strait, which was the last big battle between the American and Japanese Navies. His skipper, Ian Malcolm, called them together that morning and told them that it was a suicide mission and they didn't have to go. There were three PT boats. His PT was the first one to spot the Japanese battleships and tell which way they were going. After they spotted the battleships, the little PTs tried to get away. They all tried to use their smokescreen, but one of the PTs' smokescreen failed. Mickey's PT circled to cover the exposed PT with their smoke screen. That is when the Japanese spotlight hit them. The Japanese couldn't get their guns low enough to shoot at them because of the rails on their ship. Once they got far enough away, the battleships fired on them. Mickey's PT was hit with an eight-inch shell, which did not explode but ripped a torpedo on board in half. This is a photograph of Mickey (on the left) with some of his crew and the torpedo. (Courtesy of Clarence Edwin "Mickey" Finn.)

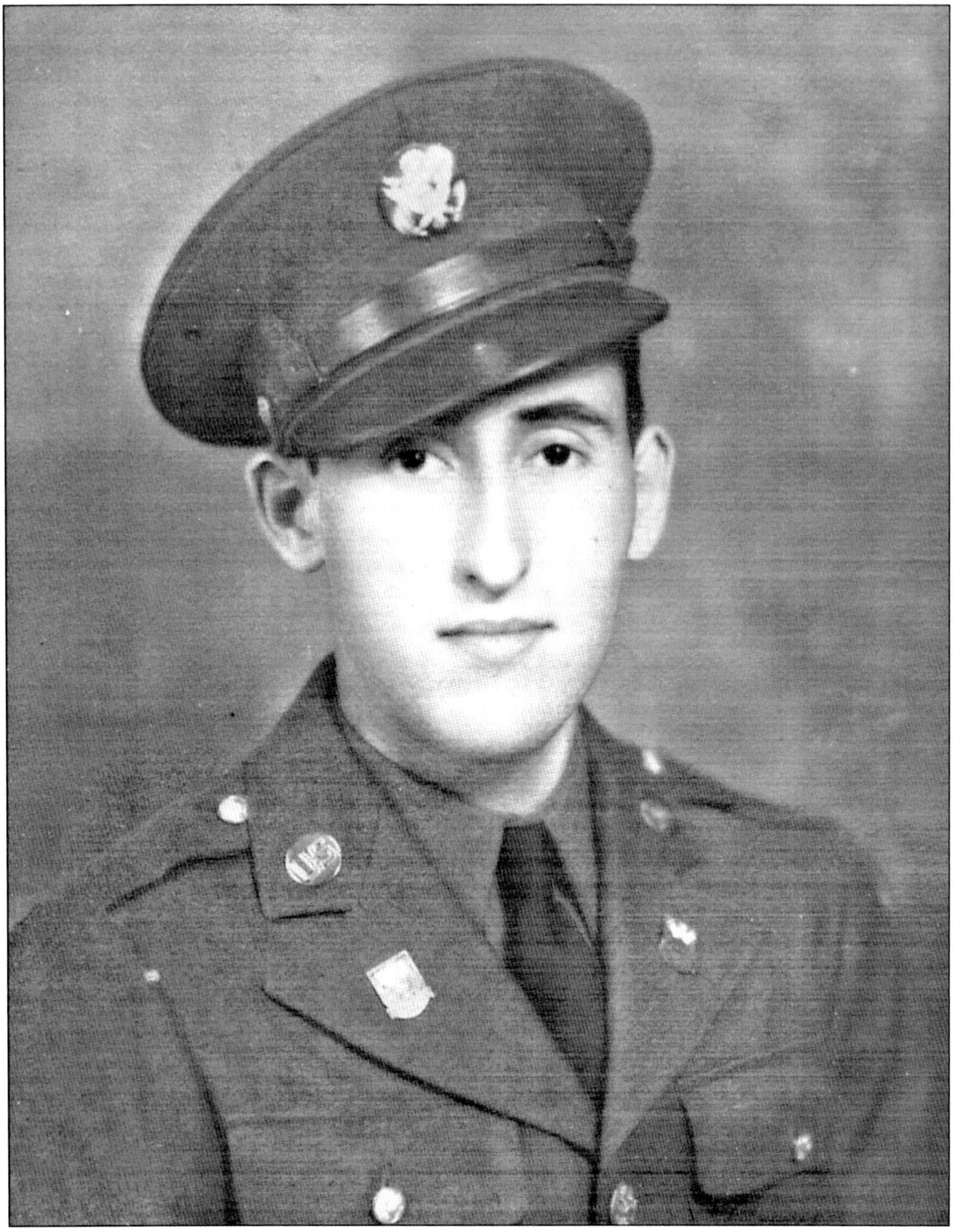

BRUCE W. MCDOWELL. Mr. McDowell served in the U.S. Army Air Force during World War II. He was a link trainer, which was an instrument flight instructor. He was based in Alamogordo, New Mexico. When the government did the atomic bomb test in the desert, Bruce was shaving in his quarters and heard the explosion. Bruce married Myrtle Leach and they had one child, Jo Alice McDowell (Carver). (Courtesy of Myrtle McDowell.)

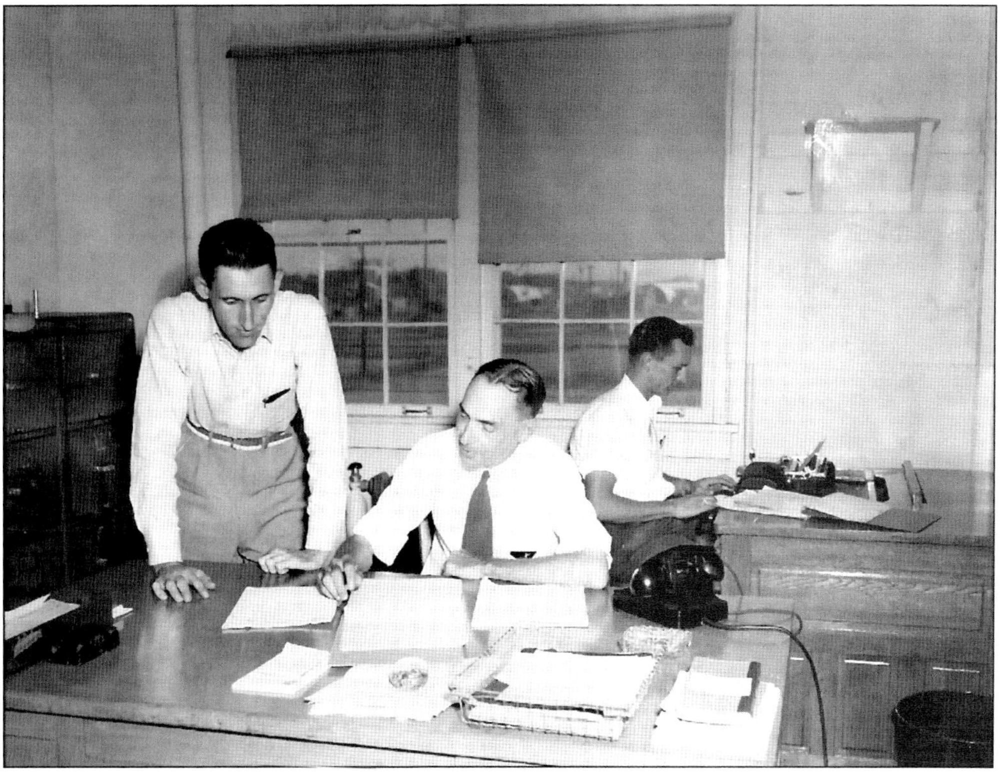

RAILROAD OFFICE AT AOW, C. 1941. Standing is Bruce W. McDowell Jr., who is at the desk of his father, Bruce McDowell Sr. (seated). The other man is unidentified. (Courtesy of Myrtle McDowell.)

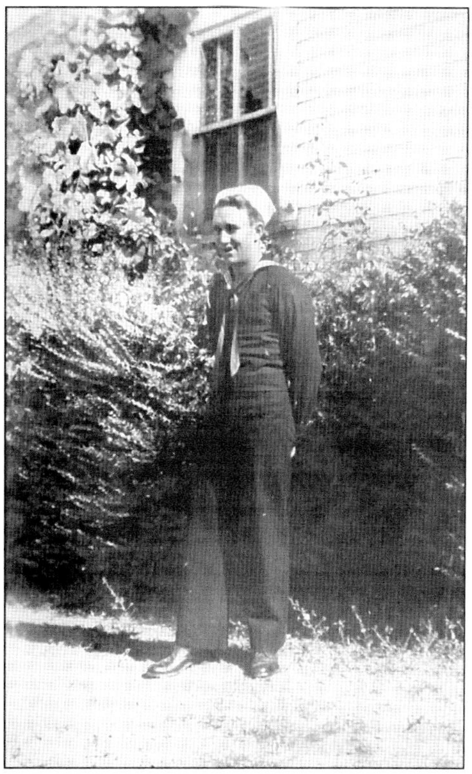

LEWIS FINN. Lewis Finn served with the U.S. Navy during World War II. Lewis was born on August 13, 1926, the son of William Michael "Bill" Finn and Stella Thomas Finn. Lewis married Janelle Fowler and had two daughters. He was a police officer in Childersburg. (Courtesy of Clarence Edwin "Mickey" Finn.)

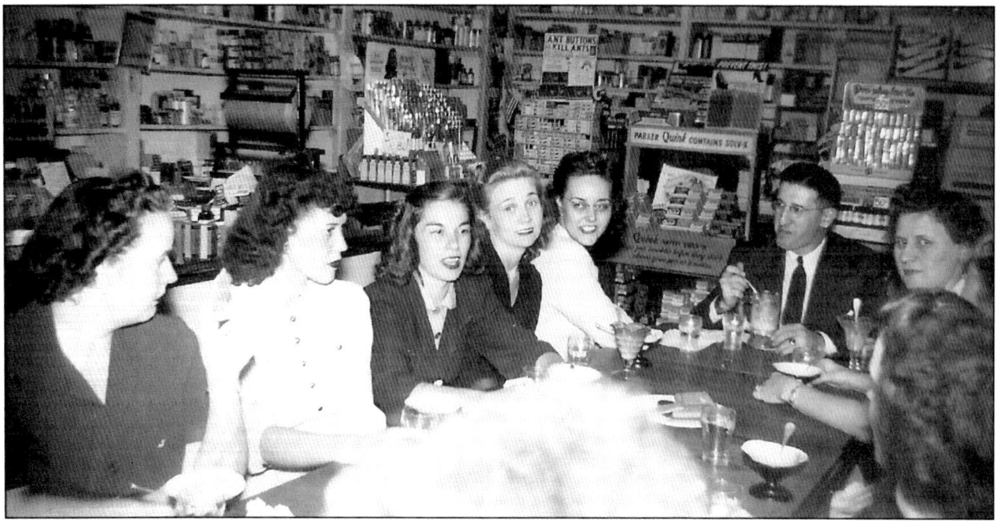

ICE CREAM AT POWELL DRUG STORE, C. 1943. Yes there was a war going on, and the ladies were working. But these ladies still made time for each other. Everyone has time for some friends and a little ice cream. Pictured from left to right are Nancy Presteria, Ruth McDowell, Hilda McGhee, Doris Richardson, Janice ?, and Mike Presteria. The two people at far right are unidentified. Powell Drug Company, located on Eighth Avenue in the Powell Building, was originally owned by druggist George Powell. He was the druggist for many years in Childersburg. George's father, T. J. Powell, was Childersburg's first physician, according to Annie Louise Ryder-Bush. In 1887, Dr. Thomas Lee came to Childersburg to be Dr. Powell's assistant and Childersburg's second physician. (Courtesy of the Earle A. Rainwater Memorial Library.)

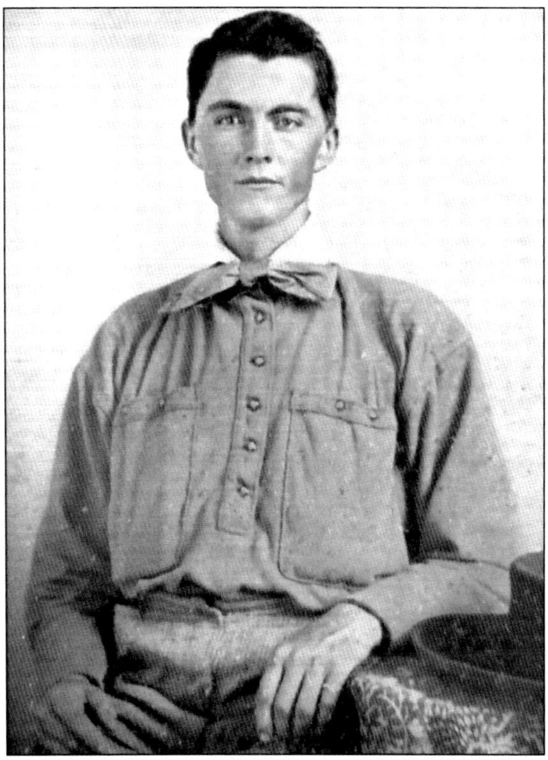

THOMAS SHEALEY, C. 1860. Thomas Shealey is an ancestor of the Limbaugh family of Childersburg. He was a Confederate soldier and was killed in action in 1863. (Courtesy of Jane Limbaugh Allen.)

GEORGE RAZMOND LIMBAUGH, C. 1863. This tintype of Confederate soldier George Razmond Limbaugh is in terrible shape. However, he is one of the oldest known ancestors of Childersburg's Limbaugh family. George was born in 1827. He and his wife, Rachel, were the parents of Jesse Limbaugh, who was the grandfather of the Limbaugh brothers. (Courtesy of Jane Limbaugh Allen.)

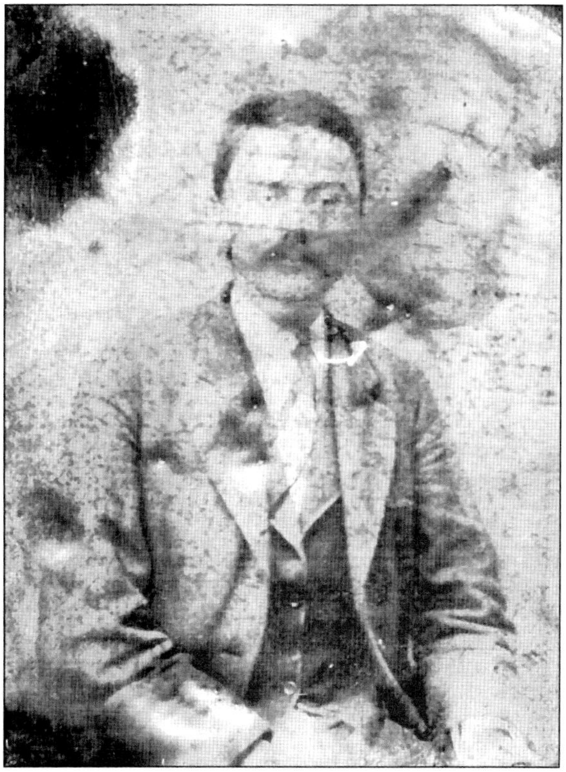

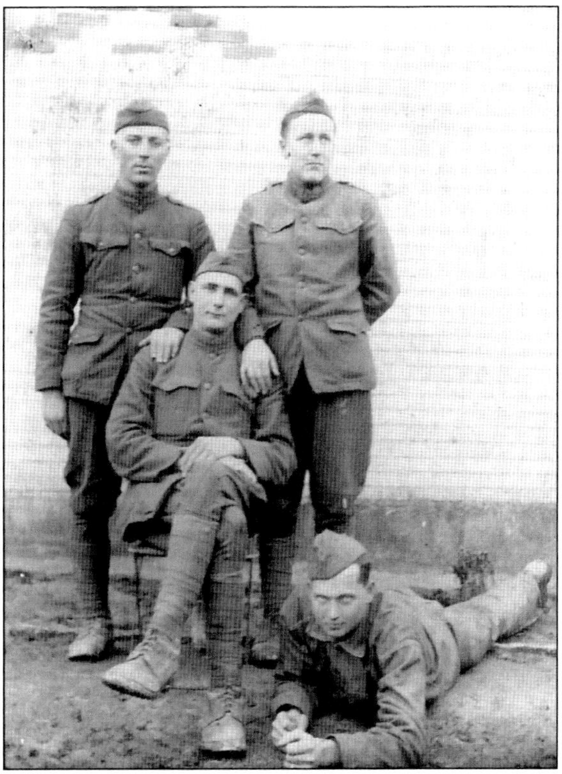

IRA FORNEY FINN OF CHILDERSBURG. Ira (seated) served in the U.S. Army in World War I. Ira was born December 23, 1890, to James Alonza Finn I and Virginia Hughes Finn. He married Elizabeth "Lizzie" Giddens. Ira taught school for a time in Childersburg and was a farmer all his life. (Courtesy of Ralph and Dolly Finn.)

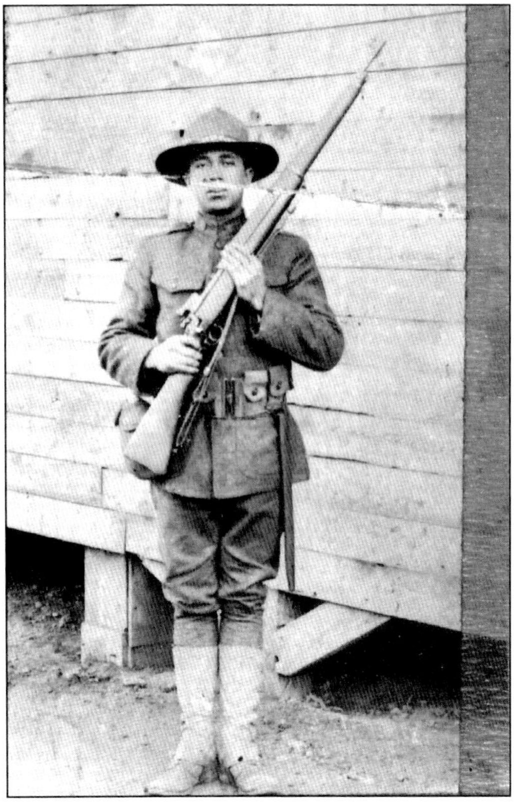

JULIUS KEMPIS MCKINNEY, 1918. Mr. McKinney served in the U.S. Army during World War I. Kempis was the husband of Callie O'Neal McKinney. They lived in Childersburg all their lives. (Courtesy of Gloria McKinney McGowan.)

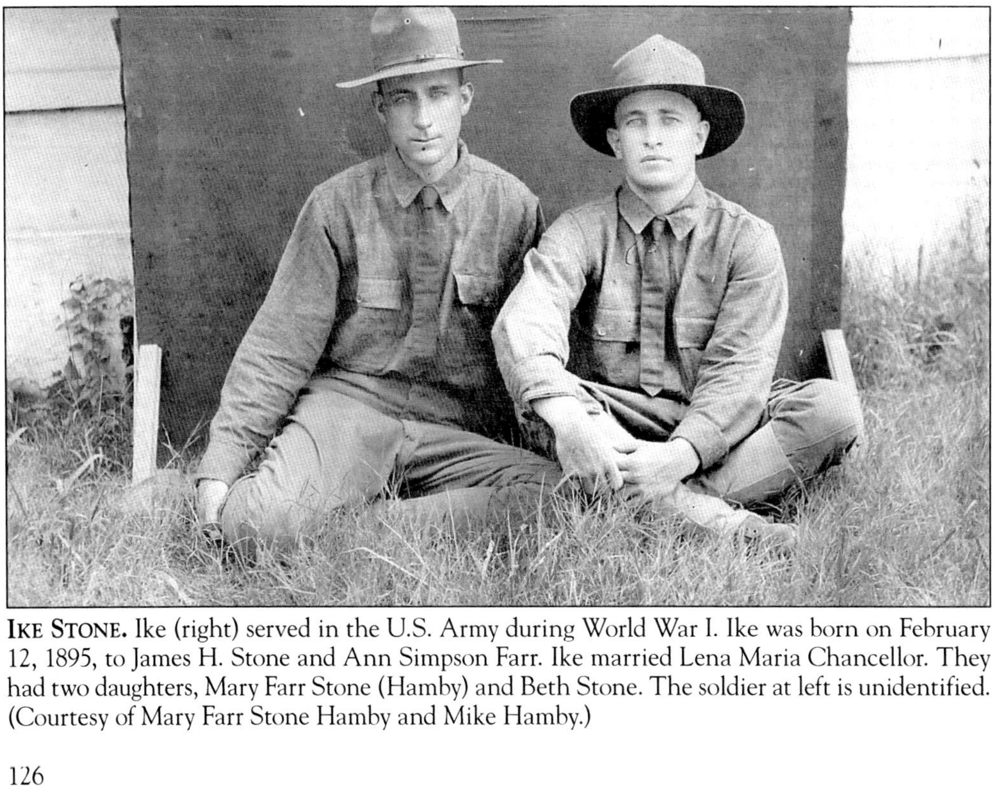

IKE STONE. Ike (right) served in the U.S. Army during World War I. Ike was born on February 12, 1895, to James H. Stone and Ann Simpson Farr. Ike married Lena Maria Chancellor. They had two daughters, Mary Farr Stone (Hamby) and Beth Stone. The soldier at left is unidentified. (Courtesy of Mary Farr Stone Hamby and Mike Hamby.)

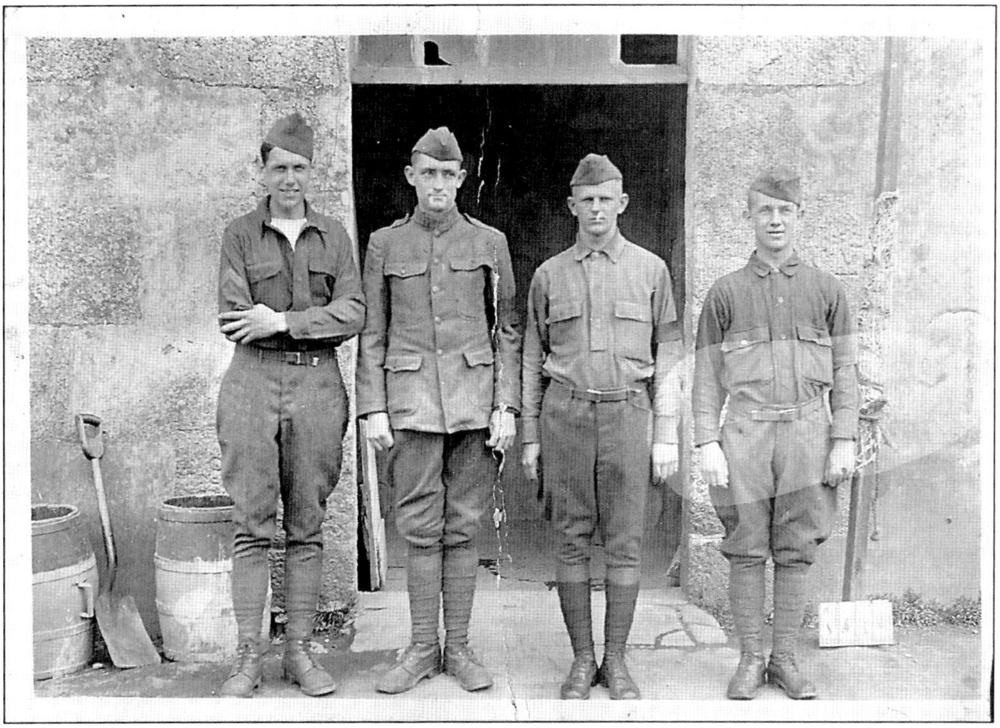

WILLIAM MICHAEL "BILL" FINN. Bill Finn (second from left) served in the U.S. Army during World War I. Bill was born on New Year's Day, 1895, in Childersburg to James A. Finn and Virginia Hughes Finn. He married Stella Thomas Finn. (Courtesy of Clarence Edwin "Mickey" Finn.)

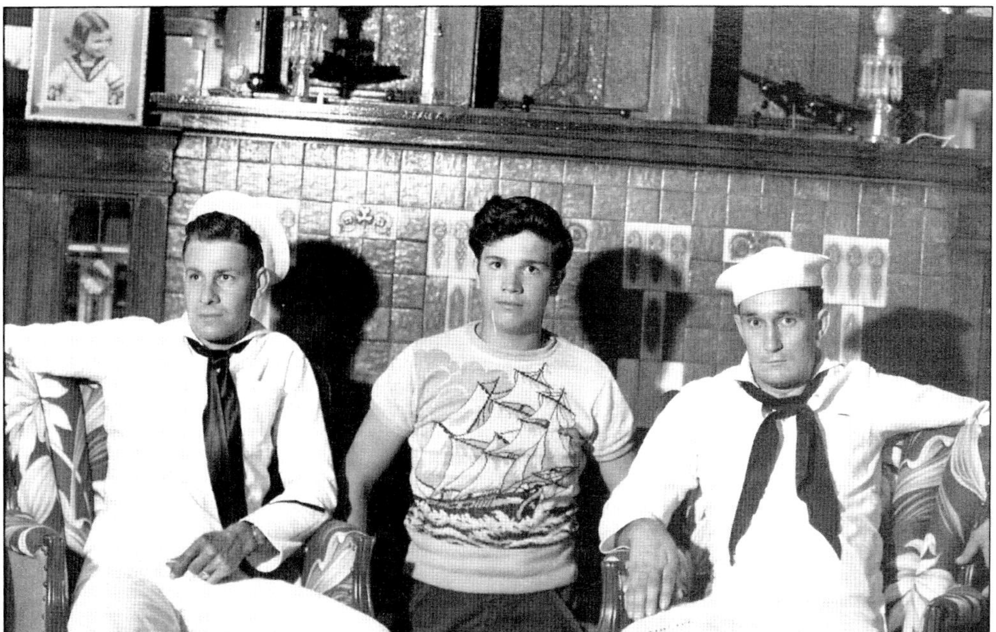

LEWIS FINN. These sailors, shown from left to right, are unidentified, Millard Herrera, and Lewis Finn. (Courtesy of Clarence Edwin "Mickey" Finn.)

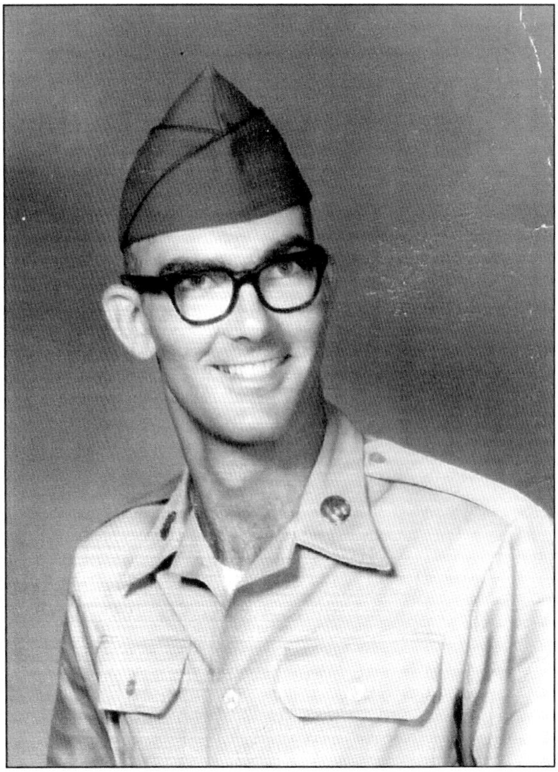

SGT. ERSKINE R. MATHIS. Sergeant Mathis was a military police officer serving in the U.S. Army at the time of the Vietnam War in Nuremburg, Germany. After the war, he graduated from Jacksonville State University and then Birmingham School of Law. He married Doris Finn in 1968, and they had one child. (Courtesy of Doris F. Mathis.)

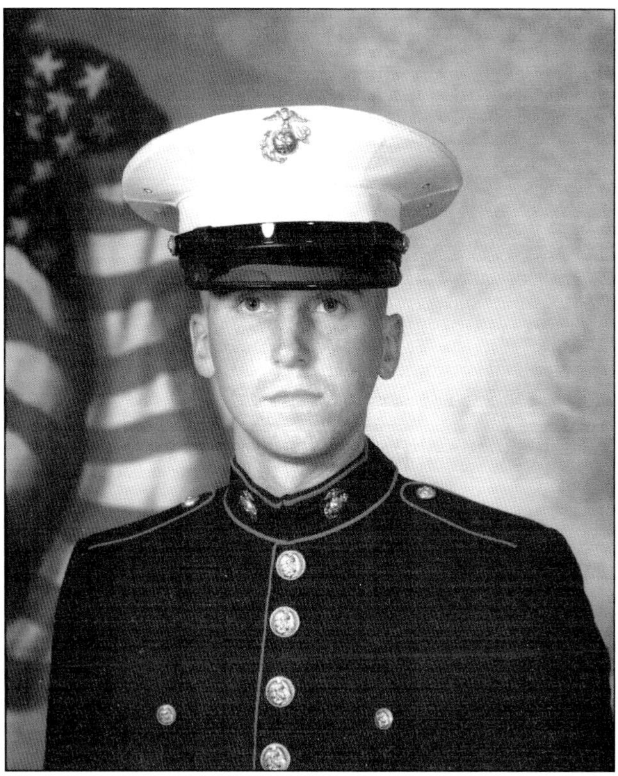

CORP. RANDY DOWNS. Randy serves in the U.S. Marine Corps in Iraq with Operation Iraqi Freedom. He is a communications specialist in COM Company and an expert marksman with the mortar, rifle, and .50-caliber machine gun.